PROSELYTISATION IN INDIA
The Process of Hinduisation in Tribal Societies

PROSELYTISATION IN INDIA
The Process of Hinduisation in Tribal Societies

Edited by
Dharmendra Kumar
Yemuna Sunny

AAKAR

PROSELYTISATION IN INDIA
The Process of Hinduisation in Tribal Societies
Edited by Dharmendra Kumar and Yemuna Sunny

First Published, 2009

ISBN 978-81-89833-74-9 (Hb)

Published by
AAKAR BOOKS
28 E Pocket IV, Mayur Vihar Phase I, Delhi-110 091
Phone : 011-2279 5505 Telefax : 011-2279 5641
aakarbooks@gmail.com; www.aakarbooks.com

Printed at
Arpit Printographers, Delhi-110 032
arpitprinto@yahoo.com

Contents

Preface

The message which a book intends to communicate can be fully comprehended with a reference to the context in which it is conceived, developed and concretised. This book is not a product of a purely academic pursuit. Nor is it a response to the much advertised issue of conversion of tribal masses by the Christian missionaries. In fact, the need for this book emerged in the course of an action research project on communal harmony. The project, **Peace and Justice Project**, was started in 2003 by a joint initiative by People's Research Society (PRS) and Action Aid India. The objectives of this project were twofold: first, to understand the reasons for the expanding base of communal ideology, and second, to develop consciousness against it through a process of constant dialogue with people. In this way it was a process of learning about the realities of communalism through a constant interaction with people. In this process, what attracted our attention was a rapid increase of the belligerent Hinduism in tribal society. We felt a need for a deeper understanding of this phenomenon with the help of a comparative understanding of this problem.

For this purpose we decided to collect papers from the experts and activists in this area. Settling down to this task, we realised that the job was not an easy one because most of the people whom we decided to approach were extremely busy persons and had many commitments to keep. Even so, they were generous enough to join us for a two-day workshop on this issue at Bhopal. We are really indebted to our contributors, not only for their valuable contributions in that workshop but also for their consent for publication of their contributions. We are also grateful to all the persons who joined the workshop and contributed through their valuable comments and questions in that workshop.

We are extremely grateful to Action Aid India for funding our project and workshop. Although it would be some kind of a thanking ourselves, we can't help thanking members of People's Research Society (PRS), particularly Deepak, Prakash, Yogesh, Deependra, Ishwar, Raghavendra, Surekha, Shivnarain and others. We are also thankful to our friends Vineet, Manoj, Asha, Sarika, Shankar, Azam and others for their valuable cooperation and support.

Introduction

In recent years, proselytisation, be it forced, allured or voluntary, has been a hotly debated issue in the Indian socio-political discourse. Not only has it attracted the attention of Indian mass media, it has also initiated the process of legislation in some Indian states. The centre of attack has been the conversion by the Christian missionaries. But what has been relatively unnoticed is another kind of proselytisation, equally real and concrete, that is the conversion of faiths of tribal masses by Hindu proselytisers. This has led to a remarkable change in the religious complexion of tribal society in India. Although this ideology (Hinduism) doesn't lay emphasis on conversion or proselytisation one can easily observe the efforts of large scale transformation of religious practices, particularly at the level of rituals and emotional association, of tribal masses. It has been argued that tribals have not to convert them. All that they have to do is to realise their real self. This ideology has concretised in the form of processes like *Ghar Wapsi* (homecoming) on the one hand and the growing religious bigotry and violence in the form of attacks on minority in tribal society, on the other.

This study doesn't aim at justifying or criticising a particular form of proselytisation. Instead an effort has been made to understand the social and historical constitution of this process and its impacts on the contemporary politics and society in India. The book is constituted of seven chapters separately contributed by seven researchers. These contributions are comprised of one theoretical chapter by Professor Virginius Xaxa and six different case studies from different parts of India where these processes are on.

The first chapter **Tribes, Conversion and the Sangh Parivar** contributed by Professor Xaxa is an effort to delineate the theoretical issues involved in the process of proselytisation. The first section of this chapter is a discussion of the very concept of tribe. To him, the term 'tribe' is a construct of colonial administration eventually added in sociological and anthropological vocabulary. However, the contours of its definition during colonial period has always been fuzzy. 'There were instances of 'tribe' and 'caste' being used either interchangeably or even in cognate manner'. It was to describe the group of people who were not dominant or the part of mainstream Indian society. Two bases for the characterisation of a section as tribe were identified; one, agricultural and pastoral castes, and two who practised animism. However, various qualifiers such as 'Hill' and 'Forest' tribes or 'primitive' and 'backward' tribes were added. What was considered common was that they all practised a form of religion that was different from the one practised by dominant sections of Indian society. Agreeing with Beteille's characterisation, Professor Xaxa explains the meaning of tribe as the social group lying outside civilisation. The significance of this characterisation is that 'conversions draws tribes to the wider aspects of civilization'.

To Professor Xaxa, with reference to Hinduism the meaning of proselytisation has been understood with reference to assimilation of tribal society into Hindu society. 'The most common terms used are Sanskritisation and the Hinduisation'. He discussed the various modes of this process of integration of tribe in the Hindu society. With reference to proselytisation by Christianity, Xaxa focuses upon the unevenness of process across the regions and communities. In relation to the modes and methods of proselytisation, Xaxa emphasises that in both Hindu and Christian conversion methods as force, aggression, inducement fraud, spiritual persuasions, and so on, have been used. With reference to Christianity, Xaxa says, 'While the employment of means considered as unfair, unethical and illegal have not been altogether absent in history and may be even practiced today, these do not constitute the dominant methods of conversion used by the Christian missionaries. The more common methods used by them have been, what may be called, developmental and social service oriented works'. Xaxa points out that conversion was often followed by great loss of much of rights that the convert had earlier enjoyed in the community. The converts were often denied food, shelter, inheritance, succession as well as participation in rites and rituals of the family and the community. They were at times excommunicated from the community.

In contradistinction to Hinduism where proselytisation is slow, gradual and staggered over many years in the conversion to Christianity, although some process is invariably involved, it is marked more by an event and hence transition from one to other can invariably be located and identified. The other interesting thing about the conversion of tribes to Christianity is that the transformation of the tribals has never been all encompassing. The change or shift was generally related with only those aspects of the social lives that were considered religious in nature or had religious overtones. However, the process of conversion clearly creates divide between converts and non-converts.

In the third section, Xaxa discusses the recent trends of conversion in the light of development of the Sangh Parivar. One such trend is aggressive articulation by the activists of the Sangh Parivar that the tribals cease to be tribes once they had become the Christians. Second, 'the advocates of Hindutva conveniently overlook the fact that tribes have distinct religions of their own. They have in fact begun to categorise them as the Hindus'. Hindutva have been building pressures, working out strategies and manipulations both at state and local levels to ensure that tribes return themselves as the Hindus and not as animists or the followers of the tribal religion in the census enumeration. Through measures such as these, tribes have been coerced and socialised to declare themselves as Hindus. Xaxa argues that it is rather absurd that one could talk of reconversion in the context of tribes as the advocates of Hindutva do. They can in fact talk only of conversion, from tribal religion to Christianity or Christianity to Hinduism.

The second chapter, **Conceptualising Religious Change Amongst Bhils of West Nimar**, contributed by Kumar Sanjay Singh is an analysis of the process of proselytisation in West Nimar District of Madhya Pradesh. Singh begins with the critique of dominant analyses which argue that religious conversion is consequence of the activities of the religio-cultural organisation. To him, adivasis are not the passive recipients of such activities. He argues that 'perhaps the most crucial problem with this approach is that while it adequately brings out the activities of the outside agencies in bringing about religious change—proselytisation, it is absolutely silent on the reasons for the adivasis to accept the change.' He argues that adivasi society has some sort of differential acceptance of the outside influences. That is to say, adivasi social formation is selective in this process.

To him this process of differential acceptance should be discussed with reference to material activities which prompt the interaction of adivasi social formation with the dominant mode of productions. He has discussed this proposition with reference to the historical specificities of the interaction between adivasi social formation and dominant social formation in Nimar region. In so doing he has discussed interaction with feudal rulers such as Rajputs and Marathas and during the British period when adivasis were used as labourers in cotton production. He has also discussed the differential influence of *Gayatri Parivar*, the *Radha Swami* sect and the *Kasturba Kanya Ashram, Niwali*. 'All these organisations aim at uplifting the adivasis from their barbarism in this pursuit they are opposed to many aspects of adivasi culture and rituals that they belief lacks temperance and moderation. Second, all these organisations are opposed to the practice of bride price and endeavour to substitute it with *Kanya Daan*. Third, all these organisations are opposed the customary prevalence of alcoholism in the adivasi community.' However, in all these efforts the organisations have not achieved equal success. The campaign against consumption of liquor and non-vegetarian food is successful. 'The impact, however, was diametrically opposite in the case of bride price where there was no significant change in spite of the activities of the ashram.'

Singh has analysed this differential acceptance on the basis of a theoretical analysis of adivasi social formation. This analysis has been carried out in four sections, Structure of Adivasi Social Formation, Dialectics of Transformation of Adivasi Social formation, Specific forms of Exploitation of the Adivasis and its Impact, Impact of Exploitation on Cultural-Religious Sphere. As to the specificity of adivasi social formation, Singh writes that 'The distinguishing feature of the adivasi social formation/ domestic community is that the community ensures its continued and future existence through production of food and products that is transformed into 'human energy'. Unlike capitalism and feudalism where different dynamics of surplus appropriation intervene between the act of production and the act of consumption, in the adivasi social formation/domestic community the production of energy and of food (i.e. consumption and production) are two aspects of the same production process; one is transformed into the other and vice versa'. This results in the dominance of elders in decision making on the one hand and the significance of bride as working hand. A balance between producers and non-producers is maintained. In the adivasi social formation this latent tenancy towards accumulation and exchange value is counteracted by the mechanism of redistribution. Customs and rituals are one of the important instrumentalities through with redistribution is achieved. As a result adivasis are reluctant to accept customs and traditions which disturb this balance.

So far as Dialectics of Transformation of Adivasi Social formation is concerned, Singh argues that autarchy of adivasi social formation is transformed through the introduction of money 'extra-economic measures, including force, by the state'. The transformation is also carried out through the introduction of wage labour and seasonal migration. He argues that 'the double labour market sets out to divide the worker into two categories corresponding to the form of exploitation which they experience: first, that of workers that are integrated into and thus reproduce wholly within the capitalist sector and second, that of migrants who reproduce themselves partly within and partly outside the capitalist sector'. While discussing specific forms of exploitation, Singh discusses various customs and rituals emerged with the interaction with other social formations. Lastly, he spells out differential impacts of these interactions on adivasi social formation and relates with the specificities of adivasi social formation. The double labour market sets out to divide the worker into two categories corresponding to the form of exploitation which they experience: first, that of workers that are integrated into and thus reproduce wholly within the capitalist sector and second, that of migrants who reproduce themselves partly within and partly outside the capitalist sector.

The third contribution, **Adivasi vs. Vanvasi: The Politics of Conversion in Central India** by Nandini Sundar examines in detail the processes by which proselytisation of adivasis are chalked out and executed by the Hindutva agenda of right-wing politics. She looks into the dynamics of *Vanvasi Kalyan Ashram's* efforts to obliterate tribal identity. Common grounds are created and propagated between tribal and Hindu religion. This enhances a myth of tribes as being part of the greater fold of Hinduism. These processes cannot be seen only as religious conversions and hence differ from, say, Christian conversion. Hinduisation is backed by the political concept of *Hindu Rashtra* (Hindu Nation). It is also examined how the state machinery has actually worked as pro-Hindutva and anti-Christian and how the BJP and the Congress has often meshed together their actions and perspectives within the state machinery.

She addresses the crucial question of tribal economy because popular notions of adivasi upliftment trickle down to cultural changes. These are devoid of access to economic and political power. Both Hindutva and Christian missions are culpable for the obliteration of adivasi identity. It is also to be noted that the Indian State privileged religious identity and belief over other forms of identity, especially those relating to economy and polity.

Thus we have a collection of six contributions focusing on the problems and dynamics of proselytisation of adivasis within the political agenda of Hindutva.

The Fourth contribution, **Proselytisation of Tribal Society: A Political Agenda** is by Dharmendra Kumar and Moirangthem Prakash. This is a study of the process of proselytisation in the Alirajpur area of Jhabua district of Madhya Pradesh.The focus of this study is the recent processes of proselytisation by Hindutva forces. The central argument of this chapter is that the process of proselytisation of tribal masses into Hinduism is closely related with the dynamics of material processes of life. That is to say, the increasing needs of modern capitalist society in the form of raw-materials sources and need for larger space leading to deforestation on the one hand and the workers in the form of dispossessed and displaced tribal masses on other, has resulted in constant intervention by the modern society into the tribal society. Through this process capitalist society tries to enclose the tribal society in the process of accumulation.[1] Here it must be pointed out that this critique of the interventions by the modern capitalistic society into the tribal society does not aim at romantic idealisation of tribal society as an ideal society. All that we want to emphasise is that the modern capitalist society has given a particular meaning to their hardships and has co-opted them into its framework by introducing its culture and ideology, thereby integrating them in the capitalist fold. Communalism being the part of ruling politics and thus the culture and ideology of modern capitalist society has played an important role in this process of co-option of tribal society into the modern capitalist society. Proselytisation, particularly, Hinduisation of tribal masses in the present context, is one such process.

The fifth chapter is by T. Kishan Singh, **Ordeals and Upheaval: A Critique of Hindu Proselytisation in Manipur** is an analysis of the relationships between Hindu and Meetei religion in Manipur. In his contribution Singh has demystified the stereotypical notion of Hindu tolerance. He has discussed it with an analysis of the trajectory of the historical development of interaction between Hinduism and Meetei. To him Meetei rituals and practices are spontaneous developments emerged in concordance with geographical and environmental specificities of Manipur. It was the migration of Hindu Brahmins due to persecutions of Mughal empire that forced an interaction and further dominance of Hinduism. In this process of creation of its dominance, Hinduism was as intolerant as any other religion.

The sixth chapter, **Conversion in Chhattisgarh : Myths and Facts** by Rajendra Sail is an analysis of the real situations of conversion in Chhattisgarh region. Sail's study is a reflection of his long-term engagement with political-social issues in Chhattisgarh. Chhattisgarh, reconstituted as a state from Madhya Pradesh, has a sizeable tribal population.

The author looks into the question of Hindu proselytisation from the offensive strategies of Hindutva employed towards the non-Hindu people. In Chhattisgarh, this strategy is overwhelmingly directed at the Christians. Historically there have been reasons like the policies adopted by princely rule like in Sarguja, which put controls on conversions. But with the formation of unified Indian state, such policies did not apply and there were increases in Christian conversions. But data shows that such increases did not carry on, there are declines at later times. Sail's main theme is the exposure of rumour strategies adopted by the Sangh Parivar and BJP in the state. There is an underlying understanding among right-wing and Fascist organisations the world over on the use of rumour as an effective strategy for partisan and dangerous political targets. The claims put forth through many such efforts focusing on Christian conversions in the state manufactured by VHP-BJP are examined against official data. It is seen that even without any complicated statistical analysis, these claims are seen to immediately wither away.

The last chapter is by Joseph Marianus Kujur, **Hinduisation Processes of Tribals: A Special Reference to the Oraons in Chhotanagpur** where he emphasises the distinctiveness of tribal identity from the identity of religion. He traces the nomenclature of many tribe names as being 'given' by the mainstream often in derogatory senses of defining the 'other'. The Constitutional provisions inherent in 'Scheduled Tribe' are also a given status that does not resonate with the self- identification of the group. The Hindutva agenda of proselytisation of the tribes is a process of co-option. We see a clash of ideology between that of domination and of equality. The mono religion and monoculture of Hindutva is pitched against that of diversity, which is represented by tribal identity. It is also noted that as Hindutva clashes with the Christian missions in tribal areas, there is also a local consciousness that strives to keep alive the original tribal identity, which is culturally defined by specific way of life and has a religious identity in tribal religions like Sarna. He argues that in a civilisational pull of the powerful and the dominant, attempts are made to pull the weaker sections into its framework. Obviously, assumption BJP and its Hindutva alliances strengthens such processes with new force and vigour. These forces of assimilation and of homogenisation are often very strong and authoritarian. But the emergence of resistance from the local level is a positive indication of the political process of democracy.

All the contributions are thus attempts to understand the process which is trying to redesign the Indian social and religious fabric. Needless to say, this redesigning has some far-reaching implications for the Indian society. This process is not only going to give new definitions to parliamentary equations, it would also have some serious impact over communal harmony.

REFERENCES

1. This process has been discussed as the movements of primitive accumulation. According to this approach, primitive accumulation is the process of separation of a group of people from their means of production and livelihood. Thus for this approach this process is not over or the accomplished fact. See "The New Enclosures" **Midnight Collective** appeared in **www.commoner.org.uk.com,** September 2001.

1

Tribes, Conversion and the Sangh Parivar

Virginius Xaxa

The issue of religious conversion has been the subject of major news headlines and controversies from time to time. Interestingly, on every occasion that such controversies have erupted in India, the population at the centre of the debate has been the communities that have generally been called 'tribes'. It was the issue of conversion of tribes in Madhya Pradesh that sparked off the first major controversy in independent India in the early 1950s. There the issue led to the setting up of an inquiry commission, more popularly known as the Niyogi Commission. The issue of conversion made major news headlines again in 1978, first with 'The Arunachal Pradesh Freedom of Indigenous Faith Bill' and later with the 'Freedom of Religion Bill' that was introduced in Parliament by O.P. Tyagi. The bill aimed at regulating conversion at an all-India level. Prior to this, the 'Freedom of Religion Bill' was passed in Orissa and Madhya Pradesh in 1967 and 1968 respectively. In Madhya Pradesh, even before Independence, some princely states had initiated enactments to ban conversion. These included the Raigarh State Conversion Act, 1936; the Surguja State Hindu Apostasy Act, 1945 and the Udaipur State Conversion Act, 1946.[1] What is interesting is that all these bills were introduced or passed primarily with a view to banning the conversion of the tribes to Christianity. Even in the 1998-99 controversy on conversion, tribes have been centre-stage of the debate.

The Concept of Tribe

In order to place the issue of conversion among tribes in the proper perspective, it is necessary to locate their social settings. The use of the term 'tribe' to describe a certain category of people in India began during colonial rule. It was, however, not clear as to what sense the term was used in, at least at the initial stage. There were instances of 'tribe' and 'caste' being used either interchangeably or even in a cognate manner. Despite the synonymous and cognate use of the term, the British viewed the segment of the population later described as 'tribe', as different from the dominant sections of the Indian society. This was evident from the nature of administration they aimed at evolving for the tribal areas. Laws in force pertaining to the general population were not usually applicable in the case of such tribal groups and communities. More often than not, special laws or laws in consonance with the traditional/'tribal' system of administration were framed for their regulation and governance.

This difference proved handy for the British administration when an attempt was initiated to provide detailed and classified information about people in India following the introduction of the census. The groups/communities regarded as different from the dominant communities were by and large categorized as tribes. Yet, when it came to the conceptualisation of the basis of such categorization, the British were far from clear as to how the two types of communities could be differentiated. This is obvious from the censuses. In the 1891 census, for example, the term used was not 'tribe' but 'forest tribe', and that too as a sub-heading within the broader category of 'agricultural and pastoral castes'. Since 1901, however, a somewhat clearer criterion began to be used. Tribes were identified and described as those who practised animism; later the expression 'tribal religion' was used in its place. The criterion so introduced was continued in the subsequent censuses, along with other qualification dimensions. Through descriptions such as the 'Hill', 'Forest', 'primitive' and 'backward' tribes, the tribes were categorized into different types. The common feature was that they all practised a form of religion different from that practised by the dominant sections of Indian society. That is, that tribes were identified as those who did not adhere to religions such as Hinduism, Christianity, Islam, etc. In the case of Hinduism, however, if groups were shown to be Hindus in their beliefs and religious practices, they were also viewed as constituting a social organisation that was markedly different from that of tribes. They were considered as parts of the caste social organisation as against those of tribes. The dimension of caste thus assumes a central place in the religious tradition of Hinduism.

With the drawing up of a list of tribes with a view to giving them certain political and administrative concessions, the consistent application of the criteria towards defining tribes took a back seat. The list of Scheduled Tribes included in the Constitution had its genesis in these administrative and political considerations. After Independence, greater attention was paid towards identification of the criteria which could distinguish tribes from others. These included one or more of such characteristic features as physical features, distinctive language, simple technology, distinct social and political organisation, geographical isolation or a combination of one or more of these. Yet, there has been no agreement over the use of these characteristics. Ghurye, for example, has shown how factors like religion, occupation and racial features have proved inadequate when an attempt has been made to distinguish tribal people from the non-tribal people.[2]

Thus, how the term 'tribe' is to be used in the Indian context and what we mean by tribal people is not easy to resolve. In general, geographical isolation—in the sense of living in forests, hills or inaccessible tracts, simple technology and modes of living—in one or more of such combinations have been taken as the criteria for identifying tribes. Despite this classification, there remain a large number of groups and communities, which are identified as tribes but do not conform to the relevant attributes. Many among them, in fact, share characteristics that approximate more to non-tribes than the tribes. Thus tribes include within them a wide range of groups and communities differing in language, technology, geographical locations, ecological settings, level of development, etc. In short, they are at different stages of social formation. And yet they have all been considered as tribes mainly because, as Beteille puts it, they have existed more or less outside civilisation.[3] They were outside civilisation at the time when attempts were made to conceptualise tribes. It is indeed important to keep note of this aspect if one is to understand the issue of conversion among the tribes. Conversion, after all, draws tribes to the wider aspects of civilisation.

Hinduism

Conversion may be viewed from several angles. Hence, it may mean different things to different people. I, however, am using the term conversion its everyday parlance, viz. change from one faith and practice to another. The transformation from one religion to another has been going on among tribes in India well before the onset of colonial rule. All the same, it was with the coming of colonial rule that the conversion of tribes gained attention. In order to get a proper perspective of conversion of tribes, we must view the issue in the wider perspective of transformation of the tribal societies.

Though there is a distinction between tribes and civilisation, the two are not treated as isolates, but in interaction with each other. Hence the dichotomy posed between tribes and non-tribes is viewed as a distortion. The changes occurring in the tribal society due to interaction with wider society, have invariably been conceived in terms of tribes moving in the direction of becoming a part of civilisations by getting assimilated or absorbed into the society the civilisations represent. Both historians and anthropologists have made such observations not only in the context of the past but also the present. Kosambi has referred to tribal elements being fused into the general society. Bose makes reference of tribes being absorbed into Hindu society.[4] Such a claim has not gone unabated, for a large amount of anthropological work of the post-Independence era still points to phenomena such as tribes being absorbed or assimilated into the Hindu society, or tribes becoming castes. In this journey to absorption or assimilation, tribes are said to stand at different levels or stages. Nowhere is this better reflected than in the classification that sociologists and social anthropologists have provided of the transformation of tribes and tribal society.

The change in the direction of absorption in the Hindu society is said to occur through certain processes that are far from uniform and identical. That this is so is evident from the range of terms used to capture the processes at work in the social anthropological literature. The most common terms used are Sanskritisation and the Hinduisation. Of course, the processes described by such terms overlap in actual emperical reality, hence there is a tendency among social scientists to use them interchangeably or synonymously. Often, the difference expressed by these terms is covered under the use of such generic terms as acculturation, assimilation, absorption, etc. It is in relation to the processes denoted by these terms that the change in tribal society has been mainly studied. And because of these processes, tribes have invariably been described or conceptualised in literature as those absorbed into Hindu society. Accordingly, they are said to have accepted the ethos of caste structure and have been absorbed within it. They are treated as hardly differentiable from those of the neighbouring Hindu peasantry.

The study of transformation of tribes to Hinduism/caste has led to a concern with other kinds of related issues, like the kinds of forces that compel tribes to come under the influence of the non-tribes and the nature and types of interaction they enter into with them. As regards the manner in which such transformation has taken place, there exists some controversy among scholars in India. The controversy has gained momentum after it has been claimed that the tribes are aggressively being absorbed into Hindu society. It is argued that there was frictionless co-existence between tribes and non-tribes until the 19th century but since then, as a result of spread of railways and roads, land-hungry peasants, traders and moneylenders penetrated into the tribal areas, exploiting them on the one hand and on the other, compelling and coaxing them into accepting their own cultural traditions and values.[5] The question that arises is whether the Hindu civilisation was tolerant up to the 19th century and became intolerant only later. Now, on this issue there are diverse views among the scholars of Indian society. Studies of the history of Indian civilisation show that the growth and expansion of Hindu society was a prolonged and complex process, both forcible and peaceful, of absorption of the tribal people into the Hindu society. In fact, history discloses various methods of tribal absorption or assimilation that was adopted by different societies at different times or epochs.[6] It was, however, not the aggressive but the peaceful process of absorption that has generally been highlighted in the literature on tribes in India.

The transformation of the tribes under this process has been conceived to occur through certain methods that have been diversely conceptualised among the scholars. Kosambi considers adoption of the technology of the Hindu society by tribes to be major methods of getting integrated into the Hindu society.[7] Bose talks of the Hindu method of tribal absorption. This, according to him, takes place mainly under the system of the organisation of production based on caste. For Bose, the system is based on mutual reciprocity, hence its characteristic feature has been cooperation and not conflict. Hence, under the caste system of production, productive activities of the various castes were protected against competition from other castes. It is this that the tribes found attractive in the system, according to Bose, and were drawn to the system, although it entailed low status for them within the caste hierarchy.[8] The other significant method of tribal absorption into Hindu society is what Sinha calls 'state formation'. He states that the processes of acculturation, Hinduisation and social stratification within the village could not be properly understood unless they were examined in the broad context of the formation of the principality. He further writes that the formation of the state provided the decisive socio-political framework of the transformation of the tribal systems into the regional caste system.[9] Some have even considered Sanskritisation as the method through which tribes are integrated into the Hindu society. To me, this seems to be more of a process than method, which occurs only when tribes are drawn into the larger society through processes that are economic and political.

Under these methods, the transformation of tribes and their absorption into the Hindu society was a long and protracted process. The process of acculturation to a new culture including religion followed as a corollary of increasing economic and political contacts of the tribes with the larger society. The process was slow, gradual and spontaneous. The term used to describe this process is generally known as Sanskritisation. It is a process whereby a group lower down the hierarchy tries to adopt the lifestyle of the group above its hierarchy. In the context of tribes, the term has been used to understand the process of acculturation to the value and customs of the dominant society. Hence it was far from easy and clear to mark when this transition could be said to have been made. There was also no intermediary or outside agency involved in this process and hence transition was said to be made without any aid from outside. The transition has therefore been broadly described as natural, given the fact that the acculturation is slow, gradual and natural and that Hinduism, besides being a religion, also represents a particular mode of social framework. In fact, it is difficult to conceive of Hinduism outside this framework. Now, the acculturation process at work among the tribes is not considered to be confined to mere lifestyle but is considered to go beyond and form an integral feature of the caste structure of Hindu society. In view of such features of acculturation processes, the term structure of conversion has hardly been used to depict changes in the tribal societies. The terms that have been frequently used in the context under reference have been 'absorption' or 'assimilation' into the Hindu society. The transformation of tribes in the context under reference has thus been in the direction of fusion with the larger society, which invariably entailed loss of autonomy and identity of the tribal society. If at all there was an identity then it assumed the form of a caste identity within the wider framework of the structure of the Hindu society.

Christianity

Next to Hinduism, it is to Christianity that one can see the phenomenon of conversion of the tribes on any substantive scale. The conversion of the tribes to Christianity is spread over the length and breadth of the country. Yet, this conversion is far from even. It varies both across regions and communities. Its presence is more strongly felt among some communities and regions than others. Excepting northeast India and, to a lesser extent, the Chhotanagpur plateau of central India, the presence of Christianity among the tribes of India is by and large not strong.

The conversion of tribes to Christianity, unlike those of the non-tribal population began during the colonial rule and continues on some scale even today. Hence considerable concern and anxiety has been shown over the matter in certain social and political circles. This concern over conversion, in fact, is the real concern but it is camouflaged under the garb of the means employed, on which Christianity can easily be attacked. It is important to note that the concern over the former holds no legitimacy unless it is shown to be linked with the latter. Hence, more often than not, concern over conversion has been attacked under the garb of methods employed by the missionaries. The Christian missionaries have been accused of using methods that have invariably been considered as bad and unjustified. These methods are cited as those of inducement, coercion, fraud, etc. Now, as was the case with Hinduism, the conversion to Christianity among the tribes too took place by certain methods. These were in striking contrast to the methods adopted under Hinduism, which have already been referred to above. The characteristics of the methods were, however, more or less similar to those at work in the context of Hinduism. They were aggressive, forceful and coercive on the one hand and peaceful, free and frictionless on the other. What, however, has been most impressed upon on the public mind in the context of Christianity is that the methods adopted by it were and are invariably one of force, coercion, intimidation, allurement, etc. While the use of such means could not be ruled out both in the context of the past and present, what is important to bear in mind is that these were and/or are not the dominant patterns of conversion of tribes to Christianity in India. If these were to be the dominant patterns, Christianity would not have been able to sustain itself among the tribes, as it has been able to do for so long. The Christian missions have also been attacked on the ground that they were/are engaged in mass conversion of the tribes. The mass conversion refers to conversion of a group, en bloc. In the context of tribe, it may mean either the whole tribe or a village or segments of it. It is worthwhile to note that until recent years, there was little differentiation in a tribal village other than those based on clans/lineage. Yet, conversion on a scale of tribe or village or clan/lineage as a whole was hardly a reality. What was a reality is that significant portions of village or group of families made a decision to join the new religion. This they did either by following a kin leader or decision arrived at democratically by a group of families. The common thing in such conversion was the desire to keep and maintain social bonds of a group or families. Such conversions assumed the form of mass conversions only over a period covering many years. It is very difficult to find a lineage/clan or village that has embraced the Christianity as a whole. One can therefore hardly talk of the mass conversion of the tribes in India.

While the employment of means considered as unfair, unethical and illegal has not been altogether absent in history and may even be practised today, these do not constitute the dominant methods of conversion used by the Christian missionaries. The more common methods used by them have been, what may be called, developmental and social service oriented works. These comprised mainly, to begin with, education, health and medicine, legal aid, agricultural-credit, etc. In more recent years, they have moved to other fields as well. These range from agricultural development and harnessing of water resources to increasing articulation of the issues of the tribal people's aspiration such as autonomy, as well as those that have been drastically affecting their life, such as displacement and rehabilitation.

The extension of legal aid, in the face of distressing land alienation, in fact was one of the main methods through which conversion was sustained in Chhotanagpur during the colonial period. In fact, these methods acted as a powerful means of deliverance or emancipation of tribes from the oppression and exploitation of the rajas, zamindars and moneylenders. The methods also emancipated them from the clutches of their ignorance, illiteracy, superstition, and diseases and opened up the way for reaping and enjoying the benefits of development and modernisation. In fact, it was this emancipatory role of Christianity, especially from the exploitation and oppression of outsiders that was the moving force behind the spread of Christianity in Chhotanagpur.[10] Only when Christianity/the Christian missionaries were perceived as not going far enough in this task, viz. deliverance from the British rule that the resentment was aired and articulated towards Christianity.[11] Birsa Munda and his movement's problem with the Christian missionaries lay precisely in this.

The spread of Christianity among the tribes of northeastern India too may, to a great extent, be explained in reference to the articulation of the similar such issues inherent in the structure of their respective societies. That this may have been the case is inferred from the fact that it was the commoners that found Christianity the most attractive in this region too. At least this was the case in Mizoram and even the Khasi Hills. In both these regions, the Chiefs were opposed to conversion. It was the commoners who embraced Christianity.[12] However, once Christianity had made its foothold, there came to be other factors that drew tribes increasingly to Christianity in the later phases. In short, the methods under which conversion to Christianity took place among the tribes in India may be better summed up in Bose's observation, viz. the Christian missionaries were perhaps the first people from whom the forest tribes of Chhotanagpur could claim their rightful status as human beings.[13]

It may further be noted that any conversion invariably entails some interests. These may be material or ideal. But even when there is pursuance of such interest, it may not be without loss of some other interests. These again may be either material or ideal. Conversion was often followed by a great loss of much of the rights that the convert had earlier enjoyed in the community. The converts were often denied food, shelter, inheritance, succession as well as participation in rites and rituals of the family and the community. They were at times excommunicated from the community. There was thus both gain and loss in the conversion to another religion. It invariably entailed weighing of the pros and cons, only after which decisions were made. The fact that conversion also entails some loss is too often ignored. Even in the context of Hinduism, Bose, as mentioned earlier, refers to tribes being drawn to Hinduism in exchange for protection and social security. Conversion hence requires to be treated more as an exchange, than pursuance of a simple one-sided self or group interest.[14]

While these constitute the method under which conversion generally takes place, the conversion in Christianity is invariably, unlike in Hinduism, effected by a priest or missionary. This is in marked contrast to the phenomenon of conversion to Hinduism. Of course, the term 'conversion' is hardly used in the context of Hinduism. All the same, in the case of the Hinduism, the transition is more of a process than event. It is slow, gradual and staggered over many years. It almost takes the form of a natural process. As against this, in the conversion to Christianity, although some process is invariably involved, it is marked more by an event, hence transition from one to other can invariably be located and identified. The other interesting thing about the conversion of tribes to Christianity is that the transformation of the tribals has never been all encompassing. Rather than entailing transformation in all dimensions of social life, as has been the case with Hinduism, the transformation is expected only in a selected or limited aspect of the total social life. The change or shift was generally related with only those aspects of the social lives that were considered religious in nature or had religious overtones. Hence, while there were changes with respect to one or more of the social aspects, there were other aspects, both structural and cultural, that were common between the converts and the non-converts. The converts, for example, continued with their languages, food habits, rules, customs, traditions, etc. that were an integral part of the social organisation of tribal society. The surrender of the old was thus never total. A tribal, even when he was converted to the Christianity and was/is expected to live a particular way of life, was/is expected to do so without surrendering his membership to the wider community, whether it is described as tribe or otherwise. The transformation thus did not lead to a total breaking away from their erstwhile and traditional community. Neither did it lead to an absorption or assimilation into an alien society. This, however is not the case with Hinduism.

Religion involves both faith and practices and binds all those who adhere to it into one moral community. Conversion, as observed earlier, hence invariably led to the formation of new social groups. This had/has certain implications for groups and communities within and outside and therefore also for relationships among them. The conversion entailed observance not only of new rules and practices but also abandonment of some of the old ones of the community. Even though converts retained much of the attributes in common with those of non-converts and maintained some continuity with their traditional social structure, the changes that were enforced following conversion brought about a rupture in the relation of the converts and non-converts. This no doubt stemmed partly from the religious teachings of the new religion but much of it was rooted in the style of life that the converts imposed upon themselves. In this they were greatly aided by the missionaries. To begin with, the converts abandoned many customs and practices. At the same time they observed many others. And while they did observe these others, they did so in total isolation from the rest of the community. The missionaries discouraged and even prohibited the converts from socialising and mixing with the non-converts. Through such exclusive living the converts completely isolated themselves from the rest and formed an exclusive group. They developed a feeling of superiority vis-à-vis the non-converts and even looked down upon them. Due to the edge that the converts enjoyed over the non-converts, in respect of education, occupation and modern values and exposure, this sense of superiority further widened the gap between the converts and non-converts. The result is there is a big divide between the converts and non-converts today. Indeed there is hardly any social space left between the two to enable them to come together to revive or evolve common ties. In fact, the only platform that the two shared together were confined to the domains of politics but even here, there has come about rupture now. Both the groups had in the past rallied strongly behind the Congress. All the same, even here differences were already visible, but it had not crystallised into a distinct identity. With the erosion of the common platform, the cleavage and antagonism that was hitherto dormant had now come to the surface and the differences are now not only ideologically being articulated but also politically exploited.

Conversion and the Sangh Parivar

At the level of politics and ideology, differences have given rise to new orientation to the conception of tribes in India. The conception, hitherto dormant and latent, came to the surface during the recent attack on the Christians in India. During the course of media coverage on attacks on the Christians, it was time and again forcefully and aggressively articulated by the activists of the Sangh Parivar that the tribals cease to be tribes once they become Christians. It was also articulated that they must state themselves as Christians and not as tribes when they apply for jobs and other benefits from the government. The implication is when they become Christians, they cease to be tribes and are therefore ineligible to apply for state benefits as tribes. Now, such a conception of tribes not only goes against the general anthropological knowledge of tribes, however diverse they may be, but also against the basic conception and spirit underlying the Indian Constitution.

Individuals have been identified as tribes because they belong to a group or community who have been enumerated as Scheduled Tribes in the Indian Constitution. The groups or communities in turn are scheduled as tribes not because they practise a particular religion but because they constitute a particular community distinct from the dominant regional community. They generally speak their own languages, have distinct social organisation and way of life that is quite different from that of the regional community. They may also happen to practise their own religions. Tribes are thus differentiated from the non-tribes not only on the basis of religion but other elements, that we have referred to above. Even when they have been drawn into the larger social structure and have become considerably differentiated among themselves in terms of income, occupation, religion world view, etc. they do not cease to be members of the community they belong to, howsoever differentiated they may be. An individual enjoys the status of a tribe by virtue of being a member of a particular community and not because of the status of being an animist or Hindu or Christian. The denial of the Constitutional provision to certain members of the community just because they have come to practise another religion goes against the very spirit of the Indian Constitution.

By bringing religion at the forefront of the conception of what constitutes tribes, the Sangh Parivar shows marked continuity with the colonial tradition. Yet, there is a departure in certain respects from that tradition. In the colonial literature, tribes were no doubt conceived of in terms of religion but they were also seen in conjunction with other dimensions. What is new as far as the advocates of Hindutva are concerned is that they have begun to conceive of tribes solely in terms of religion. Yet, even here the advocates of Hindutva are different from the colonial tradition. Under the colonial tradition tribes were classified as animists and hence belonged to the religious tradition other than those of major religions of India. The advocates of Hindutva, however, conveniently overlook the fact that tribes have distinct religions of their own. They have, in fact, begun to categorize them as the Hindus.

The tendency to conceive and identify tribes as Hindus among the Hindu right is based on the observation made many years ago on the subject by G.S. Ghurye, a noted sociologist, and the Niyogi Committee Report that endorsed the observation made by Ghurye. Since then it has become a refrain among the right-wing Hindu social and political activists. This is done on the ground of somewhat similar religious observances and practices between groups identified as tribes and the backward sections or castes of the Hindu society. Ghurye, in his book, *The Aborigines "So-called" and Their Future* made arguments in justification of describing the tribes as Hindus; the expression he used was the 'backward Hindus'. The book, since then, has come into print under several editions under a new title called *The Scheduled Tribes*. He made this argument on the ground that there was much similarity between the Hindu religion and the animistic tribal religions that the two could not possibly be distinguished from one another. He made this point based not on fieldwork data collection but on observations and comments of the Census Commissioners between the period 1891 and 1931 where they had expressed their dissatisfaction over the fact that tribes were described as animists.[15] It is of course an open truth that Ghurye made his observation on very inadequate data and very selective use of the comments and observations of the Census Commissioners.

The categorization of the tribes as Hindus leads to difficulties both conceptual and empirical. To begin with, whether tribes are to be treated as Hindus is a debatable question. There are both similarities and differences in the religious practices of the Hindus and tribes. The protagonists of Hindutva, however, have conveniently overlooked the differences. Even on similarities, it is not tenable to treat tribes as Hindus. The similarities have been drawn based on two sources. One is the influence of Hinduism on tribes and the other is similarity due to the fact that both are, to a greater or lesser extent, natural religions. There is no doubt that there has been much give and take between the two religions. However, the influence of Hinduism on tribes, though necessary, is not an adequate ground for describing tribes as Hindus. The other reference made is the dimension of natural religion. As a natural religion, tribal religion shares many attributes in common as with the religious practices of tribes in Americas or Africa as with Hinduism in India. Yet, it is doubtful if the religious practices of tribes in Americas or Africa can be described as Hinduism and tribes as Hindus. To categorize tribes as the Hindus in the event smacks of cultural and religious imperialism. Just because there are some similarities, tribes cannot be denied their distinct identity and autonomy. Second, if tribes are to be treated as Hindus, then the whole historical process depicted by the historians to understand Indian civilisation is open to contest and even rejection. And so would be the case with the conceptual apparatus such that Hinduisation, acculturation, assimilation, absorption that have been developed and used to understand the dynamics of Indian society.

Hinduism is intricately linked with the structure of caste and it is not so much against religion as against caste that the social organisation of tribes has generally been posited in social science literature. This makes it impossible for a tribal to be Hindu and member of a tribe at the same time. He can be Hindu only at the risk of losing the tribal status. The two cannot go together. He can, of course, acquire new status but that is of caste rather than that of tribe. At the same time, while tribes continue to undergo changes of many kinds, these are no longer in the direction castes. The changes in the direction of caste and therefore to Hinduism had a setback, if not a halt during the colonial period, despite the fact that it opened up the floodgates for contact with people from outside. This was so mainly because Hinduism was no longer able to give protection to the tribes that Bose has referred to in the foregoing discussion. Rather, it led to domination and subjugation of tribes on the one hand and their oppression and exploitation on the other. Instead of continuing to become cooperative, as was considered to be the case, Hinduism became competitive and exploitative. In addition, there were factors that arrested this development. Of these, the administrative and political concessions extended by the colonial state, and the spread of the modern education introduced by the Christian missionaries, often with the help of the colonial state were the most decisive. While this was the case with Hinduism, the phenomenon was quite the other way round with Christianity. The Christian missionaries addressed themselves to a great extent to problems created by the movement of the Hindu population. It was hardly surprising that the tribes were getting increasingly attracted to Christianity.

By posing the issues of exploitation, oppression and domination that had come synonymous in the relationship between tribes non-tribes and by addressing such issues of health, disease, education and language. Christianity heightened the mark of identity of tribes as against those of the larger society, especially the Hindu population. It is therefore not surprising that the Christian missionaries have been accused of depriving the aborigines of their Hindu heritage or obstructing the natural florescence of the tribes towards Hinduism.

Despite this claim of natural florescence for Hinduism among the tribes, the social and political activists of Hindutva have been building up pressure, working out strategies and manipulations both at state and local levels to ensure that tribes return themselves as the Hindus and not as animists or the followers of the tribal religion in the census enumeration. Through measures such as these, tribes have been coerced and socialised to declare themselves as Hindus. This has been done by removing primarily the separate enumeration of the category of animists and minor religions, as was the practice in the census before Independence.[16] Pressures and manipulations in this direction that began during the colonial period have been maintained in the period after Independence. By ensuring the return of religion only in terms of the major religions, tribes were coerced to return themselves as Hindus if they were not the practitioners of religion such as Christianity, Islam or any other major religion.

As observed earlier, tribes were conceived of as tribes primarily against civilisations, which in the context of India were marked by Hinduism or Islam. This being the case, it is rather absurd that one could talk of reconversion in the context of tribes as the advocates of Hindutva do. They can, in fact, talk only of conversion, from tribal religion to Christianity or Christianity to Hinduism. If one were to talk of reconversion, then it would only mean conversion from Christianity/Hinduism to tribal religion.

REFERENCES

1. A.Wingate, 1997, *The Church and Conversion*, Delhi : ISPCK, p. 35.

2. G.S. Ghurye, 1963, *The Scheduled Tribes*, Bombay: Popular, pp. 1-22.
3. A. Beteille, 'The Concept of Tribe with Special Reference to India', *The European Journal of Sociology*, 27 (1986), pp. 297–317.
4. N.K. Bose, 'The Hindu Method of Tribal Absorption,' *Science and Culture*, 7 (1941), pp. 188–194.
5. C. Von. Furer-Haimendorf, *Tribes of India : The Struggle for Survival*, Delhi: Oxford, 1982, pp. 33–38.
6. A. R. Desai, 'Tribes in Transition', *Seminar*, 14 (1960), p. 24.
7. D.D.Kosambi, *The Culture and Civilisation of Ancient India in Historical Outline*, Delhi : Vikas, 1975.
8. Bose, Op.cit, pp. 188–194.
9. S.C. SINHA, 'State Formation and Rajput Myth in Tribal Central India', *Man in India*, 24 (1), (1962), pp. 35–80.
10. N.K.Bose, 1975, *The Structure of Hindu Society*, Delhi: Orient, p. 54; K.N. Sahay, 'The Theoretical Model for the Study of Christianization Process among the Tribes of Chotanagpur' in B. Chaudhary I, 1992, (ed.), *Tribal Transformation in India*, vol. 5. Delhi: Inter-India, p. 75.
11. Bose, *The Structure of Hindu Society*, Op.cit., p. 56.
12. S.K. Chaube, 1973, *Hill Politics in North-East India*, Calcutta: Orient, pp. 52–53.
13. Bose, ibid, p. 52.
14. B.P. Misra, 'The Spread of Christianity in North-East India. An Exchange of Theory of Conversion' in S. Miri (ed.), 1980, *Religion and Society of North-East India*, Delhi : Vikas. Also Chaube, pp. 52–53.
15. Ghurye, pp. 1–22.
16. N. Sundar, 'The Indian Census, Identity and Inequality,' in R. Guha & J. Parry (ed.), *Institutions and Inequalities : Essays in Honour of Andre Beteille*, Delhi: Oxford, 1999.

2

Conceptualising Religious Change Amongst Bhils of West Nimar

Kumar Sanjay Singh

Stating the issue: Proselytisation is a raging political controversy in India since its inception as a country. The Indian elite has been paranoid about the infidelity of non-Hindu religious communities. The views of the lunatic fringe of Indian politics, the RSS and the Hindu Mahasabha, are well known. But the functionaries of the Indian state also exhibited the same anxiety. In the 1950s, with the increasing political significance of the petty bourgeoisie and that of traditionalism in politics, this anxiety started getting reflected in state policy. Expressing concern at the activities of foreign missionaries, the government of Madhya Pradesh constituted the Niyogi Committee. The findings of the 'Report of the Christian Missionary Activities Enquiry Committee', submitted in 1957 are instructive. The Committee concluded that the object of these activities was to disrupt the solidarity of non-Christian society; the activities were depicted as a danger to the security of the state. The demand for a separate state by the adivasis of Jharkhand was analysed in this perspective.[1] This equation of religion with patriotism was done with even greater fervour in the case of the North-eastern states. Hindu fundamentalist organisations, which clamoured for effective checks on missionary activities, sent at least three counter-missionary missions to the North-east by the early 1960s.[2] There are, however, some liberal intellectuals who do not limit proselytisation only to the so-called non-India religions but also consider the efforts by the Hindu organisation.

Though the political value slope of the two positions is not the same, they take the same theoretical position in explaining proselytisation. It is a basic assumption of both the positions that religious transformation in the adivasi community is a result of intervention by the outside agencies, viz. the church, organisations of the Rashtriya Swayamsevak Sangh (RSS), etc. Both the positions also seem to assume that the cause of religious transformation is religio-cultural; religious transformation is viewed as a result of the actions of organisations active in the religio-cultural field. The solution to this problem is then sought in the form of countering the activities of these religio-cultural organisations in the field of religion and culture. Thus the RSS sees conversions of adivasis to Christianity primarily as a result of the activities of the missionaries (church) and seeks to counter them by its own parallel activities. The liberals see the activities of outside religious agencies as a threat to the adivasi cultural and cosmological ethos and seek to combat it by trying to restore/revive the "traditional" adivasi system of beliefs. (It ought to be noted that here one is not questioning the desirability of reviving adivasi beliefs or the sincerity of the liberal position. One is simply pointing out the theoretical premises of the belief and the political practice such a position suggests.)

There are, however, several empirical and logical fallacies in the above-mentioned theoretical position. The first and perhaps the most crucial problem with this approach is that while it adequately brings out the activities of the outside agencies in bringing about religious change—proselytisation, it is absolutely silent on the reasons for the adivasis to accept the change. When they do mention this, as the organisations backed by RSS do, they lapse to facile explanations of economic inducement, chicanery of the preachers, etc. In other words, they assume that, but for the activities of the outside agencies, the adivasis would not have undergone religious change. To the students of social science, it will be immediately evident that the presuppositions lapse into the much maligned impact-response schema of explaining social change. Much ink has been poured to indicating the elitist bias that this approach entails. In this present instance of explaining religious change amongst the adivasis, too, such elitism is evident, for it portrays the adivasis as passive recipients of a new religion brought from outside.

However, there is no empirical basis to this elitist assumption of religious change amongst the adivasis. There are several instances of religious change amongst the adivasi communities where there is no active involvement of outside agencies. There have been studies where millenarian cults emerged amongst the adivasi communities that were quite different from the communitarian beliefs of the 'traditional' religious and moral value systems of the adivasis. David Hardimann has narrated the rise of the cult of the Devi amongst the adivasis of Surat district.[3] Similarly, there was the Tana Bhagat Movement[4] and Birsa Munda[5] in Chhotanagpur. Stephen Fuch's documents several such personality-based cultic movements in Western India.[6] In the north-eastern regions of the British Empire, the cult of Jadunang emerged amongst the Rongmei Nagas.

Even in instances of religious change inspired by the activities of the outside agencies, religious change is never as smooth and complete as the approaches under critique will have us believe. There are several textures and complexities in this process that underscore the fact that there is a remarkable selectivity exhibited by the adivasis in what they accept and what they resist in the new religion. To complicate matters even further, we witness that an adivasi community, after undergoing a process of religious change, frequently sustains different and at times contradictory belief systems simultaneously. You will have to pardon me for taking a departure at this point, since I believe that I can bring out this point more sharply through the case study of religious change in West Nimar, a district in the state of Madhya Pradesh, India.

Textures of religious change in West Nimar

Social, economic and administrative setting: The district of West Nimar, located in the geo-cultural zone of Malwa, is amongst the more backward districts of Madhya Pradesh. The district is historically the part of 'Prant Nimar' that has been mentioned in ancient and medieval texts.[7] Prant Nimar was initially divided into East and West Nimar. Subsequently, in 1998, West Nimar was further divided into Khargone and Badwani districts. Historians have forwarded various theories behind the origin of the word Nimar. Since the district together with East Nimar comprised the Narmada valley from Ganjal River on the east to the Hiranpal or "Deer's Leap" on the west, the word is supposed to connote the half-way mark of Narmada River. It is argued that the root word of Narmada is 'Nim', which means half. However, the area is much nearer to the mouth than the source of the river. The other view is that the name is derived from Nemawar, the capital of Prant Nimar in ancient times, which is now located in the Dewas district.

West Nimar is a relatively more rural district of Madhya Pradesh. The district has only thirteen towns. Of these, the first seven are part of Khargone district and the rest of Badwani. The urban population constitutes a small portion of the total population and the average of the district is lower than that of the state. A vast majority of the population, constituting approximately 84–85 per cent of the district population, lives in the villages. Even the increase in the number and total population of village far outstrips the growth of urban centres and urban population. In 1971, there were 2040 villages in West Nimar with a total rural population of 1,102,017. In 1981, there were 2111 villages (of these 1836 were inhabited) with a total rural population of 1,389,767. In 1991, there were 2171 villages (of, these, 1884, were inhabited) with a total rural population of 1,722,871. By 2001, rural population of West Nimar (i.e.of Khargone plus Badwani) had increased to 2,215,622.

Being predominantly rural, agriculture is one of the mainstays of the economy in West Nimar. Agriculture absorbs roughly 80–84 per cent of the population, 60–64 per cent as cultivators and around 18–20 per cent as agricultural labour. Sub-tenancy and absentee landlordism also exists albeit on a very small scale.[8] As per the district gazetteers 1991 (data for the subsequent decade is not available as yet) the gross cropped area in the district is 6,95,700 hectares and net area sown in the year 1989-90 is 6,29,300 hectares. Wheat, rice, gram, groundnut and jowar are mentioned as the main crops. Some important cash crops such as Soya bean and cotton do not figure in the list of principal crops. For the year 2000-2001 the total area under cultivation for cotton for the state of Madhya Pradesh stood at 238 thousand hectares, which is much less than the area for cultivation of other principal crops.[9] However, it needs to be mentioned that cotton cultivation is limited to the areas bordering Maharashtra. Cotton cultivation is done on the best land. Furthermore, since Madhya Pradesh is the ninth largest producer of cotton in the country,[10] there is a number of non-agricultural activities related to cotton that are carried on in the areas of cotton production.

From the above, it can be deduced that bulk of the trading and industrial activity is related to cattle and agriculture. There are no major industries in the state,[11] except small-scale industries of PVC pipe and manufacture of iron containers. There is, however, an important segment of household industries that give employment to some 4 per cent of the working force. Some of the important household industries are tailoring, dairy and cattle rearing, basketry, earthen pottery, shoe-making, carpentry, blacksmithy, goldsmithy, production of edible oil, etc. Maheshwar is an important centre of handloom industry and produces the famous Maheshwari saris. The industry, however, has been dwindling since the last half century or so. During 1951-61, several weaver families migrated from Maheshwar. This process never stopped ever since.[12] The expected displacement of population owing to the hydel projects may just prove to be the last nail in the coffin of this industry.

There is a thriving illegal and quasi-legal trade and production activity in West Nimar. The district is an important centre of timber trade that has led to large-scale felling of forest. This often transcends the legal boundaries, as the timber lobby does not confine itself to the volume of trade prescribed in their quotas. Though the tribal practice of Nawad is blamed officially for the loss of forest cover, it is illegal felling of forest by the timber lobby that is primarily responsible for the shrinking forest. Liquor trade is also a thriving business. Government as well as private liquor shops do brisk business, as excessive consumption of alcohol is an endemic problem amongst the adivasi population. Owing to the paucity of government banks and the strict rules for granting loans from government institutions, usury is a lucrative business. It is being conducted both through semi-formal institutions as well as private moneylenders. Private moneylenders charge as high as 10–25 per cent interest per month on any loan. Even the Bhumi Vikas Bank exacts very high interest on the loan advanced. In our interviews in Ojhar, we found that the bank had exacted up to twice or thrice the principal amount as interest from the adivasis in the last 20 years. Locals also spoke of a satta racket being operated in Ojhar.[13]

The district is predominantly a tribal district. Bhils are the largest social group inhabiting the region. It is the largest tribal group in India and the bulk of them lives in regions covered by the forest-clad areas of the Vindhya, Sahyadri and Satpura in the states of Rajasthan, Gujarat, Maharashtra and Madhya Pradesh. Madhya Pradesh has the largest population of Bhils; here the Bhil and related groups are mainly found in the Dhar, Jhabua, West Nimar and Ratlam district. Dewas, Khandwa, Shajapur and Indore also has some Bhil presence.[14] As per the 1971 census, tribes constituted 39.56 per cent of the population of West Nimar, Bhil and the related tribes constituted 98.71 per cent of the tribal population.

Though Nimar is an integral part of the Bhil heartland, since ancient times it has been a part of many kingdoms and empires. The area was very important, since around Sendhwa the Satpura range lowers down and provides a pass. The area thus lies on the important historic trade route to the Deccan. It appears that the areas comprising the district of West Nimar formed a part of the Chedi and Kalchuri Kingdom. Mahismati, the capital of the Kalchuri kingdom, is identified with the town of Maheshwar. From the 9th to the 12th century, we find references to the Rajput ascendancy in the area. Inscriptions found in Mandhata and Harsud in East Nimar mention that almost the entire area comprising the district of West Nimar was being ruled by the

Parmar Kings. Malcolm opines that the Tomars succeeded the Parmars. On the eclipse of the Tomars the Chauhan Rajputs ruled the area. Maldeo was the last king of the clan and on his death Malwa became a part of various sultanates.[15]

Rajput ascendancy was established in the area in several waves. The Parmars established themselves in the 9th century. Some scholars claim that the Rajput push in the Bhil territory was a result of a series of military defeats. Doshi claims that the Rajputs came to the Aravalli after being driven away by the Boudhs, the date of which is not exactly known.[16] The Chauhan push into the Bhil area is better recorded. After the defeat of Prithviraj Chauhan, the Chauhans were finally driven out of Delhi by Muiz-din in 1192 A.D.; 2,00,000 of them migrated to Mewar and settled at Chittor in Udaipur State. On the capture of Udaipur by Ala-ud-din in 1303, a large number of them fled to the Vindhaya hills.[17] Though on the one hand the Rajput push into the Bhil areas led to intermarriages amongst the two communities, it also led to the subjugation and marginalisation of the Bhils in their own land. In Rajasthan, the feudal states of Udaipur, Dungarpur, Banswara and Pratapgarh were all formed on the Bhil territory.[18] In West Nimar too we have reference of subjugation of Bhils and takeover of their territory. Enthoven mentions Chauhan Rajput Bharat Singh, who is said to have seized Mundale, an island in the Narmada about 64 miles from Bhusaval, from a Bhil chief in 1165.[19]

From the 12th century onwards, the strategic and economic significance of the area increased and the area acquired prominence because of its being on the historic route to Deccan.[20] The area became important for empire-building activity when the Delhi Sultanate began its expansion towards the Deccan. Alauddin first appeared in the district in 1294 and Malik Kafur marched through the district in 1294. In 1370, Feroz Tughlak made over the area around Khandesh and Nimar to Malik Raja Faruki. Since 1401, the sovereign kings of Mandu and the Faruki kings of Burhanpur held most of the district. Southward expansion of the Mughal Empire under Akbar led to the inclusion of Nimar in the Subah of Malwa. In Aurangzeb's days, most of Nimar was included in the Subah of Aurangabad.

The Marathas entered the district in the late 17th century and carried depredations as far as Dharmapuri in Dhar district. In 1720, the Mughal Emperor granted to the Peshwa Chauth and Sardeshmukhi of the Deccan province, including Nimar. With the weakening of the Mughal authority, Maratha power consolidated in Malwa and Nimar, which was located between Malwa and Poona—the seat of the Peshwa. In 1738, the Nizam was forced to grant complete sovereignty of the territories between Chambal and Narmada to the Peshwa. By 1751-52, the entire southern Nimar also passed to the Peshwa. The district, in fact, had 32 *Mahals* held by the Peshwa, Holkar and the chiefs of Badwani and Dhar, though Peshwa was nominally the head. Between 1767 and 1795, Ahilyabai ruled over the *mahals* of Sendhwa and Nagalwadi. These were briefly confiscated from her in 1768 but were restored to her in 1769. By 1798, only Kasrawad Pargana remained with the Peshwa the rest of the district passed into the hands of the Holkars, Scindhias and Pawars of Dhar.

The British entered the area with the signing of the treaty of Mandsaur (1818), which handed over Mandleshwar, Kasarwad and some other portions of the district to the British. The treaty of Gwalior 1823 placed the parts of the district held by the Scindhias into the hands of the British. The district (including East Nimar) under the British had its headquarters at Mandleshwar. However, British administrative interest in the district was shortlived and between 1861 and 1968 they exchanged Mandleshwar and Kasrawad parganas with some possessions of the Holkars elsewhere in the Deccan. In the 1860-70s, however, the British developed a keen commercial interest in the area when the American civil war resulted in scarcity of cotton in Britain. During this period, the district was drawn into the vortex of commercialisation of agriculture and the vagaries of the international market in agricultural raw material, thus initiating a process of immigration of outsiders such as moneylenders, professional classes, etc. into the area. This legacy of the colonial rule still continues.

From the foregoing paragraphs, it is evident that one of the special features of West Nimar is that even though it is predominantly a tribal area where an overwhelmingly large proportion of the population is constituted of the Bhils, yet these adivasis were brought into contact with state societies from quite early times. This was largely a result of West Nimar's geological feature. The areas became a gateway to Deccan as the Satpura ranges lower down near Sendhwa and provide a pass. The geological features were instrumental once again in determining the insertion of West Nimar in the vagaries of international trade of industrial raw material and commercialisation of agriculture. Narmada Valley, which forms the central part of Prant Nimar, had the soil type suitable for cultivation of cotton and other cash crops. Hence, in the second half of the 19th century, the British colonialist chose the area along with the adjoining areas in Maharashtra to encourage cotton production.

The geological features of the district are significantly responsible in the classification of the Bhil population as well. The district has three natural divisions: (i) Parallel with the Narmada lie the well-marked belts of the Narmada valley in the centre, (ii) the Satpura range along the southern and western margins; and (iii) the narrow belt of Vindhyas scrapes along the northern boundary in the northeast. Physiographically, these natural divisions contain rich alluvial plains, forest-clad hills and also long stretches of barren plain and rocky hills. Anthropologists have used the residence of the Bhils in these physiographical features for the internal classification of the Bhils. Erskine has classified the Bhils into three categories: (i) The village Bhils (those residing in the plains); (ii) The cultivating Bhils (those residing on the fertile foothills and slopes) and (iii) The wild mountain Bhils.[21] Lok Nath Soni demonstrates how the place of residence determined the social status of the different sections of the Bhils.[22]

The importance of Lok Nath Soni's data is two-fold; first, that it is based on fieldwork, and second, it is based on the self-perception of the Bhils. Soni informs, "Bhils of Bhilkhera[23] call themselves as Tadvi Bhil and differentiate themselves from Dhankas by saying that there are two types of Bhils: (i) Bade Jati ka Bhil i.e. Tadvi; and (ii) Dhanka (bowman). The other types of Bhil are Ujale, Pitale, Langotiya, Mama, Malwi, etc. (They) have received their names through their association with areas, dress, colour and ornament worn by them. The Malwi Bhils claim to be superior to other Bhils because they are enlightened due to contact with the city people and living in the plains. They wear dhoti and shirt like the city people. They have no marital relations with the Bhils of Rath (Rath forms the greater part of Alirajpur and Jobat tehsils in Jhabua district of M.P."[24]

Religious and social reform activities: From the above, it becomes clear that West Nimar is amongst the backward districts of Madhya Pradesh. It is predominantly rural, with some agro-industries and small-scale industry. Transport and liquor trade are other lucrative businesses. The district is predominantly adivasi; dominant intruders—the Rajputs, Khaljis, Mughals, Marathas and those brought by the British, intruded through successive waves of conquest, a process that dates back to several centuries. Along with them were groups of outsiders associated with various trades and professions. Thus, the adivasis, even when they are numerically numerous, hold a subordinate position. They lack education and the cultural refinements of the dominant social groups and classes. In addition, there are certain internal social problems, the chief being the tensions and fights amongst the adivasis over *tadi, badi aur ladi* (liquor, land and women). It is these issues, viz. illiteracy, perceived cultural backwardness, and 'uncivilised' practices such as consumption of liquor and certain dietary habits that are the focus of religious and social reform activities.

During our fieldwork, we investigated the activities of three organisations working in this area, viz. the Gayatri Parivar, the Radha Swami sect and the Kasturba Kanya Ashram, Niwali. All of them are working in roughly the same area and the social base of their activities is the Bhils and their sub-groups. However, their activities give a different emphasis on religious and social reforms. The Gayatri Parivar and the Radha Swami sect are primarily religious reform movements but also include some aspects of social reform since they oppose alcoholism and practice of bride price. The Kasturba Kanya Ashram is primarily a social reform movement engaged with education of adivasi women; the ashram also opposes bride price. However, they also include Hindu religious discourses in their curriculum of activities to improve the moral fabric of their wards.

The Gayatri Parivar is a Hindu religious group. It worships deities such as Durga, Radha-Krishna and Ram, Lakshman, Sita and Hanuman. The deities are placed in temples where a priest offers worship and oblations in the prescribed manner of the liturgical texts and scriptures. The laity of the sect is considered as Brahmin. They wear a sacred thread (Ja 'Nev' oo), perform havans and recite Gayatri Mantra (a Vedic incantation) and observe ritually sanctioned fasting. Members of this sect are obliged to discard their previous religion and the rituals/ ceremonies attached to it. They have to abstain from consumption of meat and liquor and indulgence in gambling. The sect is opposed to bride price, which is considered barbaric. Instead, the sect encourages *Kanya Daan* (giving away of the girl in marriage by the father, the brother or the eldest male member in the family).

The Radha Swamy sect is also a Hindu movement but it does not believe in idol worship or in other religious practices and symbols such as sacred thread. The sect has no icons. Instead, the sect seeks spiritual guidance in the teaching of the founding guru. The members of the sect pray before the portrait of the founding guru of the sect. A Brahmin priest does not manage temples of the Radha Swamy sect; instead, a Sevak who is an expert initiate in the sect manages it. Instead of ritual and mantras, the sect emphasises guiding one's life and thought on the patterns of moral, pure and civilised society. As a sine qua non of purity abstaining from alcohol, non-vegetarian food and gambling is obligatory. As a sine qua non of civility, adivasi customs such as bride price and other forms of marriage such as *Bhagoria* (elopement) is supposed to be given up. Instead the sect encourages *Kanya Daan*.

The Kasturba Kanya Ashram seeks to turn "tribal girls into cultured ladies".[25] In this pursuit it focuses on the education, hygiene and medical care of the adivasi girls. Along with formal education, the ashram also concerns itself with the spiritual education of the girls. Prayers are an essential part of the curriculum and it figures as an important item in the list of rules of the ashram.[26] Religious festivals are celebrated in the ashram for moral and didactic purposes. "... Janmashtmi, Ganesh Chaturdashy, Dashahra, Diwali, Holi, Rakshabandhan, etc., are celebrated in the traditional way and the significance associated with the mythological tales and parables is also discussed."[27] Inmates are taken on educational trips for their greater adaptation to the outside society. The ashram also advocates vegetarianism and opposes bride price and alcoholism.

Thus in spite of the differences in the approach of the three organisations, there are some areas of consonance. The first is on the basic aim of their activity. All these organisations aim at uplifting the adivasis from their barbarism. In this pursuit they are opposed to many aspects of adivasi culture and rituals that they believe lack temperance and moderation. Second, all these organisations are opposed to the practice of bride price and endeavour to substitute it with *Kanya Daan*. Third, all these organisations are opposed to the customary prevalence of alcoholism in the adivasi community. However, in all these efforts the organisations have not achieved equal success. To some degree they have succeeded in inculcating the desire amongst their followers to identify with the markers of civilisation.

In order to gain acceptance, the adivasis of West Nimar (Bhils, Bhilalas and Barelas) are gradually metamorphosing their surnames of those groups that are considered as having a higher status. Thus, Banjirya has become Bhadle; Suliya has become Solanki; Murshya has become Mehta, Bamnia has become Brahmane, etc. However, it ought to be recalled here that such a metamorphosis of surnames is not solely a result of activities of these organisations but also the result of unequal contact between the adivasi and non-adivasi community for a prolonged period of time. During our conversation, older adivasis indicated that this phenomenon of metamorphosing surnames can be traced back to some two generations.

Similarly, their campaign against consumption of liquor and non-vegetarian food is also reasonably successful. Bishwa Bandhu Chatterjee has compiled an interesting calculation on incidence of consuming alcohol in the area of influence of the Kasturba Kanya Ashram.[28] He shows that while consuming alcohol during death feasts has not gone down substantially, yet drinking during other festivals had been reduced. Regular drinking on an individual level, while it was still prevalent, had come down amongst those influenced by the ashram. The impact, however, was diametrically opposite in the case of bride price, where there was no significant change, in spite of the activities of the ashram.[29]

Thus, we witness that the adivasi community exhibits certain selectivity in accepting the value and moral codes of the new sects. Similarly, we witness that in spite of the efforts of the sects, the adivasis do not give up every aspect of their traditional rituals and customs. Again, Bishwa Bandhu Chatterjee's work shows that while the impact on rituals associated with rain and certain forms were influenced, those rituals that were associated with the kinship structure proved more resilient. For instance, the celebration of Indal and Bhagoria went down significantly (but they were not stopped altogether). In contrast, in the life cycle rituals such as death feast, there was no significant difference.[30]

Displacing the old problematique: Even from the above critique it becomes evident that the old problematique cannot explain the different textures of religious change in adivasi community. It cannot explain why adivasis exhibit selectivity in adopting the moral and value codes of the new religion. Why do certain rituals related with life-cycle celebrations exhibit more tenacity? Why, in certain cases, do adivasis initiate millenarian and personality cults even in the absence of intervention from outside religious agencies? It follows that it is no longer sufficient to focus entirely or even primarily on the activities of outside agencies in explaining religious change amongst the adivasis. In fact, in order to take account of this phenomenon, we have to ask a new question: Why do adivasis accept/undertake religious change?

With this question we already begin displacing the first presupposition of the old problematique, which assumes that adivasis are passive recipients of religious change. There is, however, another fundamental omission in the investigation of religious change amongst the adivasis. The change is seen as a simple act of moving from one religion to another. Yet, in doing this, a much more fundamental process of the transformation of the form and function of religion is left outside the scope of analysis. When the adivasi social formation comes in contact with other social formations, what entails is not only availability of more than one religious and moral system but also the transformation of the form and function of religion in adivasi social formation. Religion no longer performs the communitarian redistribute function that is its crucial role in adivasi social formation. This transformation is so significant that it also transforms the functions of the remaining vestiges of the 'traditional' adivasi rituals.

Once religious transformation is conceptualised in this way, it is not the role of individual religious organisations that acquire analytical primacy but structural transformations that the adivasi social formation undergoes when it comes into unequal contact with other social formations such as feudalism and capitalism. It is this structural transformation of the adivasi social formation that creates the basic condition for the transformation of form and function of religion in the adivasi community. This destroys the second presupposition of the old problematique that sees religious change essentially as the consequence of activities of the outside religious organisations. Furthermore, the political prescription of this new assumption is also different now, combating religious change cannot be a cultural combat alone, but this combat has to be linked with the political struggle to transform the structures that place adivasi social formation in an unequal position.

The new problematique that we are proposing argues that the adivasi social formation and its institutions have specificity vis-à-vis feudalism and capitalism. When the adivasi social formation is brought into an unequal relationship with feudalism and/or capitalism, it undergoes a specific process of transformation that affects the institutions of the adivasi social formation. In order to understand the historical significance of religious transformation in adivasi community, we will have to take account of this transformation of the adivasi social formation. Evidently, we will have to find some criteria for the identification that fulfil four essential functions:

1. Demarcate the adivasi social formation/domestic community from other social formations.
2. Account for the various institutions/features of the adivasi social formation.
3. Account for a principle of their relationship.
4. Account for the specific dialectics of transformation of adivasi social formation.

This essentially means that I have to explain the structure of adivasi social formation and the dialectics of its transformation. This analysis will be carried out in four sections. In the first section, we will theoretically discuss the specificity of adivasi social formation and its institutions. In the second section, we will discuss the theory of the transformation of adivasi social formation. In the third section, we will analyze how the specific form that was deployed to open up the Bhils and the specific process established for their exploitation are in consonance with the theory of transformation of adivasi society. In the fourth section, we will show how this transformation impacts the social, economic and the religio-cultural sphere of the Bhils. We will show how this transformation helps us in understanding the textures of religious change amongst the Bhils and their sub-groups in West Nimar.

The Structure of Adivasi Social Formation

I believe that rather than attempting to understand a society through some formal institutions, customs or occupations, we could try to understand a society through the way it produces its material conditions of existence. For instance, in capitalism, material conditions for existence (i.e. production and reproduction of the society) are characterised by a mode of production based on a dissociation of labour from the means of production. While this definition, on the one hand distinguishes capitalism from feudalism (where labour is not dissociated from means of production), on the other it does not lead to analytical confusion when confronted with different capitalist societies with different kinds of technology used in production, or the greater or lesser preponderance of a certain sector of production.

The distinguishing feature of the adivasi social formation/ domestic community[31] is that the community ensures its continued and future existence through production of food and products that are transformed into 'human energy'. Unlike capitalism and feudalism where different dynamics of surplus appropriation intervene between the act of production and the act of consumption, in the adivasi social formation/domestic community the production of energy and of food (i.e. consumption and production) are two aspects of the same production process; one is transformed into the other and vice versa. In other words, the labourer produces food and goods that are consumed to maintain the existing members of the community and also for permitting procreation of new members.

Thus, production is carried out for the physical production and reproduction of the youth, who are the productive members of the community, and the elderly and the infant who are the non-productive members of the community. It is pertinent to point out here that the two sets of non-productive members, i.e. the infants and the elderly are not similar to the leisure class of feudalism or the propertied class of capitalism. Within capitalism and feudalism, division between the class of workers and non-workers is absolute. On the contrary, in the adivasi social formation/domestic community the division is temporal. The elderly are the past workers and the infants the future workers. A relation of reciprocal obligation exists amongst them. The past workers have earned their share by virtue of their past labour which was also used for the survival of present workers (the past infants). A share of the labour of the present workers therefore goes in fulfilling the past obligation. Another share of the labour of the present workers goes for the survival of the infants (the future workers), as an investment for the future that is to be reclaimed as an obligation. The third share goes in the continued survival of the present worker. In other words, a system of reciprocal obligation exists between the productive and non-productive members of the community.

The teleology of this mode of production is survival and multiplication of its members. However, for a domestic community to remain viable it is imperative that some sort of balance or proportion is established between the producers and the non-producers. This imperative of survival and viability presents itself as a dilemma before the domestic community. The concern of viability, i.e. the task of maintaining a balance between the producers and the non-producers means a control over human beings. In other words, there has to be a demographic regulation of the community. Demographic regulation in an adivasi social formation/domestic community amounts to a control of human energy since every human being is a repository of human energy and by virtue of that is a worker. Thus in the adivasi social formation/domestic community, demographic regulation amounts to control over production since in this mode of production control over human energy is inseparable from control of human being and by extension of production.

The concern of survival implies that food and other products are supplied adequately and regularly to the sections of producers and non-producers. Now in an adivasi social formation/domestic community, control over human energy, worker and production is the same thing; yet energy as a product does not remain tied to the individual, it takes material form in the product and circulates with it. The imperative of survival therefore requires a mechanism of redistribution of products. Thus, in the adivasi social formations there are two mechanisms at work; first, the mechanism of demographic control that structures the production, and second, the mechanism of redistribution. We will need to specify the functioning of these mechanisms. However, before we embark upon that we will take a small detour in order to specify different types of labour.

Typology of labour is a very crucial dimension in distinguishing the adivasi social formation/domestic community from other social formations. Within capitalism there are two distinct types of labour. First, socially necessary labour time, i.e. labour that is required for the survival of living labour and the repair of maintenance of existing machines, etc.

second, surplus labour time, which constitutes the profit of the capitalist and the capital necessary for horizontal and vertical expansion of capitalism. These two types of labour time are analytically distinct but they do not present themselves as such since they are included in the labour in real time performed in a single act of production.

Typology of labour under the adivasi social formation/ domestic community is distinct from this. Since this mode of production is geared towards survival and reproduction of its members, it is defined as a subsistence economy. Thus, by definition we do not have surplus labour time. On the contrary, all labour is socially necessary labour. But this labour is performed in two distinct rhythms: first, the rhythm of production and second, the rhythm of repair and maintenance of tools and other necessary conditions of production such as fishing nets, agricultural or hunting tools, build or repair dwellings, creation of bride wealth, etc. Even traditional anthropology recognises these two rhythms but demarcates them incorrectly as alternate periods of production and leisure. Thus, within the adivasi social formation we have a single labour type (socially necessary labour) performed in two distinct rhythms.

This brings us to the question of elaborating upon the mechanism of demographic control and mechanism of redistribution. As elaborated upon above, the mechanism of demographic control is linked with the question of viability of an adivasi community. The mechanism tries to retain a balance between producers and non-producers. Through this mechanism the adivasi social formation/domestic community seeks to control and regulate population. This is an imperative, since in adivasi community production can be controlled and structured primarily through regulation of demography. **How is this regulation established?**

As already mentioned above, in an adivasi social formation the relationship between producers and non-producers is based on reciprocal obligation. However, this obligation is not distributed evenly; indeed, if we analyse the chain of obligation and claims we can clearly see that the elderly, in lieu of their labour in the past, have only claims on the labour of the youth but they have no obligation. The youth have obligation towards the elderly but no claim on them; they, however, have a claim on the labour of the infants in future in lieu of the labour they perform for their survival. The infants have only obligations and no claims. Thus in the adivasi social formation/domestic community the conditions of production themselves cause the aged to be placed at the apex of relations of production, thus establishing their authority and creating a **gerontocratic** ideology. It is this structure that controls and regulates the survival and multiplication of the members of an adivasi community.

Demographic regulation requires two major operations. First, exchange of women between adivasi communities and second, maintaining the proportion between productive and non-productive members in individual households in an adivasi community. The first operation involves establishment of intercommunity relations as this underlies every marriage tie, which requires the exchange of brides between communities. The second operation sets the rules of adoption, etc. between households. In addition to these major activities that essentially ensure that some sort of equality is retained between communities and households in terms of newborns, i.e. the source of future productive members—a must for the continuation of the community; there is a third activity, that of harmonising population to production. Meillassoux has citied the work of A. Retel-Lauretin to show that most African peoples are familiar with voluntary abortion and practices of birth control. The adivasi social formation/domestic community, therefore, is not defenceless against population explosion.[32]

All these activities are linked to the basic teleology of the adivasi social formation, i.e. production of energy for survival and multiplication of its members. Multiplication of members in adivasi community is achieved primarily through biological reproduction. This necessitates marriage, which inevitably brings communities into bilateral or multilateral ties. These ties inevitably have to be based on a notion of reciprocity. Since in the adivasi social formation, human energy personified in individual person is the main motor force for production, giving away of a pubescent girl does not only amount to a loss of her labour but also of her progeny. There has to be some mechanism of ensuring that the community thus losing out on the source of labour and progeny is duly compensated. This led to the establishment of the institution of ceremonial objects that were given by the community receiving bride as a token of debt to be settled at some future date. For the community that received the ceremonial object, it became a token of claim that was to be returned to its maker once they received a bride from them. This system of exchange of bride involved individual households and community into an intricate web of relations with other communities that agree to the rule and rituals of bridal exchange. An adivasi household thus is involved in ties of relationship emerging from the father and the mother thus, providing the material basis of kinship ties, the patrilineal and bilateral relations.

Establishing this reciprocal or equivalent mode of exchange of bride is imperative for the adivasi social formation since non-egalitarian exchange of brides can create permanent asymmetries within communities. Since availability of labour is crucial for production in the adivasi social formation, a notional equality amongst communities can be maintained only if they have similar access to present and future supply of labour. In the adivasi social formation, biological procreation and economic production are closely related. Yet, they are two distinct orders of reality. Economic production is based primarily on the physical labour of the youth and is, to a great extent, predictable. Biological procreation, however, is a process that is largely unpredictable in an adivasi community. Thus, while it is possible to work out the gross output of an individual household, it is impossible for the adivasi community to reasonably predict the number of progeny per household. Since economic production and biological reproduction follow different laws, it might so happen that even though every household potentially produces the same amount of article/ human energy, it will exhibit a great variation in the number of children born.

Discrepancy between the gross output and the number of offspring in a household creates conditions of waste. As already mentioned, the distinguishing feature of the adivasi social formation/domestic community is that the community ensures its continued and future existence through production of food and products that is transformed into 'human energy'. In other words, gross production of each household gains 'value' only if it is consumed and transformed into human energy. In households with very few or no children, there will be accumulation of subsistence goods that, under the limits of the adivasi social formation, will amount to waste; accumulation means that the 'value' of the goods, since they are not being consumed, is not being realised. On the other hand, households with too many mouths to feed will not realise the productive potential of their progeny. There is amongst adivasi communities a system of moving children between households through rituals of adoption either of nephews, nieces, etc. or from households in the same community. This once again provides the basis of kinship network, lineage, etc.

Control and manipulation of population impacts every aspect of economy in the adivasi social formation/domestic community. Since human being is the source of human energy that is consumed to produce food and artefacts, control over human beings implies control over the production circuit. Since production in adivasi community is primarily aimed at production of food, etc. that is consumed to produce human energy; control and manipulation of population also ensures that wastage or under consumption does not occur. Control over population, therefore, also implies control over the consumption circuit. Control over population and production are, thus, intrinsically related processes. They are, however, also distinct. These two, admittedly related processes are in fact structured differently. Control over population is a part of reproduction relation. (This relation places an individual in ties of lineage, kinship, etc.) Elders are based at the apex of the tie; they know the order of claims and debts of bridal exchange, the rule and customs of adoption and abortion, the initiation rites (that determine the marriageable age, etc.).

Production is carried on primarily by the youth. Control over population, is an inter-generational relation, i.e. it is vertically structured. Production, however, brings into contact producers who in an adivasi social formation are of proximate age group—youth. Production relation, therefore, is laterally structured. In other words, lateral filiations allow for continuity between peoples of neighbouring age. It is these lateral filiations that provide the basis in the adivasi social formation for institutions of collective labour for achieving common goals. Indeed, according to Meillassoux,[33] institutions such as collective hunt, etc. perform the function of reinforcing collective ties and institutions in the adivasi social formation/domestic community.

Production and reproduction, therefore, even though they are related, are not co-extensive. The concern of the adivasi social formation for viability, i.e., to harmonize population to production leads to a superimposition of these two types of filiations creating conditions of a latent asymmetry in the adivasi social formation. In the adivasi social formation, harmonizing production with population is achieved through establishing control over subsistence goods, wives and children. This control, however, has an inherent and fundamental contradiction. Analysing the system of exchange of wives can best elucidate this contradiction. Women are exchanged between communities—those having surplus giving it to those having scarcity of women. This exchange has to be reciprocal if a notional equality amongst adivasi communities is to be maintained. Thus every exchange of bride creates a claim and a debt. Those receiving the bride are in debt that they have to repay in future, while those giving the bride have a claim of a bride at some future date.

Thus, like all subsistence exchange, the exchange of bride to follows the rules of reciprocity. Yet the exchange of bride is very different from other subsistence articles. In subsistence articles, the debt and claim circuit is settled almost immediately, for every exchange involves exchange of articles with similar use values. In exchange of bride this cannot happen, for unpredictability of procreation means that the possibility that at all times the two communities involving in exchange of bride will have an equal number of nubile women for exchange will be extremely remote. The cycle of claim, therefore, is stretched across time. The duration of the settlement is prolonged in direct proportion to the number of communities participating in the network of exchange. Over time, it becomes impossible to recall and/or remember these claim/debts simply from memory. Exchanges, therefore, have to be recorded in forms of materials or goods that represent the act of transfer of bride from one community to another.

These goods represent a claim. The community that gives a bride receives a symbolic good that records the transfer. At a future date, when the debtor community returns another nubile woman, the debt is settled and the role of the symbolic good as a token of claim ends. Yet, since the goods are material objects they do not cease to exist. The same good therefore can be used to procure another bride. Thereby, a situation can emerge that a community most disadvantaged in the number of nubile women could become the biggest gainer. This community has to produce the symbolic good in order to fulfil its deficiency in nubile women, but since the good does not immediately cease to exist on the completion of a claim-debt cycle, it permits a continuous cycle of transaction. Thus, communities producing symbolic goods, by reissuing the same good for bridal exchange, can acquire a wife without having to give away a woman. Furthermore, since exchange of bride is done for the purpose of procreation, the value symbolic good gets associated with the bride's potential to reproduce. Thus, the good is returned if the woman cannot have children, or returns to her parental home with her children, etc. Since the capacity to have children is limited to a period between menstruation and menopause, the family women being married for the second time are given exchange goods of a lesser value of quantity. Both these situations testify that symbolic goods have a latent tendency to acquire exchange value and do encourage accumulation. The same logic follows for storable food and cattle.

In the adivasi social formation, this latent tenancy towards accumulation and exchange value is counteracted by the mechanism of redistribution. Anthropological studies abound in examples of rituals and customs for redistribution of food and destruction of wealth. Goods that may look like treasure acquire value only if they enhance an elder's ability and/or opportunity to control and manipulate subsistence goods, women and children. These goods do not signify any real value till they are not put back into circulation for the control of reproduction, or even destruction of the goods if they seem to threaten the cycle of circulation. Thus, the mechanism of redistribution is an imperative in the adivasi social formation due to the inherent contradiction in the system of control of production and reproduction. The mechanism of production and reproduction creates conditions of latent exchange value and accumulation, i.e. wealth. However, the mode of production of the adivasi social formation is such that social control is derived not from the possession of wealth but from management of reproduction. Thus, the apparent generosity of the elders in redistribution accumulated goods and stuff through series of rituals or even their destruction.

To sum up the sketch of the adivasi social formation/ domestic community, it can be stated that the distinguishing feature of this social formation is that here community ensures its continued and future existence through production of food and products that are transformed into 'human energy'. The teleology of this community is production for survival and multiplication of its members. The process of multiplication of members, however, is not a random or an arbitrary process. In order that a domestic community remains viable, some sort of harmony has to be established in the process of production and the process of biological reproduction. This inevitably implies control and management of reproduction. Since the condition of production of the adivasi social formation/domestic community places the elders at the apex of the relation of production and paves the way for the development of a gerontocratic ideology, it is the elders who control and manage the process of reproduction. Control over reproduction implies control over human beings. Since human energy is the motor force of production and also its final product (in the from of consumption of food that is produced), control over reproduction translates into control over production in all its aspects.

Through the control over the individual, reproduction is controlled and production is structured. Thus, the process of production and process of biological reproduction are related. They are, however, also distinct. Production leads to lateral filiations while reproduction leads to vertical filiations. Reproduction relation with its vertical filiations has latent asymmetry inherent in it. This latent asymmetry does encourage accumulation. Yet, in spite of this asymmetry and accumulation, formation of wealth never reaches such a stage that it can break the subsistence nature of the adivasi social formation. This is so because accumulated goods do not signify any real value till they are put back into circulation for the control of reproduction, or even destruction of the goods, if they seem to threaten the cycle of circulation. *In the adivasi social formation, this latent tendency towards accumulation and exchange value is counteracted by the mechanism of redistribution. Customs and rituals are one of the important instrumentalities through with redistribution is achieved. Processes of redistribution are encapsulated in a series of rituals that emphasise the communitarian aspect of the adivasi community and encourage ritualised destruction of 'wealth' or its redistribution through feasts, etc. Thus, in the adivasi social formation, rituals and customs reproduce the social relations based on reciprocity and redistribution. This is the specific hallmark of religion in adivasi social formation, that distinguishes it from the religious systems of the asymmetrical social formations.*

This last derivation is important, since it establishes that while the traditional and romantic anthropological conclusion that adivasi community did not have any form of asymmetry is wrong, it also corrects the error of 'new critical' anthropology, that by indicating existence of asymmetry abdicates attempts to identify and analyze the line of demarcation between the adivasi social formation and the other social formations. The chief distinguishing feature of the adivasi social formation/ domestic community is that it is based on reciprocity, redistribution and subsistence.

Dialectics of Transformation of Adivasi Social Formation

When the adivasi social formation/domestic community is juxtaposed with feudal or capitalist social formation, the biggest challenge for these later social formations is to devise ways to break down the self-sufficiency of the former in order to incorporate it in their network of surplus appropriation. Radical anthropological literature has dealt in detail with the forms and the result of the incorporation of domestic community in the network of capitalist appropriation. In the following paragraphs, I will briefly draw upon this knowledge to elucidate the specific forms of this incorporation, the footholds that capitalism finds in the domestic community to establish its dominance and the impact of this incorporation on the domestic community.

The adivasi social formation/domestic community is articulated with capitalism in order to withdraw cheap labour and products from it. In a sense, labour is the chief product of the adivasi social formation/domestic community since the teleology of this mode of production is production for survival and multiplication of its members. The community produces products that are consumed to create human energy. The chief objective of the articulation is to harness this mechanism of production and control of human being—the agent of labour and energy—for the satisfaction of the objectives and goals of capitalism. This mechanism of production of human beings and their labour could either be harnessed in the production of industrial raw material, agro-products and 'exotica' for which there is a demand in markets, or the mechanism could be harnessed to provide cheap labour for industries. However, in order to articulate the adivasi social formation/domestic community with capitalism, the latter must break up the autarchy of the former.

Autarchy of the adivasi social formation does not dissolve automatically on contact with money based market oriented societies. On the contrary, its dissolution requires several extra-economic measures, including force, by the state. These measures, in several cases, amount to expropriation of land. Several other measures to force people to seek cash are also implemented, such as taxes, forced labour, conscription, debt, etc. These measures break the autarchy of the adivasi social formation/domestic community, force its members to look for cash that is available only in money-based economies, and establish an irreversible dependence of the community on money. There is disagreement amongst the anthropologists on the role of the state in maintaining the articulation once the autarchy of the adivasi community is dissolved. Rey is of the opinion that once autarchy of the adivasi social formation/domestic community has been broken open and capitalism takes root in the old relations, direct government coercion is no longer needed to make the adivasis produce for the market.[34]

Anthropologists who have studied tribal societies in post-colonial societies, however, do not agree to this stage-wise analysis of the role of the state in establishing and maintaining the articulation of the adivasi social formation/domestic community with capitalism. Here, the work of Geschire needs mentioning.[35] Basing his observations on the fieldwork in Makaland, Geschire emphasises the continuation of the role of the state in creating conditions of appropriation of surplus. He indicates three significant forms of state intervention:

1. Propaganda and indirect coercion.
2. Formation of marketing boards, which always manipulated prices, in order to be left with gigantic surplus.
3. Formation of co-operatives as a direct means of control, since they had the monopoly to buy up market products from tribal communities.

Geschire, thus, makes an empirical case for the continued role of state in maintaining the articulation and thereby facilitating the appropriation of surplus. There is, however, a theoretical case for this argument as well. Marx demonstrated the continued role of state and legal infrastructure in maintaining capitalist exploitation; it is therefore theoretically illogical to assume that the role of state in maintaining the articulation of adivasi and capitalist social formation will wither away once money takes root in old relations.

Even if we make a case for the continued role of state in maintaining the articulation of the adivasi social formation with capitalism, Meillassoux and Rey are essentially right in indicating that once money takes root in old relation, it leads to an irreversible dependence of the adivasi social formation on money. It pervades every aspect of adivasi social and economic life, culture, custom and rituals. Craftwork (weaving or smithing, for instance) and subsidiary activities (building, hunting, gathering) are gradually abandoned in favour of paid (or wage-earning) activities, making the domestic sector dependent for supply of essentials on market. The growth of cash economy is thus exacerbated as one item, currency, which originated in the capitalist/colonial sector and pervades every transaction even within the domestic community. This percolation of cash in the adivasi social formation shatters its autarchy, forcing the adivasi to enter the market to sell his products or his labour. Rey asserts that the dependence on cash becomes so acute that if an adivasi did not earn money, his position would become impossible, even in his own community.

As already mentioned, the compulsion to earn cash forces the adivasi to enter the market to sell his products or his labour. The form of exploitation employed in both the cases, however, is not the same. While it is true that whether the adivasi enters the market to sell his product or his labour, it in effect amounts to the transfer of cheap and unpaid labour to the capitalist sector. When the adivasi sells his product, his labour continues to be employed in agriculture or craftwork and other subsidiary activity that the adivasi engages in traditionally. However, by taking the product to the market, the adivasi transfers a portion (large or small) of his labour outside the traditional cycle of claims and obligations. In the market, the product is sold at extremely cheap prices. This happens because of two reasons.

Marx pointed out the first reason in the 1857 preface to Grundisse. Dealing with pre-capitalist peasant societies, Marx indicated that the small peasant, not subject to rent or profit limitation, exploits himself—for he is bound to sell his product below its value, even below its price of production. The second reason is that the products of the adivasi social formation are fixed at a very low price because both the capitalist market mechanism and the adivasi omit to include the labour power and value invested by the adivasi social formation/domestic community in creating a young labourer. The inter-generational costs of producing this labour are not calculated and therefore transferred free of cost in the shape of the product being sold. The cost of the good only covers the price of the individual labour. This form of transfer of free labour and cheap product is analogous to corvee labour, the capitalist replacing the feudal lord. Corvee is unpaid labour. By not paying the cost of inter-generational investment that the adivasi social formation/domestic community makes in creating a labourer, the capitalist sector enjoys a labour rent. *The mechanism of cheap sale of products is established to extract labour rent in this situation where adivasi labour continues to be deployed in its traditional sectors of production.*

The second situation is when adivasis are employed as seasonal labour in the capitalist sector. In this situation, when an adivasi is employed simultaneously in the capitalist sector, both labour rent and surplus value is produced. Empirically the labour rent does not show itself because the adivasi worker does not supply in succession his employer with one period of free labour time and one period of paid labour time. In fact rent is realised simultaneously with the surplus value and at the pro-rata of the hours of work for which the adivasi labourer is paid. Labour rent, thus is indistinguishable from surplus value but it is still there, since over a longer period than his seasonal employment the worker divides his labour power at home and the production of commodities at the factory or the workshop. The labour provided by the seasonal adivasi worker is, thus, doubly cheap. First, they are employed in sectors of production where wages are very low and they are not paid any sustenance for periods of layoff. Second, while working in a factory or workshop, the adivasi worker actually transfers that part of the labour that he would have deployed in craftwork or other subsidiary activity that is necessary for the reproduction of the adivasi social formation. Thus he transfers labour created by the generational cycle of claims and obligations free of cost to the capitalist sector.

By this migration of seasonal adivasi workers, the capitalist sector gains doubly. First, it gets cheap labour to work in areas where workers already stabilised in the capitalist sector do not prefer to work due to its low wage structure and unattractive/hazardous working conditions. Second, the adivasi labour transfers along with the paid labour time a period of free labour time, i.e. the labour that is created entirely by the adivasi social formation for which the capitalist sector does not incur any cost. But this free labour time can be extracted from the adivasi social formation only if conditions are created for simultaneous employment of adivasi labour in self-sustaining agriculture and in paid employment in the capitalist sector. *This objective is met by setting in motion the mechanism of rotating migration. Within the capitalist sector, this implies the setting of a double labour market and a system of discriminations, so that there is a systematic discharge of migrant adivasi worker back to the adivasi social formation.*

The double labour market sets out to divide the worker into two categories corresponding to the form of exploitation which they experience: first, that of workers who are integrated into and thus reproduce wholly within the capitalist sector and second, that of migrants who reproduce themselves partly within and partly outside the capitalist sector. This double labour market is sustained by a series of discriminatory practices. The first major discrimination is the distinction between direct and indirect wages. Direct wages are paid on the pro-rata of hours of work. Indirect wages are family allowances, unemployment benefit, accidental benefits and health and medical allowances, pension, etc. Indirect wages are disbursed between integrated and migrant workers in discriminatory ways. The second major discrimination is the policy of maintaining low wages in certain sectors thus making it unattractive for integrated workers, who, since they are solely dependent on market of survival, could not afford to work on such meagre wages. These avenues are then attractive only for those workers who can rely on the support of their kinsfolk for survival. Sectarian and exclusivist ideology such as racism, bigotry, etc. is used to reinforce, guide and facilitate the operation of the double labour market.

The rotation of migrant adivasi workers is thus achieved by these forms of discrimination, which by depriving them of both social and job security force them to return home. This process, even while it creates the conditions of continuous transfer of free labour time, forms the adivasi social formation to capitalist sector with every fresh cycle of migration; it also creates a deep insecurity within the adivasi migrant workers. The dynamics of rotating migration ensures that the migrant adivasi worker never gets organically integrated within the capitalist sector. Thus the worker now requires the continued presence of and production within the adivasi social formation, so as to be able to receive sustenance during the period of lay-off and to maintain the economic structures that allow him to offer his labour cheaply to the capitalist sector. This is what allows the adivasi social formation to survive, despite its low productivity, even embedded within the capitalist system.

The articulation of the adivasi social formation with capitalism is inherently unstable. It leads to the subordination of the adivasi social formation and also triggers certain mutations and transformations within it. This statement appears to be in apparent contradiction with the conclusion arrived in the preceding paragraph. But the dialectics of mutation/transformation, as inaugurated through the articulation of the adivasi social formation/domestic community with capitalism, does not lead to the liquidation or dissolution of the former. On the contrary, institutions that enable the extraction of cheap labour from the adivasi social formation/domestic community to capitalism are retained and consolidated. Other institutions, however, are destroyed or allowed to decay over time. These latter institutions are those sustaining lateral filiations and the redistribution mechanisms within the adivasi social formation/domestic community.

It will be necessary to briefly dwell upon this dialectics of consolidation and transformation. In other words, it is necessary to plot in brief the effects of the articulation of the adivasi social formation/domestic community with capitalism. The adivasi social formation/domestic community is articulated with capitalism by opening it to cash in order to extract cheap labour, either in form of products or of migrant labour. This extraction of labour and permeation of cash are the motor force of the dialectics of consolidation and transformation of different aspects of the adivasi social formation. Once the autarchy of the adivasi social formation/domestic community is broken the adivasis are forced to sell either their products or their labour. In either case it leads to the transfer of cheap labour. Such a transfer of labour is stressful for the adivasi social formation/ domestic community since, as indicated above, this social formation does not have any surplus labour—all labour is socially necessary labour.

Transfer of labour both as migrant labour or as a cheap product creates an imbalance between local subsistence resources and population of the adivasi social formation/ domestic community. The impact of migration of labour on the productivity of adivasi community, thus leading to an imbalance of subsistence resources and population is obvious. Physical absence of labour, even in the non-agricultural season, adversely impacts the production of crafts and other subsidiary activities that are required for the reproduction of adivasi society. This loss of productive capacities of an individual is never compensated by the wages earned. As we have already pointed out, the wage paid to the migrant labour only includes the pro rata payment of per hour of work of an individual labourer. It does not take into account the inter-generational investments that the adivasi social formation incurs in creating a young labourer. Furthermore, a migrant labourer spends a growing proportion of its wages in buying his daily needs in the market during his stay in the factory or workshop. The size of this portion of wage is directly proportional to the gap between the wages and prices in urban centres and the gap between the subsistence resource and population within an adivasi community arising from migration.

The impact of selling the products of agricultural, craft or subsidiary activities, however, will require some explaining. Transfer of products from the adivasi social formation/domestic community cuts into its social surplus thus undermining its capacity to sustain its population. This tendency is further exacerbated when under the compulsion to procure cash, the nature of production shifts from subsistence to cash crop. This means that now the imbalance between local subsistence resource and demographic growth can only be restored by an increased dependence for food on the market, i.e. the capitalist sector. The transfer of cheap labour either in the form of migration or product thus creates an imbalance between subsistence resource and population. The resultant food shortage pushes the adivasi into insecurity. Confronted with an insecure future the adivasi community tries to get over this through its traditional mechanism. As argued above, that future was provided for in the adivasi social formation/domestic community by procreation—children being the future producers. This hope of children providing for in the old age results in increased natality, the resultant increase in birth rate is proportionate to the crisis in domestic economy. The net result, however, is that the balance between subsistence resource and population could become so disturbed that abject poverty and shortage of food sets in to a point where physical reproduction of workers is put at risk.

The transfer of cheap labour affects the viability of the adivasi community. In order to restore the viability of the adivasi community, balance has to be restored between production and population. The historical imperative for the continuation of adivasi social formation is created by the very fact of articulation of the social formation with capitalism. Capitalism needs the available supply of cheap labour that the continuation of the adivasi social would ensure. Even the migrant labourer needs it, since the adivasi social formation provides him sustenance during periods of layoff and also enables him to sell his labour cheaply. This double imperative, which is historically determined by the very act of articulation, means that the institutions that maintain the viability of the adivasi social formation by maintaining a balance between production and population tend to be reinforced. As discussed above, balance between production and population was maintained through the mechanism of control over population. The elderly controlled this mechanism.

Let me now briefly restate the mechanism of maintaining the viability of an adivasi community. Viability in an adivasi community in the traditional situation was maintained by devising a mechanism of overcoming shortages of nubile women and children. The necessity to exchange nubile women and adoption, etc. not only established the control of the elderly over reproduction, but also involved an individual household in ties of lineage and kinship. Thus, these ties under the control of the elderly played the function of moving population in order to maintain a balance between production and population. The lineage and kinship structure, which is a vertical (i.e. intergenerational) relationship, under the control of the elderly, controlled reproduction. Since human being was the repository of human energy—the motor force of production in adivasi social formation/domestic community, control over human beings amounted to a control over production. Production and reproduction therefore are related in adivasi social formation. They are however not co-extensive. They are related but distinct; while reproduction is structured through vertical filiations of kinship ties, production is structured through lateral filiations of proximate age groups. Traditionally, balance between production and population was established by moving nubile women, progeny and by exercising control over procreation (i.e. practices of voluntary abortion and birth control).

It is this mechanism of viability of adivasi social formation/ domestic community that is retained and consolidated when adivasi social formation/domestic community is articulated with capitalism. However, in the process of consolidation, the mechanism undergoes a certain mutation. Traditionally, the mechanism of viability was constituted by the superimposition of two related but distinct relations. The reproduction relation, i.e. the vertical filiations of intergenerational ties—the kinship and lineage ties, and the production relation, i.e. the lateral filiations of the proximate age group—the workers who are drawn from the proximate age group, viz. the youth. Balance between production and reproduction was retained essentially by manipulation of the reproduction cycle so that adivasi communities did not a face population surplus or deficit. This was so because traditionally, other things remaining equal, the quantum of production could be predicted with reasonable certainty. Procreation, however, was the uncertain phenomenon in the adivasi community. Traditionally, therefore, the attempt at making an adivasi community viable focused on controlling procreation.

The process of articulation of adivasi social formation/ domestic community with capitalism alters this situation. By withdrawing cheap labour from the adivasi social formation/ domestic community, now not only biological reproduction but also production is thrown into uncertainty. For, production now no longer depends on the productive potential of human energy, it becomes dependent on the quantum of labour withdrawn from the adivasi social formation/domestic community. In this changed situation, balance between production and population cannot be retained simply by controlling biological reproduction. Indeed, in the new situation, balance between production and population becomes increasingly dependent on the capacity of an adivasi community to divide its workers between the domestic and capitalist sector of production, and to compensate for the loss of production from one sector to the other.

It entails that the control of the elders that was exercised through the vertical filiations over biological reproduction now extends over production as well. Thus, through the very act of consolidation of the mechanism of viability, we witness the increasing dominance of vertical filiations over horizontal filiations. Uncertainty of production, owing to transfer of labour either in the form of products or migration, creates the basis for increasing control over the amount of workers to be transferred to the capitalist sector. This leads to the enhanced control of the elders over production. At the same time, under the impact of migration, the lateral filiations of production relations suffer erosion. In order to make up for the deficit created by transfer of labour, either in the form of product or migration, people previously idle (i.e. children and elderly) are pulled into the production process. Thus, the act of articulation creates the condition of consolidation and mutation of mechanism of viability of the adivasi social formation/domestic community; lateral filiations of production relations are eroded, even while vertical filiations of control over population is extended over production as well.

The position of the elders, who are at the apex of the inter generational ties is therefore consolidated. Anthropological case studies demonstrate that this inter-generational relation with the elder at the apex provides the strongest foothold for capitalism in the old relations once the autarchy of the old mode of production is broken and cash permeates its various institutions and processes. With cash permeating every aspect of the adivasi community, they soon replace ritualised objects in bride prices, initiation ceremonies, rituals of birth, death, etc. The elders then use their authority to send the youth to the capitalist sectors to earn cash necessary for these functions; these functions however consolidated the authority of the elders over the community. Here it will be of interest to refer to the study of Jos M. van der Klei.[36] Van der Klei demonstrates that when the autarchy of the Diola of Senegal was ruptured as a result of the policies of the French government, the traditional cycle of exchange between the Diola and the neighbouring communities was disrupted. Consequently, the supply of prestige goods dried up as now there was no demand for the goods traditionally produced by the Diola, viz. rice and slaves. This supply was re-established when young Diola, instead of using their labour-power for producing a surplus within the traditional mode of production, were sent out by the elders to work as migrant labourers in the groundnut fields of the Gambia and Central Casamance. The money earned was partly spent on purchasing loincloth, etc. on the spot and partly to purchase cattle from the Fluani people, for which they had to walk for over two hundred kilometres. On return, these goods were handed over to the elders. Thus the supply of prestige goods was re-established.[37]

This study underscores three important processes. First, that once the autarchy of the adivasi social formation/domestic community is broken by state policies, cash takes roots within the old relations. Second, that the rupture of the autarchy of domestic community consolidates the authority of the elders, who now not only control production through the control over the reproductive cycle, but also directly control production by determining the division of youth workers between the domestic sector and the commercial sector. Third, it is the authority of the elders that provides the internal reasons for the transfer of labour from the domestic sector to the commercial sector. Thus, it can be stated with a modicum of certainty that the articulation of the adivasi social formation/domestic community with capitalism consolidates and exaggerates the asymmetries within the former. At the same instance, it erodes the institutions and practices that provide the countervailing tendency towards egalitarianism within the adivasi social formation.

The articulation of the two modes of production thus results in making the adivasi social formation/domestic community more asymmetrical. The adivasi community becomes more unequal. This tendency towards asymmetry is not confined to the internal structure of the adivasi community; even the relationship between adivasi communities becomes more unequal. This can best be illustrated in the mechanism of bridal exchange. When bridal wealth goods acquire a market value outside, as when, for example, it consists of ivory, gold or other precious materials desired by the traders, or when money becomes the medium of bridal exchange; bride wealth producers become capable of obtaining women from communities outside those that accept the rules of reciprocal bridal transfer, in exchange for merchandise circulating under the guise of bride wealth. Once the matrimonial circuit is opened up in this way through the introduction of communities increasingly foreign to it, the final matrimonial settlement is endlessly delayed. Thus the latent asymmetry in bridal exchange in the traditional system, which we had mentioned earlier, now becomes an actuality. Here, Terray's findings on the Dida of Senegal is specially significant, for he indicates that under the influence of trade and cash crop the Dida community shows signs of hierarchisation of lineages via matrimonial procedures. Exchange of bride wealth is no longer a token of exchange of women. Indeed, he points out that the supposedly 'normal' marriage procedure of returning the bride wealth received from giving a bride to gain a bride now constitute only a minority of cases (37.8 per cent).[38]

In other words, articulation of the adivasi social formation/ domestic community with capitalism breaks the autarchy of the former. In this process, cash takes root in the old mode, thereby paving the way for withdrawal of cheap labour either in form of products or of human migration. Withdrawal of cheap labour is ensured by the mechanism of having cheap prices of products of the adivasi social formation and of rotating migration, which ensures that there is a systematic discharge of migrant adivasi worker back to the adivasi social formation. This withdrawal of cheap labour creates an imbalance between production and population. This leads to the consolidation of the inter-generational relation, which has the elderly at its apex, since these relations traditionally performed the task of maintaining balance between production and population. The articulation of the two modes of production leads to the consolidation of the control of the elderly and the vertical filiations of the intergenerational ties, even as it weakens the lateral filiations of the production relations. The result is increased asymmetry in the internal structure of the adivasi community. Introduction of trade, cash and increased control of the elderly also leads to asymmetrical relationship between the adivasi communities. Inter-generational relations with the elderly at the apex prove to the strongest foothold of capitalism in the old relations and studies indicate that elderly, driven by the motive to increase the supply of cash, now a necessary medium in bridal exchange, initiation rites, rituals of birth, death, etc., provide the internal levers for initiating migration of young workers from the domestic to the commercial sector.

Impact of the transformation on religion: The dialectics of consolidation and mutation/transformation of the adivasi social formation that is dictated by the very fact of its articulation with capitalism results in the continuation of the adivasi social formation/domestic community, albeit in a transformed form. Now institutions of control are retained and consolidated while the institutions of egalitarianism and redistribution are either weakened or allowed to decay. We have already indicated that while the vertical filiations that enhance the control of the elderly are retained and consolidated, institutions and processes related to redistribution are also weakened or are supplemented. As indicated above the institutions of redistribution offset the tendency towards accumulation in the adivasi social formation/domestic community. Processes of redistribution are encapsulated in a series of rituals that emphasise the communitarian aspect of the adivasi community and encourage ritualised destruction of 'wealth' or its redistribution through feasts, etc.

The dialectics of consolidation and transformation impacts upon these rituals and we witness emergence of, within the adivasi community, rituals providing codes of existence that are antithetical to the communitarian principals of the adivasi social formation/domestic community. Several anthropological studies have indicated this development. For our purposes, the work of van Binsbergen is especially significant as it identifies the emergence of different cults, each organised differently and upholding a different set of values and activities, amongst the Nkoya people of the Litoya valley of Zambia.[39] Furthermore, he links the emergence and co-existence of this plurality of rituals and religions to the distinct logic of distinct modes of production articulated in the Litoya valley.

Based on the ethnographic data of the Litoya valley, van Binsbergen shows that there existed amongst the people of Nakoya tribe at least five major ritual forms. Each had its own pattern of activities, its own pattern of control over people and material resources, and pursued a distinct idiom featuring different supernatural entities, interpretations of human misfortune and ways of redress. Some cults stressed morality. Some had a strongly communalist view of the human individual in that the misfortune of one of the members was supposed to reveal a moral crisis affecting the entire group (ancestral cult). Others would look at misfortune as a purely individual, accidental and a moral circumstance, to be redressed by appeasing the vagrant spirit that had allegedly taken possession of the patient (non-prophetic cults of affliction). It will be different to explain the co-existence of so many cults with mutually irreducible logics in simple functionalist terms, viz. the so-called 'functions' they performed in maintaining the cohesion of society, because these cults were too rigidly compartmentalised to be seen as performing a functionally integrated role.

In fact, this religious plurality was related to the distinct logic of the modes of production articulated in the Litoya valley of Zambia. Ancestral ritual was an ideological component of the adivasi social formation (Binsbergen calls it the lineage mode), while rain ritual was the ideological component of the tributary mode. The individual-centredness of cults of affliction, prophetic cults of affliction and Christian churches and sects, their lack of reference to communitarian production activities such as hunts, etc., their veneration of invisible entities without local referents, their more or less bureaucratic organisation (esp. of the prophetic and Christian forms) and the extensive circulation of cash in them suggested a dynamic beyond the local horizon—the process of articulation of the adivasi social formation/domestic community with capitalism and the tributary mode.

The process of articulation of modes of production thus dictates every aspect of the opening up of the adivasi social formation to the logic of capitalism.

Specific forms of exploitation of the adivasis and its impact

Forms of exploitation: Bhils and their sub-groups have been opened up for exploitation since the medieval period. In the 10-11th century, when the Rajputs entered the Bhil areas, in the 13th century Alla-ud-din Khalji, subsequently the Moghuls and in the 18th century when the Marathas began to occupy Central India. This period witnessed the emergence of a relationship between the conquerors and Bhils based on tributes and services that culminated in the development of the chakrani system. This system affixed hereditary services (both material and ritual) based on birth on different communities. These services linked the adivasis in an unequal relationship. In return for his services, the person is accorded some benefits.

Some studies are available on the functioning of the chakrani system. In an anthropological study on the Bhilkhera village in West Nimar, the functions and benefits attached to different services have been elaborated upon. Patel is the post of the village headman; he is also the ritual head of the village. He also helps the government officials during their visit and collects land revenue from the villages. As remuneration he gets 6.25 per cent of the land revenue. The post of Patel in the Bhilkhera village has been continuing in a Bhilala village for past several years.[40] Similarly, the post of chowkidar is retained in a Nahal Mankar family. For the performance of his duty, he was allotted a plot of tax-free land. In British and post-British India, the modern administrative apparatus was superimposed on this pre-existing chakrani system, for instance in the Padalya village (a tribal village in Maharashtra that borders MP), Narawan Balai was the chakran. He was allotted 15 bighas of land without tax. He also assisted the government officials in the chowkidari. Similarly, the Patel also functions as a semi-government official and maintains law and order in the village with the help of the local officials.[41]

Almost simultaneously with the intrusion of the invaders from the 9th-10th century onwards, came in money economy. The moneylenders entered even the interior tribal villages. The grip of the moneylenders strengthened through the length and breadth of Bhil country and led to the origin of a system of debt bondage. This system was known as Sagri in Rajasthan, Halia in Gujarat and Naukarya in Madhya Pradesh.[42] Even though the system was initiated in the early medieval period, it has continued uninterrupted till now. During our fieldwork, one of the office bearers of AMS, Mr. Moti Ram related that he had worked as a 'Naukar' of a Bania (Ballab Das Aggarwal). He worked in his fields and did all the chores related to agriculture—ploughing, harvesting and storing seeds. For this backbreaking work, he was paid Rs. 5,500/- (five thousand five hundred only) per annum.

During the British period, the penetration of the intruders in Bhil area as well as that of moneylenders increased manifold. British interests in commercialisation of agriculture, especially in the 1860-70s for production of cotton pushed farmers from Maharashtra in the Bhil areas of Rath (Rath forms the greater part of Alirajpur and Jobat tehsils of Jhabua district, Madhya Pradesh). Inducement of debt was also used to encourage cotton production. The plight of the Bhils under debt bondage and dispossession is also noted by the Dhebar Commission (1961:11), which states, "A large number of Bhils who have no land, have migrated to nearby towns as labourers. Economic destitution has led some of them (Bhils) to work under a system of bonded labour by which not only they but the members of their families are pledged to render service to redeem their debts."

As per the recommendations of the various commissions, banks were set up to ameliorate the conditions of the co-operative. However, this did not result in securing the rights of the Bhils since the procedure for obtaining loans from the bank is slow and complicated, and securities are demanded, which the Bhils are not able to furnish. Furthermore, with the penetration of money in the Bhil social life and custom, etc. the requirement of money is not restricted to agriculture.[43] However, the bank loans are restricted to needs connected with the farm; they are not granted to help out in personal needs. Unlike the banks and the government co-operatives, the moneylender readily offers loans without any formalities and complicated paper work. Furthermore, they maintain personal contacts with the adivasi and frequently live in the same area, speak the local dialect and understand the family and cultural background for the required loans. Thus the grip of the moneylender amongst the Bhils continues to be strong.[44]

A few words of explanation on the category of the moneylender. In the adivasi area money lending is not necessarily a distinct occupational category. The major source of cash has always been the bania in the village. In fact, one can find their presence even in the most obscure villages. But they are not the only source of loan to the adivasi. The liquor seller or even the flourmill owner practises money lending. The jewellery shop owners also lend money. The category of moneylender, therefore, is a very broad one. All those who indulge in this practice, however, share some traits. Money is lent at very high rates and recourse is taken to dupe the adivasi into paying much more than the required sum.

The twin onslaught of the intrusion of outsiders and money had an interrelated but apparently contradictory impact on the Bhils. There is enough documentation and studies to show that with the penetration of the Rajputs and the subsequent invaders, the Bhils were dispossessed of land (if not entirely, at least of better quality land). Ironically, this twin pressure also resulted in tying the Bhils to the land. Competition over land from the intruders and the increased need for money in the Bhil economy resulted in the shift from food gathering, hunting and shifting cultivation economy to settled agriculture. In his study on the Bhils of Dangs, Furer-Haimendorf has stated that basically the Bhils were a tribe of food-gatherers and slash and burn cultivators. Now, however, a majority of Bhils practise settled agriculture.

Dispossession of adivasi land took three principal forms. The first was by military invasion in the medieval period. In this period, force of arms played the dominant role in pushing the Bhils off their land. The dominant intruders took possession of the better cultivable lands. The Bhils were pushed into interior forests where land for cultivation is sparse and scarce.[45] The second form was under the British who were propelled by the imperative of commercialisation of agriculture and the need for cotton. During the period of the American civil war, farmers from Maharashtra were settled in the Bhil areas of Rath (Rath forms the greater part of Alirajpur and Jobat tehsils of Jhabua district, Madhya Pradesh). The third form is the most contemporary, where dispossession of adivasi land is going on through a more roundabout way of indebtedness. In fact, Stephen Fuchs' study on Jhabua shows that indebtedness was primarily responsible for the transfer of the best fields to the non-adivasi.[46]

The above picture seems to confirm Rey's evaluation of the different forms adopted in different stages of the opening up of an adivasi community for exploitation. According to Rey, the role of state in opening up the adivasi community is short and transitional, when force is required to break open the adivasi community so that money can take root within it. Once money takes root, the autarchy of the old production community is shattered and they are automatically forced to sell their products and labour. Geschiere has opposed this stage-wise analysis of the role of the state and had argued that the state continued to play a significant role to ensure the continued subordination of the adivasi community.[47] We had stated that Marx had theoretically argued against this stage-wise diminishing of the role of the state in reproducing exploitation. The existing literature and our field work confirms that even after money took root in the Bhil community and indebtedness became one of the primary means of transfer of land from the adivasi to non-adivasi, the role of the state in facilitating this transfer is crucial.

Our field work further confirms the continued role of state in articulating the adivasi social formation with feudalism and capitalism. We find that the forms the state adopts in maintaining the articulation are primarily non-formal and extra-legal. Unfortunately, Geschiere overlooks this dimension of the state activity. While elaborating upon the forms of state's intervention, Geschiere identifies three distinct forms[48]:

1. Propaganda and indirect coercion.
2. Formation of market boards that always fixed prices below the market value of commodities so that the boards were left with a gigantic surplus.
3. Formation of co-operatives to control production and monopolise purchase of products.

In the Bhil areas too, we find such formal interventions by the state. In the 1970s the Maharashtra Cotton Federation was formed, which fixed the cotton prices. However, since the prices were below the prevailing market rates, the cotton producers began selling their products in Sendhwa. This resulted in the rise of Sendhwa not only as an A-grade Krishi Upaj Mandi (KUM), but also a centre for industries based on cotton, such as ginning mills and oil pressing mills of cotton seeds.

We find similar interventions by the state in the area of land alienation. In 1960, a land enactment was promulgated. Under 170 (b) of the Revenue Act of the Constitution of India, adivasi land may not be sold/mortgaged to a non-adivasi and all land of the adivasis, thus alienated after 1960, would be restored to them. These interventions may appear as paternalistic measures by the state to secure the rights of the adivasi. Yet they have resulted in the adivasi's getting even more marginalised. **How does one take account of this paradoxical effect of the state's intervention?** Stephen Fuchs[49] suggests that the continued transfer of the land of the adivasi community to the non-adivasi is the result of the loopholes in the land enactment of 1960. He further opines that such loopholes can be found in every law. However, he does not dwell upon the structural implication of the existence of loopholes in every law.

Here the work of Meillassoux[50] is of particular interest. In the review of his hugely significant work in the preceding section we had indicated that maintaining rotating migration is one of the chief ways in which capitalist countries ensure a perpetual supply of chief labour force from 'domestic community'. Meillassoux further argues that this rotating migration is ensured by a series of ideological and policy measures such as racism, xenophobia, temporary residence or work permit in conjugation with turning a blind eye to illegal immigration, etc. Meillassoux argues that deployment of such stated and un-stated measures "leave the immigrant worker vulnerable to the hazards of police, administrative and employers' control and make it easier to fix their length of stay in accordance with the needs of economy". Meillassoux thus emphasises that while reading state policies, one cannot simply take recourse to ad hoc arguments such as that of pointing out loopholes in a policy. Instead, Meillassoux claims that there is a structural logic that can be seen in the deployment of the combination of state policies and unstated activities of the state.

Three conclusions can be drawn from Meillassoux's analysis:

1. That state policies are there to increase the control of the state over the 'domestic community' (i.e. in our case, adivasi community).
2. That these policies have the function of strengthening the logic of economy.

3. That, in order to understand the structural logic of state policies, we have to study them thematically, i.e. study policies dealing with a particular issue in their connectedness.

Since here we are trying to understand the Land Enactment of 1960, in order to understand the ways in which it acts in cementing the articulation of the adivasi social formation with capitalism, we will have to read it with other policies that impact on the land rights of the adivasi community. The Land Enactment of 1960, though promulgated to safeguard the land rights of the adivasi, permits it under certain circumstances. Under 170 (b) of the Act, that calls for the restoration of all land alienated from the adivasis after 1960, also mentions that the land can be alienated if special permission is acquired. This Act is accompanied with two other important legal promulgations. The first is that on the event of the death of an adivasi his legal heir acquires the title to the land only if the *patwari* transfers the land in his name. The second is that the forest officials have the power to determine that whether the land reclaimed from forest for cultivation (*nawad*) is valid or not. Under a provision of the Forest Conservation (Amendment) Act of 1988, adivasis could be evicted from forestland. The net result of these policies is that not only the control of the state over the land right of the adivasis is established, but also, this allows for possibilities of manipulating the Land Enactment of 1960, thus enabling the continued transfer of adivasi land to the non-adivasis.

Provisions of these laws, together with patent illegality, are used to enable continued alienation of adivasi land. In our fieldwork, we found evidence of this on several occasions. We will elaborate upon some of the typical cases to make our point.[51] We found that indebtedness is one of the main causes of land transfer. However, this is possible on such a large scale because of manipulations in the mutation of the ownership records. Through these manipulations, the land is transferred in stages from an adivasi to a non-adivasi. Since transfer of land from adivasi to non-adivasi is not permitted, land is first transferred to a pliant adivasi, thus making the non-adivasi a *benami* holder of land. In some cases then, land is mutated to the non-adivasi in lieu of some illegal gratification. In some of the villages in our field study, land was also taken over by the forest department.

Several cases of manipulation in the mutation of the land records were narrated to us in the interviews conducted in the field. We will mention some of the cases that we came across in Ojhar. Gulal of Chaudharypura phalia of Ojhar sold 18 acres of his land for six thousand rupees (Rs. 6000 only) to the Mahajan Basantilal. However, the land was registered in the name of Nahal Singh, an adivasi of Bhorwada village. In the same village Mangilal sold twelve acres of land to Chotalal the oil merchant, which was registered in the name of another adivasi. (During the time of the fieldwork, these transfers were being challenged in the court.) The extent of corruption and official collusion in these land transfers can be gauged from a case that happened in the Chaudharipura phalia of Ojhar, some two years before the fieldwork. Here, Bhilala adivasi Situ owed the village mahajan Bansidhar Narayan some money. Mr. Narayan, in order to recover the money, got 16 acres of Situ's land transferred to another adivasi Kandu, by using an impersonator to pose as Situ. However, when the case came up, the land was reverted to Situ.

There are also cases when, subsequent to the land's being transferred from debtor adivasi to a pliant adivasi the moneylender gets the land mutated in his own name. In Ojhar, Gal Singh owed the local merchant Punya a sum of four thousand rupees (Rs. 4000 only). Consequently, in 1969, Gal Singh had to sell seven acres and 67 deci. land to Nahal Singh, who was the merchant's front man. However, in 1971 Punya got the land mutated in his own name. Under pressure in 1983, Punya once again transferred the land in the name of Nahal Singh but again, in 1988, the land was retransferred in his name. Gal Singh filed a case against Punya in 1995 but till mid January 1999 it was still going on. There are similar cases of land transfer in other villages AMS activists inform of 25 acres of land being restored to the adivasis due the efforts of the organisation in Borli and Jamli. The activists also mentioned cases where the forest department took over adivasi land. In

Sahapura, the forest department set up plantations on 15 acres of adivasi land, however this was reverted when the AMS intervened. Similarly, in Rupla, Khazan and Risla 32 acres were taken over by the forest department but once again activists of the AMS successfully intervened in the case.

Thus, introduction of money creates the condition indebtedness that leads to alienation of land from the adivasi. Earlier we had demonstrated that introduction of money led to an interrelated but apparently contradictory process; while on the one hand it led to alienation of land from the adivasi community, it also tied the adivasi to land. We demonstrated that, owing to the twin intrusion of outsiders and money, the Bhils gave up shifting agriculture and took to settled agriculture. In fact, now we will demonstrate that the changes in the nature of agriculture is not only that of shifting from shifting agriculture to settled agriculture, but also of increasing emphasis of producing for the market. Thus we can argue that introduction of money not only leads to transfer of land but also leads to a significant transformation in the nature of agricultural production of the adivasis. However, before we go into the full implication of the penetration of money it will be pertinent to point out the reasons for the penetration of money in the adivasi community.

Money was introduced amongst the adivasi community, initially to pay tribute or taxes to the medieval or modern conquerors, it soon takes root in the adivasi exchanges as well. Money, that is always a scarce commodity within the adivasi social formation and yet the primary medium for relationship and exchange with the dominant social formations, acquires a singular prominence and soon replaces the other totemic and symbolic goods as token and markers of exchange within the adivasi community. Totemic and symbolic goods are gradually replaced by money in ceremonies and rituals of marriage, birth, death, etc. In the Bhil areas, the prominence that money has acquired can be gauged from the fact it has become the prime medium on which most important rituals are based. Several anthropological works state the increasing importance of money in adivasi rituals.

In 1961, the Dhebar Commission states that bride price in Rajasthan was not less than Rs. 300 (Rupees three hundred only). For West Nimar, a very helpful table was prepared by Bishwa Bandhu Chatterjee in his study to analyse the Kasturba Kanya Ashram.[52] This table becomes especially significant since it is conducted in villages where the Kasturba Kanya Ashram along with certain other organisations such as the Gayatri Parivar and the Radha Swamy sect are influential. All these organisations have advocated against bride price. Yet, in spite of this, the table shows a secular increase in the quantum of bride price. Bishwa Bandhu Chatterjee concluded, "The most significant and unambiguous trend... is that the range or level of payment for dowry ...has registered a systematic rise from pre-1965 to post-1965 period. It has increased anywhere from 50 to 100% or even more." Once money takes root within the rituals of the adivasi community, it also permeates other spheres of economic life. In fact, it can be said that life becomes impossible without money.

Stephen Fuchs, while studying the causes of land scarcity and land hunger amongst the Bhils of Jhabua, indicates that cash becomes necessary in almost every aspect of Bhils life.[53] From his account, four prominent nodes can be detected in Bhils' life that necessarily require money. The first that Stephen Fuchs indicates is that of agriculture; Bhils require money to purchase seeds, fertiliser, etc. In the case of cash crops, the requirement for money goes up commensurately. Second, vagaries associated with agriculture in India such as drought, flood, death of bullocks, etc. Third, weddings, funeral feasts, caste trials. Three, illness in the family. Four, addiction to alcohol that is prevalent amongst the Bhils. In fact, Stephen Fuchs points to a state of affairs whereby the adivasi community is perpetually short of cash and provisions. It is this perpetual need for money that the adivasi community takes to producing for the market.

In our area of study, the adivasis are cultivating various crops meant for the market, viz. wheat, soya bean, groundnut and cotton, etc.[54] To see the increasing importance of production for market, one can refer to Table 2.1.

The increasing importance of production for market is

TABLE 2.1 : Increasing importance of production for market.

Crop	*Indigenous seed*	*Hybrid Seed*	*For Home Consumption*	*For Sale in the Mandi*
Soya bean	X	Yes	X	Yes
Cotton	X	Yes	X	Yes
Maize	Yes	X	Yes	X
Jowar	Yes	X	Yes	X
Urad	Yes	X	Yes	Some
Groundnut	Yes	X	Yes (for oil)	Yes
Wheat	X	Yes	Yes	Yes
Rice	Very Scarcely	Yes	X	Yes
Bajra	X	Yes	Yes	Yes

Source: Interview with Sitaram Bhadle of Jhiree Jhamli.

evident from the use of high yield hybrid seeds and the production of crops aimed primarily for the market, i.e. cash crops. The purpose of this shift is to earn the much needed cash; however, ironically rather than providing the adivasi community with additional cash, the shift to production of cash crops increases the requirement of cash. Increased use of hybrid seeds results in greater requirement of fertilisers and water in cultivation. Cotton requires maximum irrigation, fertilisers and pesticides. Wheat also requires good irrigation (not as much as cotton) and fertilisers. Soya bean consumes a large quantity of fertilisers (but less than cotton), but its irrigation needs are quite less compared to cotton and wheat. Chana requires a lot of water. Jowar, urad and bajra, however, are grown with nominal irrigation (mostly rain fed) and do not require fertilisers or pesticides. All this makes agriculture increasingly capital intensive. Cost of production shoots up at every stage. The cost of hybrid seeds is quite exorbitant for the adivasi. In Chatli, the farmers gave the prices for seeds as shown in Table 2.2.

This price list was also confirmed in an interview with Gendram Dawar, the Mukhiya of Sendhwa and Bhagwanpura areas. Several adivasis who were present at the time of the interview corroborated the above rates too. The use of fertilisers and pesticides further enhances the requirement of cash. Cotton requires large quantities of pesticides and urea. Even in wheat

TABLE 2.2 : Seed Prices given by Chatli Farmers.

Item	*Price of seed procured from the bania*
Wheat	Rs. 1,200/quintal
Soya bean	Rs. 1,800/quintal
Groundnut (in season)	Rs. 1,700/quintal
Groundnut (in summer)	Rs. 2,800/quintal
Cotton	Rs. 400–500/800 gm

Source: Interview with Dara Singh Brahmane of Chatli.

cultivation, around 50 kilogrammes of urea per acre is required. The cost of pesticides and urea (procured from the bania) in the first half of 1999 was Rs. 200-300 per litre for pesticides and Rs. 202 per sack (50 kg) for urea. Cost of cultivation also goes up due to the increased cost of irrigation. Fossil fuel being expensive, the adivasis depend on electricity to irrigate their crops. However, the power supply is erratic and supplied voltage is too low (160 volts instead of 240 volts) to run the electric pumps. Consequently, the motors of the pumps used for drawing water for irrigation are often burnt out.

Finally, production for the market compromises the food sufficiency of the adivasi community. This happens because of two reasons. First, increased cost of production of agriculture means that production of cash crops, rather than decreasing cash dependency of the adivasi community, in fact increases it. Thus, the need for cash keeps on increasing in the adivasi community, further propelling production for market, thus eroding the acreage under cultivation of subsistence crops. Production of subsistence crops is also adversely affected due to the change in the nature of soil, owing to the use of fertilisers and excessive watering of the fields. Evidence of this was seen in Khutwadi. Khutwadi produces cotton. Although cotton was cultivated even earlier, nowadays a hybrid seed is used, which requires fertilisers and pesticides (once in every eight days). These fertilisers have adversely affected the jowar crop, since with the use of the fertilisers the jowar crop does not ripen.

Thus, increased requirement of cash results in change in the form of production in agriculture, whereby the adivasi community takes to production for the market to augment its supply of cash. However, this shift to production for the market only results in enhancing the requirement of cash in the adivasi community. Consequently, the dependence of the adivasi community on the *saookar, bania* and moneylenders increases. In fact, now we find that an adivasi also starts borrowing to be able to cultivate cash crops. It leads to a particular kind of debt bondage. Production of cash crop requires on an average Rs. 2,500 per acre. This money is procured in most cases from *Aggarwals* and *banias*. The moneylender charges an exorbitant rate of interest of 50 per cent at quarterly rates. Hence if an adivasi borrows Rs. 5,000 in June, by harvest time in October/November it becomes Rs. 7,500. Furthermore, the debtor adivasi is obliged to sell his produce only to the moneylender or his representatives at the *mandi*. Thus production for market further increases the dependence of the adivasi community on the moneylenders.

The cumulative effect of enhanced requirement of money, increased production for the market and the growing indebtedness of the adivasi community results in the rupturing of the autarchy of the adivasi community and its greater insertion into the market. However, it needs to be pointed out that this insertion of the adivasi community in the market does not mean that the adivasi social formation gets assimilated or dissolved in feudalism or capitalism. On the contrary, this insertion is very specific, whereby the adivasi social formation is locked in a subordinated position with the market-based social formations (feudalism and capitalism). This specific relation then permits the extraction of products of adivasi social formation at a very cheap rate.[55] Thus market, rather than becoming a space where adivasis are integrated in the money economy, becomes an asymmetrical space which permits the extraction of cheap labour (in the form of products) from the adivasi social formation. This happens because, owing to their weak resource position the adivasis have at best an imperfect insertion in the market whereby every level of the market system is not available for their access. More important, the moneyed interests, here the *Aggarwals, banias*, etc. control the levers of the market and manipulate it in fixing the prices, etc. in their favour.[56]

In the case of cash crops such as cotton this was seen in

different mandis. At Balwadi the *Seths* sell everything (seeds, fertilisers, pesticides, grocery). Most of them have formed a cartel. They have kept alive the tradition of *Aadat* (auction) and control the prices artificially, and so the adivasi gets short changed. Licensed merchants auction the cotton at Balwadi Mandi, but the buying merchants 'fix' the price. Although the weighing fee is Rs.10 and the auction fee too is nominal, the auctioneer/*dalal* demands and receives 2 per cent of the total sale of the produce. This surcharge of 2 per cent and the cost of transporting their produce to the *mandi* become prohibitive for the adivasi. The result is that several adivasis, to avoid paying this 2 per cent have stopped taking their produce to the Balwadi *mandi*. Now the merchants buy the products directly from the village at rates that are Rs. 50–100 quintal cheaper than that at the *mandi*.[57]

The asymmetrical structure and pricing in the market is evident in every transaction involving the adivasi and the outsiders. Stephen Fuchs mentions that the merchants buy the farm products of the adivasi at a cheap rate and sell their own merchandise at a higher rate (cf. fn. 104). Even though one disagrees with the theoretical reason forwarded by Stephen Fuchs for this, one agrees with the empirical veracity of the statement. During the fieldwork, we prepared a chart of the price difference in the products being sold by the adivasi and the merchants in the local mart at Segbi[58] and the primary market in Sendhwa. We found that the products of the adivasi were cheaper in the local mart while the products of the merchants were more expensive in the local mart relative to the primary market in Sendhwa. Since the bulk of the adivasi community transacts mainly in the local mart, it results in remittance of cheap labour (in the form of products) from the adivasi social formation.

TABLE 2.3 : Agricultural Products of the adivasi

Item	*Segbi mart*	*Sendhwa KUM*
Soya bean	Rs. 5/kg	Rs. 7-8/kg
Groundnut	Rs. 12-13/kg	Rs. 14/kg
Cotton	Rs. 12/kg	Rs. 15/kg

Certain other food items that are not grown in Segbi are also more expensive in the local mart than in Sendhwa. Rice is not grown in Segbi. The cost of rice in Segbi is Rs. 14/kg. In Sendhwa, the same quantity and quality of rice costs Rs. 11/kg.

TABLE 2.4 : Merchandise of the traders

Item	*Segbi Mart*	*Sendhwa*
Salt	Rs. 2.30/kg	Rs. 2/kg
Kerosene	Rs. 15/litre	Rs. 10/litre
Soap (Nirma)	Rs. 7/pack	Rs. 5/pack
Biscuits (Parle)	Rs. 6/pack	Rs. 5/pack
Clothes (shirts and trousers)	Not available	Rs. 300/pair
Baskets	Rate variable	More expensive here
Utensils	Approx. Rs. 75/wt. measure	Approx. Rs.50/wt. measure
Groundnut oil	Rs. 60/litre	Rs. 50/litre

Alienation of resources, indebtedness and continuous remittance from the adivasi community, owing to the asymmetrical nature of the market, creates a massive resource deficit. The adivasi community is compelled to take recourse to exceptional methods. There are two prominent measures that the adivasi community takes to replenish its resource position: first, it attempts to increase its source of income by reclaiming land from forest. This process is called *nawad*. Second, the community in order to earn much needed cash, takes to migration to seek cash-bases employment. Both these measures are taken recourse to in drastic proportions.

Nawad has been an emotive issue in the adivasi community and has been cashed by mainstream parties for electoral gains. The right-wing Hindu party the Jana Sangh affiliated to the Rashtriya Swayam Sevak Sangh consolidated its electoral base in Sendhwa by supporting the issue of *nawad*. The extent of *nawad* can be gauged from the fact when the Congress government[59] invited applications to regularise the *nawad* before 1,980 lakh applications were filed. In Badwani, 4,074 persons filed application for 99,942.755 hectares of land. In Khargone and Sendhwa, 93,399 persons filed applications for regularisation of *nawad*. Similarly, in Barwaha several hundred people filed for regularisation of *nawad* of which government accepted the regularisation of 60.223 hectares.

Migration is also resorted to on a regular basis to offset the cash crunch. From Chatli, people go to work in the ginning/ spinning mills at Sendhwa, which is 8 km away from the village. Migration to seek employment begins, for an adivasi, from the age of twelve. Entire families migrate to Sendhwa for work. Similarly from Sakad, which is 9 km away from Sendhwa, entire families migrate to work in the spinning/ginning mills of Sendhwa. From Badwani, adivasis migrate to Bankaner, Dhar district, Maharashtra, to work in the mills. Even at the time of the fieldwork, we found two operational ginning mills in Badwani.

These measures are adopted to alleviate the resource crunch bearing upon the adivasi community. But, these measures are akin to burning the candle at both ends. Although *nawad* increases the acreage under cultivation, it seriously depletes the availability of forest-based resources that are so crucial for the sustenance an adivasi family. Similarly, migration in the non-agricultural season may gain some additional money for the adivasi family, but it also deprives the adivasi community of able hands to replenish the resources such as repairing house, agricultural and other tools, etc. that is crucial for the survival of the adivasi community as an economically viable entity.[60]

This system, however, benefits the market-based social formations immensely. Migration opens up a supply of very cheap labour. The adivasis migrating to work as seasonal labour in the ginning/spinning mills are paid a very meagre salary. Adult male workers are paid Rs. 42 while females and children are paid Rs. 37 per day for 12 hours a day. The payment can be made on a daily or weekly basis. They have to work for 6 days a week without any breaks or half day. As is evident, this rate is far below the government prescribed rates. Migration does not only makes cheap labour available, there are cases where migration offsets the shortage of labour. If migrant adivasis were not there, it could have resulted in hike of wages. Bankaner that is situated in the Dhar district of Maharashtra abuts

Badwani. During October-November, i.e. the cotton season, there is an acute labour scarcity in Bankaner. In the absence of availability of local labour, the labour agents from Bankaner endeavour to direct adivasi labour from Badwani to Bankaner. Labour agents of mill owners of Bankaner advance loans to the adivasis in the summer season when the adivasis are faced with a severe financial crunch. These indebted adivasis are under obligation to migrate to Bankaner to work for the mill owners in the cotton season in October-November.

The benefit of supply of cheap labour is compounded by the fact that the adivasi labour is employed as seasonal labour. Labour is required in the ginning/spinning mills for only four months in a year. The mill owners, rather than appointing a permanent labour force opt for seasonal labour. They have encouraged the development of a temporary labour market. Indebted adivasis, who have been working in the mills are obliged to provide more workers to the mill. These adivasis are called *muqaddam* (labour agent). A labour agent is bound to supply labour to a mill on a weekly basis. In the course of our interviews, we met Har Das of Achli village. Har Das is currently involved with the Nimar Mazdoor Sangh, but earlier was a *muqaddam* who used to supply labour from the cotton and groundnut belt of Balsamer, Dalsamanda, Chatli, Kheri and Achli.

Employment of labour on a seasonal or weekly basis means that the mill owners do not have to make provisions for maintaining the labour round the year. Thus the mill owners can afford to scale down the salaries and the adivasi labour has to depend on the adivasi community for maintenance for the period when he/she is not working in the mills. In other words while mill owners benefit from the cheap supply of labour, they spend nothing for its upkeep. The expenditure for the upkeep of the labour continues to be borne by the adivasi community. Thus the mill owner not only gets cheap labour but labour that does not require any additional expenditure for maintenance. (In the preceding section I have argued that this leads to the double exploitation of the adivasi labour, please refer to the section on dialectics of transformation and consolidation.)

Seasonal employment of workers has political benefit as well since this makes formation of trade unions commensurably difficult. This is evident in the attempts of the Nimar Mazdoor Sangh, which faces an uphill task in organising since the labour is seasonal in nature, only four months in a year.

Impact of exploitation on the socio-economic sphere: We have demonstrated above that in order to exploit the adivasi social formation it has first of all to be opened up. This was achieved by a series of invasions first by the Rajputs and subsequently by the Khalji, the Mughals and Marathas. This military subjugation was followed by the imposition of tribute and taxes collected in cash or kind. Once cash was introduced in adivasi social formation, it took root in it and gradually replaced exchange and barter from cultural, ritualistic and economic relations. Thus, first force and then cash opened up the adivasi community for exploitation. Cash gradually replaced military subjugation as the chief means for articulating the adivasi social formation with the succeeding feudal and capitalist (under the aegis of colonialism) social formations. Yet this does not mean that the role of the state in maintaining the subordinate articulation of the adivasi social formation has been eroded. State policy measures, informal actions as well as patent illegality and corruption of the state functionaries and institutions continue to play a significant role in maintaining it.

Once adivasi social formation was opened up and thus articulated with the succeeding social formations, special forms were deployed to enable continuous remittance of resources from the adivasi social formation. The chief object of this process is remittance of cheap labour and its products. We have demonstrated that in West Nimar, cheap labour is withdrawn from the adivasi community by developing a temporary labour market and seasonal employment of adivasi labour in the ginning/spinning mills. Remittance of cheap products is ensured by asymmetrical structure of the market. Thus, the exploitation of the adivasis in West Nimar follows two distinct processes, first of opening up of the adivasi community and second, deployment of specific forms to remit labour and resources from the adivasis. These specific forms are deployed to enable remittance are in consonance with the specific structure of the adivasi social formation.

Hence the process of exploitation has two distinct impacts: First those transformations that are necessary to open up the adivasi community, i.e. transformations in the internal structures of the adivasi community to break its autarchy; second, to consolidate those aspects of the adivasi social formation that enable remittance of cheap labour and products. These two processes together determine the trajectory and direction of mutations within adivasi social formation when it is articulated with feudalism and capitalism. Amongst the Bhils, these two transformations can be briefly stated as follows:

1. The process of opening up of the adivasi community by military conquest of the Rajputs, Khalji, etc. and by the introduction of cash in the community has led to increasing stratification within the community. This stratification is not only within individual adivasis (creation of rich and poor) but also between lineages that has resulted in the stratification of Bhils among Bhils, Barelas and Bhilalas, the Bhilalas being the most influential and the Bhils the least. Furthermore, different clans of the Bhils, Barelas and Bhilalas are being placed increasingly into an unequal relationship.
2. The process of consolidation of the structures that enable remittance of cheap labour and products has led to the consolidation of the kinship structure and the position of the patriarch.

One of the logical corollaries of insertion of adivasi community in the market economy is emergence of stratification in the community. In the section dialectics of transformation and consolidation (above), we had argued that there are some latent asymmetries in the adivasi community, as per Meillassoux the system of bridal exchange epitomised this latent asymmetry. But this asymmetry remained latent since in adivasi community channels and mechanism of redistribution existed.[61] Once the autarchy of the adivasi community is broken, this mechanism of redistribution breaks down and the latent asymmetry is actualised. Amongst the Bhils and its sub-groups too such latent asymmetry existed both in the politico-economic and the cultural levels.

At the politico-economic levels, power was unequally distributed; political power rests with the council of elders (roughly translated as panchayat) that is controlled by the headman. Amongst the Barela, Bhilala, Patelia, etc. the headman is called Patel. Amongst the Bhil, the headman is called Tadvi. The post of the headman is hereditary. In larger villages, every Phalia has its own headman. Besides the headman, there are few other positions of authority and respect. Among the Bhils, Bhopas or Dewalo is a religious person who acts as a priest, medicine man and witch finder. The Bhopas have a hierarchy; some are of a superior order than the rest. But, all of them are seen as religious leaders[62] and are objects of reverence, respect and fear.

There are several privileges attached to the post of headman. The headman presides over various religious and cultural rituals. He is given the responsibility to collect land revenue and gets 6.25 per cent of the revenue as remuneration.[63] He also has the right to distribute the land reclaimed from forest i.e. *nawad*.[64] All this vests considerable power in the hands of the Patel. In the present money-based economy control over political and land resources has translated into relatively better economic position of the Patels.[65] The economic and political position of the Patels is also consolidated due to the superimposition of modern political structure over that of the adivasi community. The Patel now acquires a semi-government official status. He helps government officials during their visit and maintains law and order in the village with the help of other local officials.[66] In this capacity, the Patels develop close links with the local administration and the police. The PUCL report elaborates upon the close link between Mr. Jhagadia Patel and the police.

Consequently, the power vested traditionally in the hands of the Patels, etc. consolidates and creates the condition of increasing stratification in the adivasi community, a condition that is further exacerbated by the insertion of the adivasi community in market economy. Over time, differences in resource position of the adivasis increase. Though the community still does not have a significant presence of landless adivasis, the fact is that now the landless labourers and adivasis with considerable land holdings, both appear at the opposite end of the spectrum. (There is a word of caution, however; degree of affluence in adivasi community is less dramatic than in the non-adivasi community since there is widespread indebtedness in the community, even amongst landholders.) Bishwa Bandhu Chatterjee has prepared an interesting table (Table 2.5) with a sample base of nine villages.[67]

TABLE 2.5 : Land Holding Patterns (acres per family)

Sl. No.	*Village*	*Land-less*	*Up to 5*	*5-15*	*15-25*	*25-40*	*40-100*	*<100*	*Total*	*Average size*
1.	Kusmiya	13	25	16	—	1	1	—	46	10.8
2.	Zhakhar	14	13	17	7	4	—	—	35	15.7
3.	Jamniya	11	15	40	2	1	3	—	62	12.7
4.	Sulgaon	11	32	53	—	1	—	—	97	7.6
5.	Mansor	1	18	26	2	2	—	—	49	9.6
6.	Mogrikheda	—	27	19	6	3	1	—	56	10.6
7.	Salon	15	35	23	1	4	—	2	80	11.5
8.	Chatly	3	41	45	14	2	—	—	105	10.7
9.	Kunjary	2	34	64	11	9	—	—	120	10.9
	Total	50	220	303	43	27	5	2	650	
	Total cases	50	270	573	616	643	648	650		

The above table shows the opening up of differentiation in resource position and emergence of a small section of landless families in the adivasi community and an even smaller section of rich peasants (however, it has to be borne in mind that this table was prepared in the early 1970s, during our fieldwork we came across instances of landless labourers Burapani, Segbi, Ojhar and Khutwadi). One of the corollaries of variation in land holding is that sharecropping and agrarian labour has emerged in the adivasi community.

Though sharecropping is not as prevalent as self-labour, it is also practised amongst the adivasis in this area. There are two types of sharecropping that are predominantly practised. In the first type, the yield is divided into two equal parts after taking out the seeds. In this case, the sharecropper supplies the labour-force and other equipments needed for agriculture. The second type is called *Batai* or *Teesari Pati*. In this type the owner of the land provides all the agricultural implements required except labour. The owner of the land gets 2/3rd of the yield and the worker gets only 1/3rd of the yield.[68] Incidence of landless labour is even less but exists none the less. Landless labour does all kinds of chores. Gend Ram Dawar, one of the prominent activists of the AMS, is a landless labourer. He used to chop wood in the forest and also did odd jobs for a living. There are also incidences of deployment of landless labour in agriculture. We witnessed this in Jhiree Jhamli, where landless adivasis work as agricultural labour. Agricultural labour is paid much below the official wages. The existing rates during the duration of the fieldwork were Rs.15–20 per day for harvesting and Rs. 30–40 for ploughing. Unlike the wage structure at factory where men and women are paid different salaries for same work, in agriculture both men and women are paid Rs. 15–20 for harvesting. However, ploughing, which fetches Rs. 30–40, is done only by men.

Earlier we had stated adivasis acting as fronts to enable transfer of land to the non-adivasi. The incidence of sharecropping and employment of agricultural labour is a much more direct case of exploitation of adivasi at the hands of another adivasi. (It has to be borne in mind, however, that this is not very prevalent even now.) Other than the sphere of agriculture, there are evidences of this kind of exploitation in loan transactions. Anthropological studies demonstrate that in the majority of the loan transactions presence of a witness is mandatory. This witness is held responsible if loan is not returned. Advantage to the witness is that he also derives some benefit out of the deal. Many of the witnesses, who are Bhils themselves, exploit other needy Bhils, for whom they stand witness.[69]

Invasion from more stratified social formations and penetration of money led to the disintegration of the Bhils into various independent groups and sub-groups. Certain clans and lineages that gained prominence owing to the contact with the invaders or due to better adaptation to money broke away from the main Bhil community and claimed independent identity. Furer-Haimendorf has indicated this process of assertion of independent identity by the Meenas. He shows that till as late as 1921 census, Meenas were mentioned as Bhils, but since then have repudiated that identity.[70] Similarly, the Bhilalas emerged as a result of marital union between the Bhils and the Rajputs. They now repudiate all connection with the Bhils. These new groups enjoyed a better social status than the Bhils.[71] Thus, invasions and penetration of money led to asymmetrical stratification of the Bhils that had a very significant impact on the future course of development of these communities. It disrupted the relation of reciprocity between the sub-groups which at one time were clans of the larger Bhil community involved in a network of economic and social exchange. Tribute, taxes and rent exacted from the subordinate groups and unequal access to resources did not only create unequal relationship amongst the sub-groups, it also created a condition where survival for the marginal groups is becoming increasingly nonviable. I will elaborate upon these issues to better explicate the point.

Asymmetrical stratification of Bhils into sub-groups began with the advent of Rajputs. The Rajputs took women from the Bhil community that led to the creation of distinct sub-groups of Bhilalas, Patalias, etc.[72] The superior sub-castes, due to their proximity with the Rajput rulers, had the right to exact tribute and levy labour or money rent on the other sub-groups. In turn, they had to pay tribute to the ruling Rajput rulers called *Darbar* (royalty or prince). For instance, the Bhil sub-groups that were created due to intermarriage with Rajputs, could exact labour rent from the other Bhil groups. The Chaukhariya Mankars were employed to bring drinking water and also to do other domestic chores during marriage and other social functions. The Nahal Mankars are engaged for grazing cattle, as labourer and as watchmen.[73] In return, these superior sub-groups had to pay the *darbar* a fixed amount as a token of their allegiance.[74] When Allauddin Khalji conquered this area and later, with the Mughal rule, Muslim officials were posted in the region, some of whom got married to Bhils, thus creating a new sub-group of Tadvi Bhils. The Muslim sub-groups of Tadvi Bhils and Nible reside in those parts of Satpura range that forms a hedge between the Narmada and the Tapti rivers.[75] These Bhils claim descent from Pathan ancestry. The superior status of this sub-group vis-à-vis the Bhils is evident from the appellate Tadvi, which means headman.

This asymmetry between the sub-groups disrupted the patterns of exchange of products and labour between clans and lineages. The disruption of exchange of goods is relatively obvious. With the exaction of tribute and taxes, the system of exchange as reciprocity, the chief basis of all exchange in adivasi social formation, is destroyed since now the movement of goods and money is unidirectional and obligatory. In the same vein, exchange of labour is also disrupted. In the previous section, I had argued that adivasi social formation maintains the balance of labour supply through exchange of nubile women, adoption and birth control. Amongst these, reciprocal exchange of women is one the chief ways of maintaining reciprocal exchange of labour force. However, with the emerging asymmetry amongst the Bhils and its sub-groups, this system gets disrupted. Marriage, dining, etc. between the sub-groups is stopped. The Bhilalas do not admit the Barela and Bhil women in their group. If a Barela man brings a Bhil wife, he can be excommunicated until he leaves his Bhil wife.[76]

With the impact of trade, cash crops, etc. this hierarchisation becomes even more pronounced and we find that asymmetry emerges even within the different clans of a sub-group, leading to disruption of reciprocal exchange even amongst them.[77] In West Nimar, this process of asymmetry within sub-groups is fairly advanced too. Amongst the Bhilalas, we find that there is an unequal marital exchange between the Bhilalas of Nimar and that of Rath. Though the Bhilalas of Rath have affinal relation with the Nimari Bhilalas the exchange of bride is unidirectional. Women from Rath are accepted as brides by the Nimari Bhilalas but they rarely marry off their daughters to the Rathwas. Similarly, the Baria Bhilalas of Mathwar (South of Alirajpur) rarely marry into Rath.[78]

Exaction of tribute, taxes, etc. and unequal exchange of products and labour has created resource asymmetry amongst the Bhils and its sub-groups. Some village case studies available indicated a fairly unequal distribution of resources amongst the different sub-groups. Lok Nath Soni has done a village-based study of Bhils and their sub-groups and has provided a table on ethnic group-wise landholding pattern in the Bhilkhera village of Khargone.[79] The study suggests that Bhilala have the maximum resources under their command.

TABLE 2.6 : Landholding in the village Bhilkhera (landholding per family in acres)

Ethnic groups	*0-5 acres*	*6-10 acres*	*11-15 acres*	*16-20 acres*	*21-25 acres*	*< 26 acres*	*Landless labour*	*Total*
Bhilala	20	18	9	12	6	4	2	71
Bhil (Tadvi)	4	–	–	–	–	–	6	10
N. Mankar	2	–	–	–	–	–	25	27
C. Mankar	–	–	2	–	–	–	–	2
Bharud	–	–	–	–	–	–	5	5
Nai	–	–	–	–	–	–	1	1
Bairagi	–	–	–	–	–	–	1	1
Total	26	18	11	12	6	4	53	130

Our own fieldwork also suggests that on the whole the Bhilalas control maximum resources, followed by Barelas and the position of the Bhils is the most precarious.[80] Uneven access to resources has impacted on the capacity of the Bhilalas, Barelas and Bhils to reproduce themselves. That the capacity of the Bhils to sustain themselves is diminishing can be seen in the declining demographic growth rate of the Bhils vis-à-vis Bhilalas and Barelas. As per the 1931 Census of the Central Indian Agency, there were 76,149 Bhilalas in the entire Holkar state; the population of Bhils was greater and stood at 83,232 persons. By 1971 the position had reversed, in the 1971 Census the population of Bhilalas in West Nimar stood at 1,41,997 while the Bhil population was only 71,866 persons. Similarly, Barelas were not even mentioned in the 1921 Census; however, by 1971, we find that their population that stood at 1,58,706, was twice as numerous as that of the Bhils.[81]

Though Bishwa Bandhu Chatterjee sees this as "indicative of existence social currents leading to the diminution in the ranks of the Bhils and their absorption in the Barela and Bhilala tribe who are considered more respectable...," the reason for this is essentially demographic. Given the ritual and social codes of distancing between the Bhils, Bhilala and Barelas that has been stated above, it would appear implausible that Bhils would be accommodated amongst the Bhilalas and the Barelas. In fact, the slow demographic growth of the Bhils is a result of the decreased capacity of the Bhils to sustain large families. The AIBAS data shows the average family size for Bhils of Madhya Pradesh in the year 1981 was 5, while that of the Bhilalas was 6.[82] Since there is a correlation between average family size and demographic growth, it appears more plausible that the decline in the demographic growth of the Bhils vis-à-vis the Bhilalas and the Barelas is due to demographic reasons and not because of the assimilation of individual Bhils into the Bhilala and Barela fold.

This brings us to the second impact of the exploitation on the Bhils and their sub-groups. We have demonstrated till now that by increasing stratification between clans, lineages, sub-groups and individuals, the lateral filiations of the Bhil community was broken. With it, institutions of collective labour, redistribution of resources and reciprocity in exchange either became weak or were disrupted. However, contrary to this, the position of the elders, i.e. fathers, and the kinship structure was consolidated. While discussing the latent asymmetries in adivasi social formation in previous sections, I had indicated two major nodes of latent asymmetry in adivasi community: first, in the exchange of nubile women and second, in the concentration of rights of decision making and the unilateral claim on the labour of the youth by the elderly. In fact, gerontocratic ideology is the dominant ideology of adivasi social formation. I have demonstrated that with the weakening of the lateral filiations of the adivasi community, the latent asymmetry in exchange of nubile women is made manifest. Now I demonstrate how kinship structure that is vertical filliation and sustains gerontocracy, gets further consolidated owning to the special forms of exploitation of the adivasi community.

There are at least three important reasons as to why kinship structure is consolidated. I have already mentioned one of them while discussing the specific forms adopted for the exploitation of the adivasi community. While discussing this I had indicated that the ginning/spinning mill owners have encouraged the development of a temporary labour market. By doing so, they gain a cheap labour force without the responsibility of maintaining them in the periods when work is not available. For this, it is imperative that even when the adivasi community is opened up, it is not completely destroyed; if the adivasi community is completely destroyed, it will no longer be possible to push the workers back to it in the lean periods. Thus, for successful remittance of cheap labour from the adivasi community, it is necessary that even though the lateral filiations, are ruptured in order to open up the community the vertical filiations i.e. the kinship structure remains intact.

For the migrant adivasi workers also, it is beneficial that the kinship structure remain intact. Though by working in the spinning/ginning mills the adivasi worker is doubly exploited, he gains cash that is scarce in the adivasi community. This in turns enables him to increase his income; thus, even though the adivasi is exploited, he improves his position within his own community. But the labourer can gain in this way only if the kinship structure is there in order to subsidise the labour. If kinship structure were to break up, such low wages will become absolutely non-remunerative. Thus a kinship structure is required to provide security and succour in times of need. This is true even in the non-economic sphere, since kinship structure is seen as a place for shelter and protection in moments of danger. We came across this function of the kinship structure in the unfortunate Uma, who was the wife of late Kalia. She was raped, stripped naked and thrown out of Julwania village. In the situation of crisis, she fled to her natal home in Kabri and sought refuge. Her kinsfolk were determined to take revenge.[83]

The third reason is that kinship proves to be one of the levers for penetration of cash in and for pushing labour out of the adivasi community. Earlier, we referred to Jos M.van der Klei's work to show how the kinship structure pushed the adivasi youth to migrate as seasonal labour. In West Nimar too we find that kinship structure is one of the chief conduits through which cash took root in the adivasi community. We had argued that cash took root in the adivasi community initially to pay rent, taxes and tribute. But soon cash replaced symbolic goods in rituals and ceremonies. One of the chief institutions that got so transformed was marriage, where cash has become the predominant form of bride price. Amongst the Bhils, marriages involving bride price[84] are fixed by a middle man, i.e. *Bhandgidi*. Once the marriage proposal is accepted, bride price is paid. This is in the sole custody of the father of the bride. Thus gerontocracy has gained from the monitisation of relations. Kinship structure is thus consolidated since gerontocracy the dominant group in kinship structure is strengthened by penetration of cash. Since kinship thus provides ground for cash to take root with the adivasi community, it becomes an aid rather than obstacle to the feudal and capitalist social formations. Therefore, later these are also interested in its consolidation.

From the above account of forms and impact of the exploitation of the adivasi community we can briefly summarise the dialectics of transformation and consolidation of adivasi community. With the impact of invasions in the early medieval period by the Rajputs and subsequently by the Marathas, the Bhil community was opened up. This also led to the introduction of money since this was the medium to pay revenue and taxes. The opening up was furthered under capitalism (inaugurated under the aegis of British colonialism). Thus the adivasi social formation was articulated with feudal and then capitalist social formation. This opening up led to the rearticulating of the internal structures of the adivasi social formation. The lateral filiations within the adivasi social formation were either disrupted or weakened and were replaced by relations that reflected the stratifications appropriate to the social formations with which it was articulated. Articulation with feudalism led to the disintegration of the Bhils into asymmetrically related sub-group where rigid hierarchy and social distancing was maintained based on birth and feudal privileges. Articulation of capitalism led to the emergence of economic stratification within these sub-groups and also the beginning of the process of individuation within the sub-groups.

Impact of exploitation on cultural-religious sphere: Specific forms adopted to open up and exploit the adivasi community means that the lateral filiations of the adivasi social formation were disrupted or weakened; however, the vertical filiations get consolidated since they rather than being obstacles for the articulation are one of he principal institutions that create conditions for cash to take roots in the adivasi community. This specific dialectics of transformation-consolidation results in determining the contemporary mutated form of the adivasi social formation. The articulation of the Bhils with the succession of invaders and market economy has resulted in its recasting, whereby the community now incorporates three kinds of relations:

1. Asymmetrical relation between the Bhils and their sub-groups.
2. Economic stratification within every sub-group.
3. Vertical filiations of kinship ties.

Thus the dialectics of trasformation and consolidation impacts upon the social and economic structures of the Bhil community. However, it impacts upon the religious and cultural structures as well. In adivasi social formation that is based on reciprocity and redistribution, rituals and culture act as mechanisms of reciprocity and redistribution. Once the adivasi social formation mutates and reciprocity and redistribution are disrupted, the form and function of religion and culture mutates as well. Now, rather than acting as institutions that keep the latent asymmetry in adivasi social formation in check, the religious and cultural practices act as the mechanism for legitimising and reproducing the new relations within the adivasi social formation. In the case of the Bhils, we find that the religious and cultural practices now reflect the three relations that exist in the community after undergoing mutation.

This is what explains the co-existence of different rituals and customs which are so varied in their form and ideological content that it will be impossible to club them together on the basis of similarity of function. On the basis of the three types of relations that the rituals, religion and culture seek to reproduce we can distinguish the range of religious and customary practices into three types.

1. Those religious and customary practices that seek to reproduce the structure of the kinship.
2. Those religious and customary practices that seek to reproduce the asymmetrical relations between the Bhils and their sub-groups.
3. Those religious and customary practices that seek to reproduce the individuation of the adivasi community.

There are several festivals and customs and rituals amongst the Bhils and their sub-groups that seek to reproduce the structure of kinship. These festivals and rituals reflect the communitarian belief which is the most solid foundation on which kinship ties are based. The festival, rituals and customs reflect equal affliction of entire kinsfolk in ritually prescribed moments of moral crisis, danger or happiness. Two such practices are very important in the ritual calendar of the Bhils—Kavad and Indal. Kavad is a wooden/bamboo staff with two wicker baskets slung on either ends and carried over the shoulder. The adivasis have a tradition of carrying a Kavad from house to house, collecting any object, totem, livestock supposedly infested by evil/spirit/disease and then taking all these out in a procession through the villages and dumping them outside the precincts in order to exorcise the evil/pests/disease. Indal is an adivasi festival, which is organised by individuals whenever they worship the God of Rain (Indra) for favour/boon, and these are realised. Indal is organised by that family subsequently in honour of Indra, and the whole village and surrounding villages join in all-night revelry. Since everyone does not ask for boons at any regular self-appointed time, nor are the boons all fructified, Indal is consequently not celebrated in the same village every year.

Similarly, the kin also shares grief. On the event of any death, the kinsfolk are invited on the day of the first festival falling after the death. They go there with colour and gulal. Colour is poured on the door of the house and gulal is sprinkled on that. Then colour and gulal is sprinkled on the male members of the family. The women of the family weep on this occasion. They also weep on the festival days early in the morning. The guests are offered water to drink and *bidi* and *chilam* to smoke. The guests take their food and return the next day. The food is made from contributions of flour and jaggery made by the close relatives. Thus kin share the grief. In these life-cycle rituals, participation of the agnate and cognate kin is ritually prescribed. For instance, other than the husband and the wife, the core of an adivasi family presence of the *Jawai* and the maternal uncle is essential in a number of life-cycle rituals. *Jawai* is a classificatory term and it includes husbands of the sister, father's sister and daughter.[85]

The second type of festivals, customs and rituals reproduces the asymmetrical relations between the Bhils and their sub-groups. These are mostly in evidence in nucleated type of villages that are mostly inhabited by the Bhilalas and the Patelias at the core with the Bhils and the other groups on the fringes. According to Aurora, in village rituals the Patelias, Bhilalas, Bhils, Balais and Mankars are kept into hierarchy on the basis of ritual distances between these groups. According to the rules of ritual, Patelias are followed by the Bhilalas, Bhils, Mankars and Balais, in chronological order. The Bhils must maintain a distance of one arm's length and the Mankars two arm's length during any ritual or ceremonial occasions.[86]

The third type of festivals, customs and rituals reproduces individuation of adivasi community. These are essentially rituals and customs practised by the followers of the Radha Swamy sect, the Gayatri Parivar and the Kasturba Kanya Ashram. Though there are differences within the form and practices of these groups, all of them lay emphasis on individual effort for social upward mobility. The Gayatri Parivar emphasises the observations of ritual and dietary probation of the follower to become the Brahmin. Here an individual's performance of *havans*, recitation of *Gayatri Mantra* (a Vedic incantation), wearing of sacred thread (by men), adopting vegetarianism, abstaining from alcohol and bride price and observing fast transforms him into a Brahmin. In the Radha Swamy sect, paying obeisance to the founding guru of the sect and following the path laid down by him makes the follower an enlightened soul. The Niwali Kanya Ashram lays emphasis on observance of personal hygiene, morality, abstaining from bride price, and alcohol and non-vegetarian food for the enlightenment of the individual.

These rituals and customary practices lack reference of adivasi communitarian principles. They advocate veneration of entities without local referents, entities that have their roots outside of the adivasi community. The ritual practices are therefore part of the opening up of the adivasi community by the other social formation. This perhaps explains why these ritual practices while they have succeeded largely in prohibition of alcohol and meat, have failed in the issue of bride price. It is pertinent to recall here that money is one of the chief instruments for opening of the adivasi community. Furthermore, it is the penetration of money in adivasi customs and rituals such as that of marriage that has made kinship structure one of the main anchors of the articulation of the adivasi social formation with feudalism and capitalism. It stands to reason then that intent apart, these new rituals and customs are structurally impotent to prevent the percolation of money in the adivasi community.

Thus, the opening up of the adivasi community and the special forms deployed for its exploitation mutate the adivasi social formation whereby its egalitarian and lateral filiations are disrupted. On the other hand, it consolidates the latent asymmetries in the adivasi social formation by consolidating the vertical filiations of kinship structure that has the elders at its apex. This affects every aspect of the adivasi social, economic and cultural-religious sphere.

REFERENCES

1. Christophe Jafferlot, *The Hindu Nationalist Movement in India* (New Delhi, 1996), pp. 196–97.
2. Jafferlot, op. cit. p. 203.
3. David Hardiman, 'Origins and transformations of the Devi', in Ranajit Guha (ed), *A Subaltern Studies Reader: 186–1995* (Minnesota, 1997) pp. 100–139.
4. S.C. Roy, *Oraon Religion and Customs* (Calcutta, 1972).
5. K.S. Singh, *Birsa Munda and his Rebellion* (Delhi, 1988).

6. Stephen Fuchs, *Rebellious Prophets* (Bombay, 1965).
7. Bishwa Bandhu Chatterjee, *A Candle in Woodland: Kasturba Kanya Ashram, Niwali – Past, Present and Future*, Bombay / Delhi, p.24.
8. Bishwa Bandhu Chatterjee, *A Candle in Woodland: Kasturba Kanya Ashram, Niwali – Past, Present and Future*, Bombay / Delhi, pp. 28–29.
9. *Basic Rural Statistics*, (Ministry of Rural Development, 2001) p. 23.
10. Ibid., p. 26.
11. *The Encyclopaedic District Gazetteers of India*, p. 386.
12. Bishwa Bandhu Chatterjee, op. cit., p. 29.
13. For details see the appendices on the profiles of the villages and towns surveyed.
14. Lok Nath Soni, 1993: pp. 3–4.
15. C. Payne (ed.) *Malcolm's Memoir of Central India*, New Delhi, 2002, pp. 7–9.
16. J.K. Doshi, *Social Structure and Cultural Change in a Bhil Village*, Delhi, 1976, p. 6.
17. Venkatachar, 1935, p. 58.
18. James Tod, *Annals and Antiquities of Rajasthan*, Vol. I. See also S.C. Varma, *The Bhil Kills*, Delhi, 1978, p. 6.
19. R.E. Enthoven, *The Tribes and Castes of Bombay, Vol. I*, Bombay, 1920, pp. 151–78
20. Bishwa Bandhu Chatterjee, ibid., p. 24.
21. K.D. Erskine, *Rajputana Gazetteers*, Vol. II-A. Ajmer, 1908.
22. Lok Nath Soni, ibid., pp. 7–13.
23. Name of a village in West Nimar.
24. Lok Nath Soni, ibid. pp. 8–9.
25. Bishwa Bandhu Chatterjee, *A Candle in Woodland: Kasturba Kanya Ashram*, Niwali (New Delhi, 1973) p. 45.
26. Bishwa Bandhu Chatterjee, ibid., p. 51.
27. Bishwa Bandhu Chatterjee, ibid., p. 53.
28. Bishwa Bandhu Chatterjee, ibid., p. 189
29. See footnote 53.
30. Bishwa Bandhu Chatterjee, ibid., p. 190.
31. The arguments elaborated upon in this section is derived from a reading of radical anthropologists such as Rey, Meillassoux, Greschire, etc.
32. Meillassoux, C., ibid. p. 130, fn.7.
33. Meillassoux quoted in Hindess, B. and Paul Q. Hirst, *Pre-Capitalist Modes of Production*, London, 1975, p.55.
34. Rey, P.P., 'Class contradiction in lineage societies', *Critique of Anthropology*, 13–14, (1979) pp. 41–60.

35. Geschiere, P., 'Imposing capitalist dominance through the state: The multifarious role of the colonial state in Africa', in Wim van Binsbergen and Peter Geschiere, *Old modes of production and capitalist encroachment: Anthropological explorations in Africa*, (1985), pp. 122–126.
36. van der Klei, Jos M., 'Articulation of modes of production and the beginning of labour migration among the Diola of Senegal', in Wim Van Binsbergen and Peter Geschire, ed., *Old modes of production and capitalist encroachment: Anthropological explorations in Africa*, London, 1985, pp. 71–93.
37. van der Klei, ibid., p. 89.
38. Quoted in Meillassoux, ibid., p. 74 (fn. 7).
39. Wim van Binsbergen, *Religious Change in Zambia*, London, 1981.
40. Headmen of all the tribes are called Patel. However, amongst the Bhils they are called Tadvi. The post of Tadvi or Patel is hereditary in all the groups. See also Lok Nath Soni, ibid. p.69. NN Vyas, 'Bhils', p.100. ST Das, Life Style: Indian Tribes (Location Practice), 1989, p. 272.
41. Lok Nath Soni, ibid., pp. 29–30.
42. S.P. Sharma and J.B. Sharma, *Culture of Indian Tribes*, New Delhi, 1998, p. 312.
43. In fact the study of S.P. Sharma and J.B. Sharma shows that even in cases where Bhils got loans or Taccavi from the government they did not spend it on the allocated head but on customs such as marriages and festivals. S.P. Sharma and J.B. Sharma, *Culture of Indian Tribes*, New Delhi, 1998, p. 325.
44. Stephen Fuchs, 'Land Scarcity and Land Hunger among some Aboriginal Tribes of Western Central India', in K.S. Singh (ed.), *The Tribal Situation in India*, New Delhi, 1972, pp. 368–369. S.P. Sharma and J.B. Sharma, *Culture of Indian Tribes*, New Delhi, 1998, pp. 317, 324–325.
45. Stephen Fuchs, 'Land Scarcity and Land Hunger among some Aboriginal Tribes of Western Central India', in K.S. Singh (ed.), *The Tribal Situation in India*, New Delhi, 1972, pp. 367–368. S.P. Sharma and J.B. Sharma, *Culture of Indian Tribes*, New Delhi, 1998, p. 312.
46. Stephen Fuchs, 'Land Scarcity and Land Hunger among some Aboriginal Tribes of Western Central India', in K.S. Singh (ed.), *The Tribal Situation in India*, New Delhi, 1972, pp. 368, 371.
47. The discussion is conducted in the preceding sections.
48. Geschiere, ibid., pp. 122–126.
49. Stephen Fuchs, ibid., p. 368.

50. Claude Meillassoux, ibid., pp. 121–123.
51. Data was collected in 1999 form Jamnia, Segbi, Borli, Jamli, Sahapura, Rupla, Khazan, Risla, Ojhar and Warla.
52. Bishwa Bandhu Chatterjee, *A Candle in Woodland: Kasturba Kanya Ashram, Niwali—Past. Present and Future* (Allied Publishers, New Delhi, 1973) p. 188. For a slightly more updated list of bride price see Lok Nath Soni, ibid., pp. 85–88.
53. Stephen Fuchs, ibid., pp. 368–69. See also, SP Sharma and JB Sharma, ibid., pp. 319–321.
54. There is a geographical scattering of the type of crops grown in Chatli, Niwali and Sakar groundnut is the major cash crop. In Sendhwa area, groundnut and soyabean are the major cash crops. In Ojhar, Chachria Khutwadi and Warla area cotton is the major cash crop.
55. For a detailed theoretical discussion on this point, please refer to the section on dialectics of transformation and consolidation.
56. Although anthropologi cal and economic works mention this point, they do not see it as a structural trait of the market. They rather see it as absence of equal opportunity to the adivasi. See, for instance, Stephen Fuchs' interpretation. While analysing the reasons for adivasis being compelled to sell their crops cheap to the merchants he states, "...tribal regions (are)... so remote from larger business centres, market places and railway lines...the tribal farmers are obliged to sell their crops to the merchants who visit them. These often offer a cheap price for the farm products the tribals have to sell, while they sell their own merchandise at a higher rate." Stephen Fuchs, ibid., p. 369.
57. Information gathered in an interview with Sumli Bai, a landless labour and activist of AMS in Khutwadi.
58. Segbi is approximately 8 km from Sendhwa.
59. The attempt by the Congress government is not bereft of politics. After inviting the application for regularisation of *nawad* in 1994 the case was allowed to hang at the Centre for four years. Finally, when elections drew to a close, the Congress government decided to distribute land under the special powers of the Governor under which a new provision was drafted. This proposed law declared that as per the survey of 1994, 2 hectares land per family would be given to 77,964 adivasis.
60. For the discussion on the impact of withdrawing of cheap labour force from adivasi community see the section on dialectics of transformation and consolidation above.
61. Cf. section on dialectics of transformation and consolidation.

62. N N Vyas, ibid., p. 100.
63. Lok Nath Soni, ibid., p. 29.
64. PUCL report, appendix II.
65. The PUCL report documents that Shri Bhim Singh, a Patel, possesses some 80 acres of land.
66. Lok Nath Soni, ibid., p. 29.
67. Bishwa Bandhu Chatterjee, ibid., p. 187.
68. Lok Nath Soni, ibid., p. 38.
69. SP Sharma and JB Sharma, ibid., p. 321.
70. C. Von Furer-Haimendorf, 'Foreword', in T. B. Naik, *The Bhils*, a study, (Delhi, 1956) p. 6.
71. Bishwa Bandhu Chatterjee, ibid., p. 31.
72. AM Shah and RG Shroff, 'The Vahivanca Barots of Gujarat: A caste of genealogist and mythographers', in *Journal of American Folklore*, Vol. 71 (1958) p. 258. RE Enthoven, The tribes and castes of Bombay, (Bombay, 1920). JK Doshi, *Social Structure and Cultural Change in a Bhil Village*, (Delhi, 1976) p. 6. Venkatachar, ibid., p. 32. Varma, *The Bhil Kills*, (Delhi, 1978) p. 6.
73. Lok Nath Soni, ibid., p. 7.
74. JK Doshi, ibid., p. 6.
75. MKA Siddiqui, 'Islamization among the tribes of Central and Western India', in *Bulletin of the Anthropological Survey of India*, Vol. 25, Nos. 3 & 4, pp. 46–72.
76. Lok Nath Soni, ibid., p. 68.
77. This has been indicated by Terray in his study of the Didi in Africa.
78. GS Aurora, ibid., p. 64.
79. Lok Nath Soni, ibid., p. 27.
80. cf. also Bishwa Bandhu Chatterjee, ibid., p. 31.
81. Bishwa Bandhu Chatterjee, ibid., p. 32.
82. KS Singh, *India's Communities* (Delhi, 1998). pp. 431, 434.
83. PUCL report.
84. Every type of marriage amongst Bhils does not involve bride price. However the prevalence of bride price over other types is well established. For the different types of marriages and the rates and form of bride price in them, see Lok Nath Soni, ibid., pp. 83–89.
85. Lok Nath Soni, ibid., p. 52.
86. GS Aurora, ibid., p. 46.

3

Adivasi vs. Vanvasi: The Politics of Conversion in Central India*

Nandini Sundar

If adivasi lands and resources have come under sustained attack by the forces of organised capitalism over the past hundred years or so, their beliefs too have had to face a determined war of attrition by organised religions. The two processes, in fact, feed off each other, with a growing commodification of life seeming to require a portable, commodified religion.[1] However, unlike the 'adherent-centred view' adopted by much of the recent literature on conversion,[2] which seeks to explicate the multiple processes by which conversion occurs or its meaning in the life of those converted,[3] this paper studies the campaign process as competing religions seek to establish hegemony on adivasi soil. Competitive proselytisation is primarily a political phenomenon, aimed at expanding numbers and keeping alternative religions out. If converts find solace in religion, or if new forms of religious and social imagining emerge, this is quite incidental to the purpose for which programmes of conversion are undertaken. Following Saberwal, the attempt here is to understand the ways in which resources and person-power are deployed to crystallise religious identities, and the implications of this process for adivasis in particular and for citizenship in

* This article has earlier appeared in Satish Saberwal and Mushirul Hasan (eds.) *Assertive Religious Identities*. New Delhi, Manohar, 2006, 357–390.

India more widely, as the state reifies religious identity at the expense of other identities.[4]

Jashpur District in Chhattisgarh (on the border with Jharkhand, sharing a common culture and people) is a useful site for such a study, since it has one of the oldest and largest Catholic communities in Central India. Not coincidentally, therefore, the *Rashtriya Swayamsevak Sangh* (RSS) front, the *Akhil Bharatiya Vanvasi Kalyan Ashram* (henceforth VKA) was first established here, to counter Christian missionary activity and to 'awaken tribals to their true Hindu identity'. The population of Jashpur is predominantly Oraon, followed by a number of 'OBC' (other backward classes) groups like the *Rautia, Mahakul, Teli,* and *Gosain. Marwari, Jain* and Muslim traders dominate the district and block headquarters. In broad-brush terms, the Catholic Church has its 'field' among *Oraons,* while the OBCs and upper castes form a potential Hindutva base. However, the RSS is also seeking to expand among unconverted *adivasis.* While the first half of the paper looks at the establishment of the Catholic Church in Jashpur, its perceived connections to the demand for an independent Jharkhand state, the setting up of the Kalyan Ashram and the politics of the Niyogi Commission, the second half of the paper examines the everyday working of the VKA.

Unlike conversion to Christianity, conversion to Hinduism has been much less studied, leave alone recognised,[5] except under the gradualist, anonymously authored processes termed 'the Hindu method of tribal absorption' or '*Sanskristisation*'.[6] For instance, both the Arya Samaj and the RSS describe their conversion merely as 're-conversion' as '*shuddhi*' (purification) or '*gharvapsi*' (homecoming). Hindu conversions are helped by the unmarked Hinduism of the state which treats Hinduism as the default religion when it comes to classifying adivasis in the census or other government records. Both Christians and Hindus see Freedom of Religion Acts in MP and Orissa as targeted primarily at Christian conversion.[7] However, state practice is contradictory in that judicial pronouncements on adivasi personal law have distinguished them from Hindus.[8]

Insofar as conversion is not just about a quantifiable change in religious belief, but a change of lifestyle, it is often hard to distinguish from other processes of change. Indeed, much change occurs through the process of 'uplift' or absorption into the 'mainstream', which are terms characteristic of state discourse towards adivasis. If the mainstream is defined as the path of capitalist development—Christianity in this area has long served to bring adivasis into the mainstream, through its emphasis on education for a middle class lifestyle,[9] even as it owed its initial success to its stand on behalf of the adivasis against a mainstream represented by landlords and officials. When the VKA or other Sangh associates talk of the 'mainstream', however, they additionally define it in terms of Hindu religion and 'culture'. By equating nationalism with 'Hindutva', the RSS portrays conversion to Christianity as an 'anti-national act', drawing spurious links between conversion to Christianity and separatism.

In every case, however, the real casualty is a pluralist idea of society and polity, in which adivasi religion and modes of resource use are celebrated and recognised in their own right. While a study of conversion would require a detailed description of the religion that existed before, my focus here is more on the politics of conversion campaigns than on actual processes of religious change. Adivasi religion, like any other, has never been static and what comes to us today as 'authentic' is necessarily filtered by a variety of influences and perspectives. For instance, much of Sarat Chandra Roy's classic study of the Oraon religion and custom is taken up by trying to trace the various influences on Oraon religion from outside.[10] But in its bare bones, as described by Roy, Oraons had two main classes of deities—nature spirits and human spirits, but within them there were hierarchies. *Dharmes* or the creator of the universe, earlier known as *Biri-Belas* or the Sun-God, was the most important. In addition, Oraons made offerings to village tutelary deities and to spirits inhabiting particular rocks and trees. Each lineage or khunt, as also each household within the lineage, had its own ancestor spirits.[11] Oraons had no temples, except a shrine for *Devi Mai* (which Roy presumed was borrowed from the Hindus) and their deities were usually represented by stones, or wooden pegs. A sal tree or grove known as *sarna* served as the site of worship. There was no separate priestly class and the *Pahan* performed the ceremonies. His office was hereditary in some villages and elected in others.[12]

The ongoing movement in Jharkhand to have adivasi religion recognised as '*sarna dharm*' or '*adi dharm*', and classified as such in the census, itself represents a systematisation of a variety of practices. Yet it is perhaps the only alternative to the religious imperialism of both Hindus and Christians. Indeed, even when Hindus and Christians are willing to concede the existence of such a thing as a distinctive adivasi religion, their descriptions involve acts of appropriation. A VKA pamphlet claims that adivasis are part of a wider Hindu family because Hindus also worship nature (*Tulsi*, *Ganga*, *Nag*, etc.).[13] Christian propagandists, like John Lakra, on the other hand, argue that Oraon religion is similar to Christianity in that it too is founded on belief in *Dharmes* or one Supreme God.[14] Ultimately, all religions (like languages) are products of a particular politics of classification, and the recognition accorded to their gods depends on the economic and political power of a people.

PART I: COMPETING BIOGRAPHIES

Establishment of the Jesuit Mission in Jashpur

> With a mission school there immediately follows a Sunday school and out of that grows a church. The history of many a Church in Assam can be traced back to an investment of say, forty dollars per year and the placement of a Christian teacher in an otherwise unevangelized village.[15]

The early histories of mission stations in Asia or Africa usually read as biographies of dedicated and self sacrificing priests, who went out to the furthest corners of the world and liberated their benighted denizens from the spiritual and civilisational darkness in which they lived.[16] The first mission in the Jharkhand region was the German Gossner Evangelical Lutheran Mission in 1844, followed by the Anglican Mission or the Society for the Propagation of the Gospel in 1869, and then the Catholic Mission. All of them were first set up in Ranchi District.[17]

Internal Jesuit explanations for the phenomenal success of the Catholic mission[18] usually centre around the charismatic figure of Constant Lievens, a Belgian Jesuit who came to Chhotanagpur in 1885. Realising that the main problem the Mundas faced was economic, he helped them fight their cases in court.[19] As his biographer Clarysse notes, while Lievens may have been more interested in the 'eternal happiness' of the Mundas, for them, the hope he held out for 'happiness in this life' by taking up their legal rights far overshadowed the other as a motive for conversion.[20]

Missionary entry into the princely states was faced with greater obstacles than in British India, in part because of the need to keep native rulers intact as figureheads, even as colonial administrations introduced changes in the tenurial system which meant higher rents, restrictions on access to forests and more forced labour (*begar*).[21] Conversion invariably involved a break in the traditional paternalist relations between rulers and their subjects, a relationship which was buttressed by the interpenetration of state ritual with local religion in the form of Dussehra celebrations, in which the king played a leading role. Being part of an alternative religious organisational structure emboldened adivasis to protest against existing political and economic structures. Missionary activity thus often worked at cross-purposes with the colonial administration's need to maintain the status quo. Paradoxically, Independence and a Constitutional right to propagate proved more congenial to Christian missionary activity (and even more so, of course, to Hindu missions) than colonial rule.[22]

Caught between the need to maintain law and order in the states and a professed policy of religious neutrality, eventual outcomes usually depended on the predilections of particular colonial officials.[23] For Christian-minded officers serving in Hindu-ruled states, enforcing 'freedom of religion' often translated as unofficial pressure on the Rulers to allow Christian missionaries in.[24] In Jashpur, this resulted in the Raja being forced to allow the German Lutheran Mission and Catholics into the state in 1906-07, despite his fears of subversion. However, in later years, the missionaries were also warned not to allow their preachers to mobilise peasants against the king.[25]

Friction between the Raja and the missionaries continued till Independence, necessitating periodic government enquiries. In 1913, Blakesley, the Political Agent, found that most of the conversion was due to material incentives on the availability of easy loans, help with marriage expenditures, free legal services by the catechists and the belief among some Oraons that their land revenue would be settled and they would be free from *begar,* as in Chhotanagpur. However, the Central Provinces Government did not accept Blakesley's recommendations, and the Jesuits who were hitherto operating from Ranchi district now moved into Jashpur.[26] The colonial state's frequent application of the Defence of India rules to extern rebels or Congress protestors during the World Wars suggests that it did not subscribe to the freedom to propagate all ideologies in its territories. This also meant that those with economic grievances had no choice but to express them in religious terms.

Matters came to a head in 1922 when villagers in *Uparghat* (the portion of Jashpur state above the ghats), encouraged by Lutheran preachers, refused to perform *begar.*[27] Soon after, the movement spread to Nichghat, with Lutherans playing the leading role, but both Catholics and non-Catholics joining in. Here too, the cause was excessive *begar* for zamindars and state officials which interfered with the peasant's own cultivation, the Raja's proposal to tax uplands and homestead plots, increases in rents, and oppression by state and police officials. Forest rights, e.g. contractor monopolies on lac, were another issue.[28] Large meetings were organised across Nichghat. In one incident, a constable was killed, following which, the Raja summoned forces from neighbouring Sarguja state. Several people were arrested and beaten, including 12 Catholic *pracharaks*. However, the Raja's demand for expulsion of the missionaries met with little success, and on the contrary, the joint outcry of the Lutherans and Catholics against 'human rights abuses' in Jashpur led to the Raja's being deposed.[29]

The Belgian Jesuits maintained that they had nothing to do with the protests and had in fact asked their flock to keep away from such activities. Indeed, the Catholics opposed the total abolition of *begar* because it was a Lutheran demand, and as a report by Father Vandendriessche to the Archbishop of Calcutta shows, rejoiced when Lutheran meetings on the issue were a failure. On the other hand, one Tana Oraon of village Barangjori told the Diwan that the *Bara Padri* had allowed them to attend the meetings and told them that if they attended church regularly they would be let off *begar*. What perhaps was equally likely was that the Belgian fathers had lost control over both their local *pracharaks* and their converts: as one convert told Fr. D' Alcantara: "Father, we shall remain Catholics of course, but with regard to these social affairs, we will no more listen to you because you are sitting with the Raja." If the Jesuits allowed their flock to attend political meetings, it was so as not to lose them altogether.[30]

These 'disturbances' provide a clear sense of the way in which conversion was rooted in agrarian discontent as well as the extent to which adivasi religious identity was as yet fluid, with individuals changing from one sect to another depending on the perceived benefits. Further, what European missionaries sanctioned and what their local preachers understood as the appropriate means and ends of conversion often exhibited significant divergences. We also get a sense of the schisms within Christianity with both Catholics and Lutherans contesting for souls. Supporting peasants against the state was often less important than ensuring they did not fall into the clutches of the other church. Equally, we see how the Raja preferred to blame missionaries for incitement rather than address people's complaints regarding economic exploitation.

Similar pressure resulted in the Raja of Gangpur giving the Lutherans and Catholics extensive plots of land on perpetual lease.[31] World War I, however, ensured a Catholic advantage over the Lutherans. In W.G. Archer's words: "In the first place, the access which the Catholic Mission has achieved has been secured by the methods of commercial competition. It has under-cut its rivals and has not hesitated to poach on other sportsman's grounds. Its main rival has been the Lutheran Mission, which prior to the War was a fighting alternative to the Jesuits. The War, however, sent the German missionaries into liquidation and although some of them returned when the hostilities were over, they found that the Catholics (mainly the Belgian Jesuits) had made similar annexations in the field of converts to those secured by the Allies in the German colonies."[32]

The mission question was revived in 1927 following reports of extensive proselytisation in Khuria Zamindari. The mission was found to run a virtually parallel administration, compounding minor offences and paying the fines into the mission account, concealing crimes, boycotting non-Christians, recruiting labour for the tea gardens, sugar plantations, and for the army, and running co-operative banks into which their remittances were deposited.[33] Catholics were asked to attend mission schools rather than state schools,[34] and on occasion seem to have received preference in the land settlement.[35] In 1936, the Bishop of Ranchi asked permission to erect schools and chapels in Udaipur state (neighbouring Jashpur), on the grounds that there was a huge demand for it. This was discovered to be somewhat fraudulent. It was a drought year, and people had heard that loans were easily available at Tapkara mission, provided they cut off their top-knots. The numbers too were much lower than the Bishop claimed: when one member of the family took a loan, the entire family was shown as having converted. The Bishop's justification, when confronted with this evidence, was a marvel of sophistry: "the taking of loans is not a motive of conversion, but it is in the eyes of the Aborigines a sign of adherence and a pledge of earnestness and sincerity."[36] The enquiry resulted in the missions being asked to maintain registers of converts, missionaries and preachers, and to notify the government of changes, not unlike the measures required by the contemporary Orissa Freedom of Religion Act 1967 and the MP Dharma Swatantraya Adhiniyam 1968.

If, in 1929, the Secretary of State could cite greater Christian sensitivity in England and America against bans on missionary activity,[37] by the mid-1940s, various Hindu groups had become equally sensitive. Theble Oraon, the first president of the Chhotanagpur Kisan Sabha, who then joined Congress, and the

Hindu Dharma Rakshak Sangh held meetings along the Ranchi-Jashpur border, warning adivasis about Bible teaching by the missions.[38] In Mandla, another adivasi-dominated part of the Central Provinces, Elwin had joined hands with his former adversary A.V. Thakkar of the Adimjati Sevak Sangh to counter the Catholic mission's unethical practices and claimed that along with the Arya Dharma Seva Sangh and the Gond Seva Mandal set up by P.G. Vannikar, one of Thakkar's trusted aides, he had been able to shut down 25 mission schools.[39]

The Demand for Jharkhand

Through the late 1930s up to the mid-1940s, one of the issues of consistent concern to the colonial authorities in the Eastern States, was the agrarian unrest in Gangpur, which bordered both Jashpur and Ranchi districts in British India.[40] Under a revised settlement in which lands reclaimed from the forest were taxed, rents went up by 44 per cent. Lutheran Mundas then embarked on a no-rent campaign, in some cases took forcible possession of lands from which they had been evicted, broke forest laws, held large meetings armed with bows and arrows, acknowledged Jaipal Singh as their leader and refused even to listen to their pastors. The Catholics, although present in larger numbers in Gangpur, were not part of the campaign.[41] Although the movement was eventually suppressed, and counter meetings of "anti-adibasis" were organised in Gangpur, professing loyalty to the state,[42] the demand for Jharkhand was identified by adivasis across the eastern states with a restoration of control over land and forests, and against the arbitrary power of thekedars, forest guards, etc.

Although non-Christian movements like the Tana Bhagats who operated along the Ranchi–Jashpur border, also refused to pay rent, or obey forest laws, until they were persuaded to by Gandhi[43], and both the Chhotanagpur Unnati Samaj and the Adivasi Mahasabha cut across religious boundaries, the movement for Jharkhand was identified by the RSS and the Congress government in Madhya Pradesh as a Christian inspired separatist movement similar to the Muslim demand for Pakistan.[44] A publication of the Vanvasi Kalyan Ashram, titled *Friends or Foes of Adivasis and Dalits*? begins:

> The elements who had not reconciled to the nation's independence continued to conspire to weaken and fragment the country further. A little known event of those days was a conspiracy hatched by Christian missions to carve out, with the help of Mohammed Ali Jinnah and the Nizam of Hyderabad, an independent Christian country comprising Chhota Nagpur (Bihar) and parts of Madhya Pradesh, Orissa and West Bengal, which was detected and foiled by our government. Because of this conspiracy the then State Government of C.P. and Berar was faced with a critical situation in the tribal areas of the province. The tribals, mostly Christian converts under the tutelage of Christian missionaries had revolted and the hostility of these tribals to India's new independence and the provincial government of the day was so strong that when late Pandit Ravi Shankar Shukla, Chief Minister (then known as Prime Minister) of the province toured the area, he was greeted with black flags and cries of 'Jai Jesus' in response to the slogan of Jai Hind raised from the dais.[45]

The founding narrative of the Vanvasi Kalyan Ashram takes off from this moment. Insulted on being greeted at Jashpur with slogans demanding Jharkhand and asking him to go back, Shukla asked the Gandhian, A.V. Thakkar, well known for his work among adivasis and dalits, for advice on tackling the 'missionary menace' and growing separatism. Thakkar advised taking the help of 'nationalist social service organisations' and on the recommendation of P.G. Vannikar, appointed Ramakant Keshav Deshpande of the RSS as Regional Director of the Tribal Welfare Department.[46] Deshpande's biographer, K.D.Sapre, comments on the irony of a Congress government about to arrest Deshpande as part of its sweep against the RSS after Gandhi's murder, sending him instead to Jashpur as a government servant.[47] Yet, this was not so surprising after all, considering that a strand of the Congress was sympathetic to the Hindu Mahasabha, and had been open to members of the RSS also joining the Congress.[48] The Madhya Pradesh branch of the Congress was dominated by the 'Hindu traditionalist faction' and Shukla, in fact, had been introduced to the Congress through Moonje of the Hindu Mahasabha.[49]

Indeed, Shukla's experience in Jashpur forms the starting

point for the Niyogi Commission too.[50] In the chapter, 'The circumstances leading to the appointment of the committee', the Commission devoted several pages to the demand for Jharkhand as a Christian-inspired separatist movement:

> In view of the political bias with which Christian missionaries had carried on proselytism during the last half a century in the merged territories and in view of their active support of the dangerous Jharkhand movement Government considered it necessary to put down the activities which led to fissiparous tendencies.[51]

Elsewhere of course (p. 50), the Commission recognises that at least one strand of the movement was demanding merely merger of some states with Bihar rather than with the Central Provinces, or at most a separate Jharkhand state within India. Yet the treatment of the Jharkhand movement by the States Reorganisation Commission and the Congress betrays total contempt for the right and capacity of adivasis to govern themselves, a right that they were happy to grant to much less culturally homogenous linguistic groups.

The Niyogi Commission

The Niyogi Commission was one forum when the interests of the RSS and the Congress government of Madhya Pradesh meshed rather well. Set up by the Shukla government in 1954 under the chairmanship of Dr. Bhawani Shankar Niyogi, retired justice of the Nagpur High Court, the Commission's mandate was to enquire into complaints that Christian missionaries used force or monetary incentives to convert people. The Commission also ostensibly broadened the scope of its enquiry to look into complaints by Christian missionaries of harassment by local officials and non-Christians.[52]

However, both in terms of its composition with only one Christian whom the Christians regarded as non-representative and in terms of its mode of operating, it was clear that the cards were stacked against the Christians. Sapre describes the close links that Niyogi and other Commission members like Ghanshyam Singh Gupta had with the RSS: Niyogi apparently took up the task only after Golwalkar reassured him that the Vanvasi Kalyan Ashram and other RSS workers would represent the Hindus.[53] While the Commission toured 14 districts and visited a number of institutions, it also relied heavily on a 99-question survey, in which, as the Catholics quite rightly complained, "most of the questions were veiled accusations against the Missions". Out of 385 replies to the questionnaire, 55 were from Christians and 330 from non-Christians, of which significant numbers were members of the Arya Samaj, or RSS.[54] While noting that the activities of the Arya Samaj and RSS in countering missions had led to tensions, the Niyogi Commission blamed this on the "objectionable methods followed by missionaries", who also initiated false complaints against others.[55] The Catholics argued that enumerating adivasis under the Hindu column in the 1951 census, when they had previously been classed as animists, was also a form of mass conversion to Hinduism[56]. Yet this cut little ice with the Commission which instead cited the problem faced by earlier census commissioners in distinguishing animists from Hindus.[57]

The Commission found that with Independence, American missionary evangelisation had increased,[58] and that the bulk of external money went towards paying *pracharaks*.[59] Methods of evangelisation involved both coercion and inducement: changing names of students and giving them Christian names, holding compulsory Bible classes for non-Christians attending mission schools, giving witness and preaching in hospitals, moneylending and waiving interest if the borrower turned Christian, running orphanages, using Christians in government departments like the police, education or forest department, to hold meetings, organising bhajan mandalis where yeshu *bhajans* were sung and the Yeshu Bhagwat was recited, and abusing Hindu gods.[60]

The recommendations of the Commission in response to what they pictured as a worldwide Christian conspiracy to 're-establish Western supremacy' and threaten 'the security of the state'[61] were to ban all mission activity in labour recruitment, place controls on the entry of foreign missionaries and conversions, and increase government involvement in the running of orphanages, schools, hospitals, etc.[62] They also recommended, quite gratuitously, that the Indian churches establish a 'United Independent Christian Church in India without being dependent on foreign support', a suggestion voiced again by the RSS after the then Prime Minister Vajpayee renewed the 'national debate on conversions'. And then, in language that would be echoed by the RSS some 50 years later in its 2003 conference, the Commission noted:

> In the present secular state of India, the best safeguard any minority could have, is the goodwill of the majority community and the right attitude of the minority is one of trust and confidence in the fair sense of the majority.[63]

Battling Christian Missionaries: Ramakant Keshav (Balasaheb) Deshpande

> Different kinds of activities are necessary for the all-round development of the country. The Sangh aims to cover all fields through its work. The Vishwa Hindu Parishad has its own distinct objectives to bring all the Hindu sects on to a common Hindu platform and to revive all the temples that were destroyed and ruined.... The task of the Akhil Bharatiya Vidyarthi Parishad is to bring direction to the country's youth. The Bharatiya Janata Party is the political wing... Today there is a concerted effort to separate the vanvasi samaj from the Hindu samaj and make them think they are not Hindus. Our effort is to awaken the vanvasi regions and remove this feeling of difference. For this we have to unite the Vanvasis. That is the Akhil Bharatiya Vanvasi Kalyan Ashram's work. That is its major role. We will do all sorts of work, and try and fill all kinds of gaps such as lack of health facilities or drinking water but at all times our objective must be clear.[64]

If Lievens was the heroic figure of Catholic perseverence in evangelising the vast field that the adivasis of Chhotanagpur represented, the RSS equivalent is the figure of Ramakant Keshav Deshpande, who, by setting up the Kalyan Ashram, stemmed the seemingly unstoppable march of the missionaries and reclaimed souls or bodies for the Hindus. Like Lievens, the inspiration for his presence in Jashpur came not from a curiosity about adivasi life and conditions or a desire to help them, but from an organised system whose driving force lay elsewhere in the RSS case, the establishment of a Hindu Rashtra, in which members of all other religious communities would have second class status.[65]

KD Sapre's *Shri Balasaheb Deshpande: Jeevan aur Karya* (life and work), might be read as a classic Sangh biography of a classic Sangh figure. The hero of such biographies is inevitably born to a Sangh or at least a conservative middle-class Maharashtrian family, has contact with the leading ideologues of the Sangh, is the innocent victim of police or government accusations, is arrested for terrorist and disruptive activities, acquitted for lack of evidence, and finally graduates to become a 'respectable' figure of society with wider acceptance among a Hindu public.

Born on 26 December 1913 at Amaraoti to Keshavrao Deshpande, a government karamchari, Ramkant was one of four brothers, all of whom did law. His maternal cousin was Murli Deoras, the third RSS *Sarsanghchalak*. When visiting Nagpur, Deshpande attended lathi sessions, was introduced to Dr. Hedgewar and became a Swayamsevak.[66] After finishing a BA and law degree, Deshpande started practising law in Ramtek with his uncle. He also became the *karyavah* or leader of the Ramtek Sangh. In those days, Golwalkar lived in Ramtek and had a library which Deshpande frequented. In this way, we are told, "the stream of his life and that of respected Guruji met and Balasaheb's life of national service began".[67]

Deshpande, says his biographer, was a dedicated freedom fighter, and patrolled the streets during the Quit India Movement to maintain law and order, along with his band of RSS associates. Unfortunately, his sterling qualities were not recognised by the Muslim police officer in charge of Ramtek, who arrested him and sent him to Nagpur for trial on charges of looting and arson. Despite extensive eyewitness evidence, he was acquitted because the Ramtek tahsildar, Harkare, whom he had once saved from lynching by a mob, refused to testify against him. The evasions in this account are almost as fascinating as what Sapre actually tells us such as the RSS's lack of involvement in the Quit India movement, or the strong likelihood that Deshpande was in fact engaged in communal and disruptive activities.

Deshpande then got married and got a job in the ration department, but soon resigned, ostensibly due to a stand against profiteering. He returned to law. After Gandhi's death, when the public was 'being incited' against the Sangh, Deshpande's house too came under attack. He was saved by the appearance of his brother. Soon after this, the incident at Jashpur with Ravi Shankar Shukla occurred and Deshpande was posted to Jashpur as Director of the Tribal Welfare Department.

The Battle over Schools

When Deshpande reached Jashpur, he found that the missionaries had a hundred primary schools. At once, so Sapre's story goes, he asked the government for permission to open a hundred government primary schools. Wherever there were mission schools, Deshpande set up one of his own, appointing teachers on the basis of their *chotis* (topknots) and their physical strength. The teachers were warned that they would have to defend themselves. Some of them had only passed the fourth grade.[68]

In a remarkable section titled: *Bhai Bin Hot na preet* (without fear there is no love), Sapre approvingly recounts instances when Deshpande employed physical violence to cow the missionaries down, including filing court cases against them. For example, he went to a village which was a Christian stronghold, accompanied by eight or ten lathi-wielding youth. Having gathered the villagers together, he instructed them to say 'Jai Hind'. When they allegedly replied 'Jai Ishu', he threatened to beat them all up. This tactic, Sapre tells us, worked wonders. But it was only after an incident when he beat up Father Mews at the Ginabahar Catholic school, for ostensibly stopping an Ashram boy using the mission compound as a thoroughfare, that Deshpande claims he realised how important the schools could be as fighting centres.[69]

Given this unabashed account, the Catholic complaint that the teachers were not there so much to teach tribal students but to harass and threaten Christians, seems a reasonably correct one. In his reply to the Niyogi questionnaire, the President of the Raigarh Catholic Sabha explained why they refused to co-operate with the Adivasi Welfare department:

> From the day of merger, the Madhya Pradesh Government declared a fierce war on our schools. All our Primary schools lost their recognition and none received a grant-in-aid. The Adivasi Welfare Department tried to open rival schools next to every Catholic school at least in areas that were not inaccessible. In these rival schools, teachers were paid fabulous salaries, at least three times the amount paid in our schools; the pupils were charged no fees, received books and stationary free, and also a daily meal into the bargain. And very severe pressure was put on non-Christian parents to induce them to withdraw their children from our schools.[70]

The Catholics sounded entirely aggrieved, complaining that the inspectors were failing their children.[71] However, their own reaction was of equal belligerence. Father Vermiere of the Jashpur Roman Catholic Mission wrote in a letter to one of his Superiors:

> You may have read in the *Herald* some very spirited answers purported to come from Jashpur Christian students against the vile slander by one who came with a large retinue to spy [on] our institutions at Gholeng and Ginabahar. He dares call himself a member of the much esteemed Servants of India Society. He and his colleague have nearly wrecked the nascent Mission of the Norbertine Fathers in Mandla, District Jubbulpore. They were sent here by the Prime Minister, but if they hope to ruin this Mission, they are very much mistaken. Our Catholics are too advanced to be taken in, or frightened by such slanderers. Protest meetings against their vile report continue to be held, chiefly to wreck their treacherous machinations. As one of the two is a sort of Minister for the uplift of the backward people, he has a considerable government budget to dispose of. Their aim is more to prevent us from converting, than to care for the uplift of those they used to keep them in bondage (sic). Just now they are starting 40 new schools for these backward adibasis. The third I hear of is in a village where we possess a school since 30 years. But knowing that many pagan children come to our schools and that we had sent a petition for a building to enlarge that school, they surreptitiously try and draw away the pagan children from us. But we are ready for them. Today my men are gone there to attend a big panchayat to draw up a protest, and get all the pagans to refuse withdrawing their children from us. I am giving you all this for the sake of those in the community interested in Jashpur affairs.[72]

The Central Provinces Government, not surprisingly, came down on the side of the Tribal Welfare Department in the schools matter, noting that "the duty of Government being to provide non-sectarian educational instruction for the people, no legitimate objection could be taken against it".[73] Indeed, there could indeed have been no objection, and given the sectarian nature of Catholic schooling, they would have had little right to complain if the schools run by the Tribal Welfare department had been truly neutral. Instead, however, under Deshpande they functioned not merely as pro-Hindu but anti-Christian institutions.

Some 50 years later, the setting up of schools is still a matter of fierce competition, but this time, it is the Vanvasi Kalyan Ashram, which is resisting government schools coming up in its vicinity. At a meeting in Chatori village in 2001, the headquarters of Manora block, inhabited primarily by Pahari Korwas, officially a 'Primitive Tribal Group', the Tribal Welfare Secretary from New Delhi, S.K. Naik, on inspection of the area, dusted down the teacher of the government school for having only three students while the Kalyan Ashram school had 62. K.P. Singh, General Secretary of the VKA later told me that the government school had been set up by the Christian Tribal Welfare secretary of Chhattisgarh State in order to attract children away from the Kalyan Ashram school with the promise of mid-day meals. But the plan, he gloated, had backfired because the Hindu Tribal Welfare Secretary at the Centre decreed that the children in the Kalyan ashram school should also get mid-day meals, because it didn't matter where they studied. The meeting at Chatori ended with Naik ordering more funds to be given to the Kalyan Ashram so that they could expand their hostel.[74]

But schools were not the only arena in which the Catholics and the Sangh clashed, and Deshpande seems to have been assisted by other Hindutva forces, in addition to the state. For instance, in its response to the Niyogi Commission, the Catholic Sabha of Jashpur described the activities of the Arya Samaj, Deshpande's Ram Rajya Parishad and "the All-India Vaidik Shuddhi Samaj of a certain Swami Ramanuj Saraswati" which involved "spreading of the most shameless lies in the press and through fly sheets; for instance, that the Christians are gathering and hiding in the woods, arms and ammunition, against an eventual rising; frightening poor people into reconversion by threats of loss of land; also offering to give land; offering fabulous salaries to would-be converts to Hinduism".[75] One Boko Sardar, under the guidance of Swami Ramanuj, urinated on the walls of a Christian chapel at Tangergaon and sang Hindu *bhajans* in another chapel.[76] The methods of the Christian missionaries, according to the Catholic Sabha, were in contrast, "service of the neighbour, persuasion, never force or fraud".[77]

Both sides disrupted intra-village relations, but each attributed it solely to the other. Deshpande's response to the Niyogi commission emphasised the fact that Christian converts were not allowed to participate in village festivals and instead celebrated agricultural rituals like *nayakhani* in their churches. Dussehra was replaced by a festival called Jubilee. He also reported frequent village conflicts when Christians tried to bury their dead on *sarna* grounds or otherwise encroach on it. The Catholics, on the other hand, claimed that conversions made no difference to their way of life, other than renouncing idol worship and gram devatas ("we would deem it a grievous sin, if, knowing the one true God we went and gave worship to idols, devatas and bhuts").[78] Instead they blamed Deshpande for ruining relations between the two communities, which had hitherto been harmonious.[79]

PART II: THE VANVASI KALYAN ASHRAM

> *We want the kind of vanvasi leadership which can bring Hindu unity. We need to erect a society which is proud of Hindutva... Our work is to bring about awareness and create leadership.*
> *Balasaheb Deshpande, Sanstha, Shasan aur Karykarta. 1990: 17*

Deshpande resigned from government service after two years, because the changing political exigencies meant that the Government no longer gave him full support. While he had been successful at countering the Catholics, government rules prevented him from achieving his other major objective giving tribal boys *Hindutva sanskars.*[80] He then set up the Vanvasi

Kalyan Ashram along with another Swayamsevak, Morubhau Ketkar, and financial and moral help from the Maharaja of Jashpur.[81]

For a long time, no students came to the *ashramshala*. Sapre's narrative goes on to relate, in tones strongly reminiscent of Catholic primers on the lives of saints, how God's grace worked to bring students to the hostel. Just as Ketkar was about to give up, he dreamt of the RSS founder, Hedgewar, who advised him to carry on. By coincidence, (read divine intervention), six boys came to the ashram to study that day and after this miracle, the ashram soon came into full swing.[82]

As Sapre tells it, local traders and sadhus played a significant role in the expansion of the Kalyan ashram.[83] *Yagyas* and *Dharam Jagrans* were especially useful occasions for mobilising both while traders contributed money and materials, local sadhus like Gahira Guru, Rambhikshuk Maharaj and Swarupanand helped them in their mission of 'dharm jagran'. One such event was the inauguration by Golwalkar of the new Kalyan Ashram buildings in Jashpur in 1963. Traders like Bhimsen Chopda, who felt threatened by the Jharkhand movement introduced Kalyan Ashram to larger magnates like Hanuman Prasad Poddar of Gorakhpur who, in turn, helped them raise money from his Marwari contacts. Sympathetic government officials also helped. Thousands of adivasis, according to Sapre, participated in these events, and Ramayan and bhajan mandalis were established in some 114 villages.

Relationship with Government

A significant part of the early history of the Kalyan Ashram centres on its uneasy relations with Congress governments. As with Christian missionaries under colonial rule, much depended on particular officers or politicians, and even as it officially eschewed dependence on government funding, efforts were/are constantly made to get legitimation from senior politicians and functionaries as a 'non-political' organisation doing 'good work' for 'adivasi uplift.' In the process, links with the Sangh may be downplayed. In the early years, or so Sapre claims, both A.V. Thakkar and U.N. Dhebar accorded them significant recognition.[84] Later, when charged with a Jansangh association by Shankar Dayal Sharma (then Education Minister in the MP government), Deshpande reports telling him, "If I had come to you with a white cap, you would have funded me. It is because we are far from politics that you don't want to fund me".[85]

On the other hand, in internal pamphlets designed for Kalyan Ashram workers, the organisation emphasises its Sangh identity:

> Once the Speaker of the Madhya Pradesh assembly Shri Ghanshyam Singh Gupt came to the Ashram. He said you are branded with the Sangh stamp, which is why you are not able to get government aid. So just change your board slightly. Put up an Arya Samaj board, but continue to do the same work. I'll make sure you get government aid. We said we are what we are. It is essential to retain our identity or the source of our inspiration will dry up and we will be able to do no work.[86]

The Ashram's official line is that dependence on government funding saps the spirit of voluntarism, and restricts recruitment or the kind of work done,[87] and indeed, efforts are made to raise money from the 'public'. While locally, business families are a prime source,[88] non-resident Indians also contribute significantly through the US-based India Development Relief Fund (IDRF), and the UK-based Hindu Swayamsevak Sangh.[89] Not all the donors are necessarily, however, Sangh supporters. Following a critical investigative report on their activities, the IDRF attempted initially to deny that the VKA was a Sangh organisation and later, when it was forced to admit this, tried to emphasise its 'service activities'.[90]

At the same time, it is undeniable that having the BJP in power at the Centre (1998–2004) involved substantial payoffs for Sangh organisations.[91] KP Singh, General Secretary of the VKA was appointed on the board of CAPART for the eastern region, in charge of funding NGOs, and Juel Oram ensured that funds from the Tribal Welfare Ministry he headed went to RSS NGOs.[92] Financial support from TRIFED, the Ministry of Tribal Welfare, the Ministry of Rural Development, and the Ministry of Youth and Sports, enabled the Kalyan Ashram to organise a Swadeshi Vanvasi Mela at the Nehru Stadium in Delhi from

February 11 to 14, 2001. A seminar on adivasi issues, which was held on the premises was aimed at gaining public acceptability, with participants like the well-known administrator-turned-activist B.D. Sharma or N.C. Zeliang of Nagaland speaking on the same platform as known RSS activists like Mahesh Chandra Sharma, BJP appointed head of the Khadi Gramudyog Commission, Shree Basant of the Karigar Panchayat or K.P. Singh of the Vanvasi Kalyan Ashram.[93]

The VKA stand on 'indigenous peoples'

The Kalyan Ashram is now trying to appropriate the concerns taken up by non-party social movements like land and displacement, though much of it appears instrumental. For instance, as Raghav of the Vanvasi Kalyan Ashram in Lohardaga (Jharkhand) confessed, a survey they conducted which raised the issue of restoration of alienated tribal land, was really aimed at Muslims, even though there are as many Hindu money-lenders.[94] Any contradictions that might arise between the BJP's support for multinationals or its base of exploitative traders and the VKA's constituency of adivasis is reconciled by claiming to be two different organisations, by attributing it to the BJP's need to govern or get votes, and finally, by the understanding that ultimately the agenda is really the same the building of a Ram temple and the establishment of a Hindu Rashtra.

At the same time, the VKA resists the terminology of 'indigenous peoples' and even the term adivasi, which grew out of the Jharkhand struggle. Instead, it prefers to call them '*vanvasis*' or forest dwellers as against '*gaonvasis*'(village dwellers) and '*shahrvasis*' (city dwellers), on the grounds, shared by many post-colonial critics, that the distinction between tribes and castes is a colonial product. Any attempt by Indian adivasis to take their concerns to international forums on indigenous peoples is seen as contributing to the break-up of India. A letter from R.K. Deshpande to the Prime Minister, Narsimha Rao, warned the Government of India about the representations to the UN by the Indian Council of Indigenous and Tribal Peoples. After having pointed to the Church connections of some of the members of the delegation like Bishop Nirmal Minz, the memorandum warned of the "nexus between the Church-backed separatists, insurgents and other disintegrationists like the ULFA, Khalistanis, Pak-aided Kashmiri militants and other similar outfits.'[95]

While the Kalyan Ashram blames Christian missionaries for changing adivasi culture, it does little to protect it either, other than promoting their dances. Local languages are not forbidden in their schools and hostels but Sanskrit and Hindi are glorified. There is a real reluctance among Kalyan Ashram students to admit to knowing Kurukh and my attempts at getting assembled children in Chatori to sing a Pahari Korwa song while waiting for the Tribal Welfare Secretary were contemptuously discarded by one of their ideologues, Avadh Bihari, who asked them to recite a Sanskrit shloka instead.[96] However, if they see Christian competition in the use of local adivasi languages, the VKA is not averse to using them either.

Although the Kalyan Ashram publicly claims that one-third to half of its workforce is 'vanvasi' and the ceremonial positions like that of the President and Vice Presidents are filled by tribals, the organisational positions which hold real control are in the hands of non-tribal, upper caste RSS men. As of 2001, the VKA had 842 male and 210 female full-timers, out of which approximately half were 'vanvasis'.[97]

The VKA claims to have over 10,000 projects including *satsang kendras* and *lok kala mandals*, schools, *ekal vidyalayas, bal sanskar kendras*, libraries, dispensaries, hospitals, agricultural development and vocational training centres, and sports centres, and contacts with over 35,000 tribal villages.[98] However, as one ideologue put it, "whatever we do is only a means to an end".[99] There appear to be three major ends: 'dharm jagran' (literally, religious awakening) or conversion in order to expand numbers, recruitment of full-time workers for the Sangh, and fomenting violence against minorities.

Education as Dharm Jagran

> *Avadh Bihari*: The main aim of *Kalyan Ashram* is *Dharam Jagran*. This is the cheapest and most effective way of mobilising people. Schools and hospitals are just means towards this end. This is why VKA doesn't have too many schools and isn't entirely focused on

education like the Ramkrishna Mission.[100]

Ramesh Upadhya: *Dharam Jagran* is the ultimate and real objective. Schools, etc. are an easy way to draw people the cheapest way to mobilise people is through *dharam*, by running *bal sanskar kendras* etc.

Rathi: The main difference between us and the Ramakrishna Mission is that they want perfection in what they do. We are not interested in horizontal achievement but in vertical spread. The more ground or people we cover, the better.

NS: So your main aim is *Dharm Jagran*?

Rathi: Not even that. Our main aim is to keep Christians out.

Ramesh Upadhya: This was always the aim—that our numbers, which had gone down due to theft by other faiths, should go up again. But for strategic reasons, we don't want to do it publicly under the *Kalyan Ashram* banner. Swami Amaranand organises the events and then calls Dilip Singh Judeo for publicity. Judeo gets lots of publicity, which is good for his career, and we get his support.

Much of the media coverage of the VKA has focused on the public 'reconversion' ceremonies.[101] In Jashpur, these are organised by Swami Amaranand who lives on the campus, and while the number of converts involved may be debatable, they are useful as public spectacles. VKA members simultaneously play on fears of increasing conversion, as well as boast of having stemmed the tide.[102] In fact, however, as the above conversation shows, much more lasting conversion to Hindutva occurs through schools and hostels.[103]

Deshpande's early insight that schools could serve as incubators of physical violence was extended to seeing hostels as nodal points for Sangh extension activities in the villages:

> *We know that not all students of our chatravas [hostel] will become fulltime workers. But all of them will have received our sanskars... of all our activities, the most important one is the running of the hostels. The rationale behind our hostels is different from the usual ones. We want to make our hostels the focus or centre of attention for the region. Through this medium we want to bring about awareness in the whole region.*[104]

Accordingly, a handbook for the private use of Kalyan Ashram workers notes that in addition to the hostel warden, an additional worker should set up a centre in or near the *chatravas* to keep in touch with a circle of 20–30 villages around and organise them through *eklavya khelkud kendras, gram samitis,* dramas, etc.[105] Children are trained to hold *bhajan mandalis, satsang kendras, shakhas* and other activities when they go home for the long summer vacations.

The hostels are in much demand and even some Christians apply.[106] Although the surroundings are shabby (especially in the girls' hostel), and food is basic, these hostels provide a totalising and intense experience. There is a proliferation of Hindu visual imagery—all of which is part of a carefully planned design to expose children to Hindu idioms.[107] The daily routine at both the girls' and boys' hostels stretches from early morning prayers to *shakha* attendance to an evening *shakha* followed by *arti* and *bhajan,* which appears to create an almost trancelike impact on the students. The students also read the *Hanuman chalisa* or *Ramayan path* together in the mornings.[108] In addition there are weekly discourses on national events (from a Sangh point of view, of course), annual days at which the leading people of nearby villages are invited, and celebrations of Hindu festivals. Girls are more involved in ritual activity than boys, especially on occasions like *janmashtami* and *rakhee.* Rakhee has a special meaning in the Kalyan Ashram calendar—with *vanvasis* tying *rakhees* to non-*vanvasis,* thus establishing a bond between the communities. In short, whatever time is spent away from studying goes into Sangh-related activities. Needless to say, this routine is quite different from their daily lives at home. The prayers and the *bhajans* too are quite different from their own religious practices.

It is the everydayness of school and hostel life, however, and not just the exposure to rituals, which has the most lasting effects. Assi Zilya, from Kohima district studying in her final year of the BA degree in Raipur and living in the VKA hostel described how she only 'discovered' that she was really a Hindu when she came to the Ashram in Raipur:

Assi: "Before that, we always thought we were different from Hindus. We worship the Sun God.'

NS: So how did you know you were Hindu?

Assi: "We also believe in the Sun, Hindus also believe in the Sun, and our ways of worship are similar. We also pray to God at sowing or harvest."

The North-East girls reported that when they go home, even if as Kalyan Ashram workers, they resume praying in their own languages and to their own local gods. But they say that a sense of identity with Hinduism as against the locally dominant Christianity remains.[109] A number of students in the Jashpur Chatravas had also been to mission schools at some point in their lives. Bima Bhunkar and Asha Chakris, two college-going students at the girls' hostel in Jashpur had both been at Mission schools till the 12th. They told me they had not seen it as a problem then, but after coming to the Kalyan Ashram and learning about their Hindu *dharm*, they began to see how bad the Christians were for converting.

Apart from schools, the VKA runs pre-school centres for children (Balwadis or *bal sanskar kendras*) to teach them the rudiments of reading, writing and *sanskar*. These *sanskars* include learning to say *pranam* instead of their own adivasi greeting *johar*, touching the feet of their elders and shouting slogans like *Saraswati Mata ki Jai, Mahapati Ram ki Jai, Brindavan Krishna Ki Jai.* Not every child understands what they are chanting and the littler ones often fall asleep, but sustained exposure to these centres inevitably inculcates respect for Sanskrit as a language worth knowing, and a belief that 'civilisation' consists in Hindu markers of behaviour. More important than the actual information that children may or may not remember is the symbolic message transmitted.

'Keeping in mind the love of youth for sports' there are 'Eklavya khel kud centres' for older youth. The idea is 'through that medium to attract them to the Kalyan Ashram and Sangh' and having thus attracted them, 'to use the power of organised youth to bring about a change in society.'[110] Before and after the game, children are expected to greet the motherland, shouting *Bharat Mata Ki Jai*. The games are designed to be indigenous, with names like '*Agnikund*' and Ram–Ravan. Here, as in the *shakhas*, the referee calls out directions in Sanskrit, and while not all participants may be Sangh supporters, this enjoyable activity generates considerable goodwill for the ashram. Every four years the Kalyan Ashram holds an all-India sports event, and while there is an attempt to get children from schools other than simply Kalyan Ashram or RSS schools, Christian children are definitely discouraged.[111]

For older people, the VKA runs *satsang kendras* or religious gatherings in villages where villagers are taught Hindu *bhajans* and *kirtans*, and given discourses. Like the Catholics before them, who set hymns to local tunes, the Sangh may keep in references to the Singbonga or local gods, but Hindu gods like Ram and Krishna inevitably involve pride of place. VKA newsletters also serve an important proselytising function, especially in a situation where reading material and alternative sources of information are scarce. Each branch of the VKA brings out its own newsletter for instance, the Jharkhand branch brings out *Ekal Varta*, the Jashpur unit brings out *Vanvasi Darshan*. One issue of *Vanvasi Darshan* had accounts of Christians who had 'reconverted' as well as an article on the universal importance of Lord Ram. They claimed this was shown by the fact that towns were named after him all over the world, such as Rampside, Ramsbottom and Ramsgate in England, Ramtuel and Rambert Viliers in France.[112]

Recruitment of full-timers

> The true test of how successful a hostel is the number of full-time workers it generates for the Sangh and the Kalyan Ashram and only then does a hostel become meaningful.[113]

Judged by the standards of how many full-timers it generates, the Kalyan Ashram is a rather successful institution, with several of its hostellers going on to do *seva* for a couple of years before they take up normal lives and occupations. Some of these students go on to summer camps run by the RSS where, apart from more physical training, they also get ideological training.

When Avadh Bihari, an old *pracharak* and joint organising secretary of the VKA, visited Jashpur he went on a recruitment round of all the hostels.[114] His discourses combined a grandfatherly interest in the futures of the children with inspiring examples of Sangh volunteers who had devoted their life to service. Each sermon ended with his asking how many students were willing to join the Sangh, warning them that they would have to give at least two years as full-timers after finishing their education. Each session generated some half a dozen volunteers from Classes 11 and 12, and he encouraged them to write to him about their aspirations. At the girls' hostel, the conversation was appropriately tailored to his idea of female future. After solving an internal hostel dispute, he claimed that this was the decade of women's empowerment and they should go forward just as "Jijabai gave birth to Shivaji and Kausalya to Ram. Behind every great man is a mother who gave the right *sanskars*, and sacrificed her life to bring the great man up". He then told the girls 'the story of Itwari' who had been saved from being a nun and had joined the Ashram. Only one of the girls present had been to a Rashtriya Sevika Samiti camp, so the others were advised to join. Finally, Avadh Bihari asked how many of the girls wanted to do *samaj seva* (social work). At that point only one stood up but two others later said they had felt shy and asked for their names to be given to 'Dadaji'.

Much recruitment also happens through personal contacts in the villages. Somvari, a woman *pracharak* in Lohardaga, for example, comes from a family in Angul. She took quiet pride in the fact that her family knew Dara Singh, the killer of Graham Staines, and Jual Oram, the Tribal Welfare Minister. Male *pracharaks* used to come to their village to teach and she was attracted by the idea of doing *samaj seva* and *dharam raksha*. Somvari said she was also very keen to learn Hindi as it was the *rashtra bhasha*.

While Jashpur had no women *pracharaks*, Jharkhand had some 14 full-timers. Although the image of the ideal woman promoted by the RSS is of someone who takes care of the home and brings forth fighting children who will defend Hinduism, in practice the VKA women *pracharaks* are empowered women. While there is a clear internal gender hierarchy, the familial idiom in which the organisation is run means that the relationship between senior VKA men and the younger women *pracharaks* is a relaxed, even joking one. In part this may also be due to the fact that adivasi women are used to a relatively non-hierarchical structure in their villages. At the same time, the leadership of the VKA, as of the RSS more widely, is obsessed with sex—particularly the idea that 'Hindu' women are sexually exploited by Muslims and Christians and makes much of this propaganda in adivasi areas.

Living conditions in the Kalyan Ashrams are both spartan and egalitarian, providing a sense of community, with elders referred to in familial terms (Dadaji, Bhabhi, etc.). Every worker is paid according to their needs—single *pracharaks* (male and female) get just enough to cover their living expenses, but men with families are paid on the basis of dependents. Unlike the 'Westernised' lifestyle of the Jesuit priests, which students in their schools are led to aspire to, the Kalyan Ashram purposely keeps its surroundings in tune with existing conditions.

Inciting violence against others

The Kalyan Ashram runs a variety of other programmes each of which is carefully described in the handbook. Yet, even such a seemingly innocuous activity as organising health workers in each village can serve as a site for mobilisation against mission activities, as the following incident shows. A meeting of VKA village workers, balwadi workers and village-level health workers at Sanna started off with Avadh Bihari asking questions on how many *satsang kendras* had been held and what kind of prayers had been conducted. The health workers were asked how many patients they had catered to and whether the patients were able to pay the five rupees charged per visit. The discourse then slowly shifted. They were told to look out for other organisations, which were evangelising, and to tell the Kalyan Ashram so that it could be stopped. One by one, men got up to report the events in their area, mostly to do with religious issues the visit of a 'German' preacher (from the German Evangelical Lutheran Church), a conflict in a village with the '*Adi Dharm party*' (followers of original Oraon rituals). The *Kalyan Ashram* followers had prevented the *Adi Dharm* villagers from planting the *karma* in the *akhara* and they had taken the matter to the police. The villagers were told to go easy with the Adi Dharm as it was an internal fight between Hindus, and watch out for the Christians. Another man reported a dispute with a Christian farmer who owned a borewell but diverted water to the river instead of to others' fields—clearly a local quarrel which had little to do with religion. He was advised to get the villagers to sign a petition against the man. Differences with ordinary Christians were thus encouraged and turned into major religious difference, while differences between others, including Adi Dharm followers, were minimised.

While maintaining that they are a distinct organisation from the Vishwa Hindu Parishad, in practice, relations are close, and while visiting the VKA in Lohardaga, I was taken to meet the RSS *karjwa* there, who runs a sweet shop and coordinates all the RSS organisations in the area. Together, the VKA worker and the RSS head told me of their activities during the *Ramjanmabhoomi shilanyas*, when videos dramatising the alleged destruction of the original temple, the construction of the *Babri Masjid*, and cow slaughter were taken around all the neighbouring villages. The VKA worker said he had taken part in the demolition of the *Babri Masjid* and had taken many people from Lohardaga.[115] There also appear to have been sporadic incidents of violence against Christian evangelists and some ordinary Christian villagers.[116]

Given the strength of the Catholic community in Jashpur, the priests there are less worried about the growing influence of the Kalyan Ashram than elsewhere and tend to dismiss their 'reconversion' activities as vote building performances.[117] Most of the RSS envy and anger is directed at the Catholic Church, perhaps because its substantial buildings and estates visibly embody strength. Ironically, however, Catholic expansion in India has more or less levelled off and the Church is pre-occupied with maintaining its flock against the depredations of rival Christian denominations, particularly American evangelicals. Post-Vatican II, the Catholic Church has also attempted to 'indigenise' itself, e.g. by reviving festivals like *sarhul* which do not directly contradict Christian tenets, and using *Kurukh*.

While the Catholic Church and the *Kalyan Ashram* battle it

out, a third force (the *Parha Samaj*) attempts to retain and strengthen the old *parha* system and indigenous religion, but with little support from government or anyone else. As Surya Oraon, a Professor of Kurukh at the BS College Lohardaga and Secretary of the District Parha Sabha said, "Once the Christian missionaries had finished pulling us towards Christianity, the Kalyan ashram began pulling us towards Hinduism." There have been tensions between the *Kalyan Ashram* and the *Parha Samaj* over the holding of the *sarhul* festival—with the *Kalyan Ashram* celebrating it with a *havan* instead of the traditional way, and holding it on a different day. In many ways, however, the *Parha Samaj* and the Kalyan Ashram share a common agenda—for instance, the *Parha Samaj* has also tried to take on Christian evangelicals, and one of their demands is that Christians should not get reservations, as they benefit doubly-from being minorities (with their own educational institutions) and Scheduled Tribes.

Conclusion

While the sequence of the paper may seem to 'explain' the working of the *Kalyan Ashram* as a 'reaction' to missionary activities, or appear to be drawing equivalence, this is not the case. The notion of a Hindu *rashtra* (Hindu nation) has had an independent trajectory which makes it coeval with Muslim separatism and Christian conversion and not a mere consequence, much as the RSS would like us to think otherwise. The two forms of 'welfare conversion' cannot be equated in terms of their ultimate effects on *adivasi* society, at least in part because of the numerically marginal position of Christians within Indian society today.[118] It is also important to remember that the RSS is not simply converting people to Hinduism but to *Hindutva*, which is a political rather than spiritual affiliation. What does emerge clearly, though, is what Jaffrelot has identified as the key strategy of the RSS–'stigmatization' and 'emulation'.[119] Even while aiming to counter Christian missions, the VKA, not surprisingly, draws upon the organisational forms earlier developed and practised by the Catholics.

In either case, it is the economic and political problems of the *adivasis* coupled with state indifference, which have provided the ground for religious mobilisation. While high rents, *begar* and restrictions on forest produce drew people to the Catholics and Lutherans, who offered a means of resistance, in the post-colonial period, it is the *Sangh's* welfare activities in the field of education and health which draw people into its orbit. For many of those thus associated with the *Kalyan Ashram*, its discourse then begins to seem empowering, with its admission of 'neglect' by the Hindu upper castes, its call to primordial defence of religion, and its increasingly skilful use of mainstream development discourse on tribal land alienation and poverty.

The state's acts of omission and commission are central to the enterprise of religious mobilisation. Quite apart from the unmarked religious practices of the state, both the colonial and post-colonial states have enabled conversion through their absence in the fields of education and health. But, more subtly, the state also enables religions to convert by, on the one hand, refusing to recognise ordinary political protest as legitimate and, on the other hand, legitimising religious violations as acts of conscience. In the past, while the colonial state routinely expelled people it thought guilty of political propaganda, it went out of its way to ensure freedom of conscience to those engaged in religious propaganda. In the present, state discourse through the media depicts the destruction of the Babri Masjid as something more than a pure act of vandalism, while political organisations fighting for the economic and political rights of workers or peasants are seen as mere terrorists. The same demand when couched in religious terms, receives greater state attention than if it had been made in purely secular terms.[120] In other words, the Indian state has routinely privileged religious belief and identity over other forms of belief and identity, which inevitably has the circular and reaffirming effect of strengthening religious affiliation. Finally, insofar as the state, Christians and Hindus share a vision of 'adivasi uplift' that involves cultural changes without accompanying access to economic and political power, they are all equally culpable for the obliteration of adivasi identities.

REFERENCES

1. For instance, displacement and migration make it harder to worship localized dieties in particular natural phenomena.
2. For the term see Sathianathan Clarke. ' Transformations of Caste and Tribe' in Rowena Robinson and Sathianathan Clarke. eds. 2003, *Religious Conversion in India: Modes, Motivations and Meanings*. Delhi: Oxford University Press, p. 218.
3. Recent studies have emphasised the political agency of converts, and conversions as the fashioning of new syncretic identities. See essays in Rowena Robinson and Sathianathan Clarke, eds., 1998, *Religious Conversions;* Gauri Visvanathan, *Outside the Fold : Conversion, Modernity and Belief* (Princeton University Press); Richmond M. Eaton, 'Comparative History as World History: Religious Conversion in Modern India', *Journal of World History*, 8(2), 1997, pp. 243–271.
4. Saberwal, Satish 2004, 'Anxieties, Identities, Complexity, Reality', In Mushirul Hasan, ed. Will Secular India Survive? Gurgaon: Imprint One, pp. 93–124.
5. For exceptions, see Sumit Sarkar 'Hindutva and the Question of Conversions' in K.N. Pannikar ed. 1999, *The Concerned Indian's Guide to Communalism*, Delhi Viking, Arvind Sharma 1977,'The place of conversion within Hinduism', *Contributions to Indian Sociology*, 11(2), 345–254.
6. N.K. Bose, 1941, 'The Hindu Method of Tribal Absorption', *Science and Culture*, 8, pp. 188–194; for Sanskritisation, see M.S. Srinivas, 1961, 'Hinduism', in *Encyclopedia Britannica*, 12 Chicago.
7. In the *Constituent Assembly Debates* too the 'Right to Propagate'' was left in as a 'concession' to Christians.
8. Julian Saldhana, 1981, *Conversion and Indian Civil Law*, Bangalore: Theological Publications in India, pp. 47–56; see also Kumkum Sangari, 1999, 'Gender Lines; Personal Laws, Uniform Laws, Conversion', *Social Scientist*, 27, (5-6), pp. 17–61.
9. Fieldnotes on Loyola School, Kunkuri, January 2002.
10. S.C. Roy, 1928, rpt. 1972, *Oraon Religion and Customs*, Calcutta: Editions Indian.
11. Ibid, pp. 11–12.
12. Ibid, pp. 4–8.
13. Surya Narayan Saksena, 1994, *Vanvasi Kalyan Ashram Kya Or Kyon*? Delhi, Akhil Bhartiya Vanvasi Kalyan Ashram, pp. 5–6.
14. John Lakra, 2000, 'Tribal Culture and tribal Christians', *Sevartham*, Vol. 25, p.18.

15. Senior missionary at Kohima, 1937, cited in Eaton, *Comparative History*, p. 254.
16. See accounts in Felix Padel, 1995, *The Sacrifice of Human Being*, Delhi: Oxford University Press, pp. 199–206.
17. K.S. Singh, 1983, *Birsa Munda and his Movement* 1874–1901, Delhi: OUP, pp. 20-21.
18. They numbered some 71,200 by 1900. Singh, Ibid, p. 21.
19. L.Clarysse, S.J., 1985, 'Lievens and the Zamindari System', in *Sevartham*, p. 6.
20. Clarysse, Ibid, p. 15.
21. See Nandini Sundar, 1997, *Subalterns and Sovereigns*, Delhi: Oxford University Press, H.S. Kamath, 1941, *Grazing and Nistar in the Central Province Estates : the Report of an Enquiry* Bhopal: Government of the Central Province, R.K. Ramadhyani, 1942, *Report on Land Tenures & the Revenue System of the Orissa and Chhattisgarh States*, Berhampur: Indian Law Publication Press.
22. See Padel, Sacrifies Op.Cit., p.189, on post-Independence Christion Conversions of Gonds; Frederick S. Downs, 'Christians Conversion Movements in North East India' in Robinson and Clarke, eds. *Religious Conversions*, pp.381–400; Eaton, Comparative History, 'Move for North India Church Union' *Glasgow Herald*, 14 October 1948, which reports the Indian tour of Rev. Dr. Nevile Davidson and optisim of missionaries regarding their prospectus under independence.
23. File No. 268-P1929, For & Pol, *National Archives of India*, New Delhi (NAI).
24. FILE No.233-P (S)/36, for & Pol. Dept (Pol Branch) , NAI. The bulk of this report is reprinted in the Report of the Christian Missionary Activities Enquiry Committee, Madhya Pradesh (henceforth referred to as the Niyogi Commission, 1956), Nagpur: Government Printing Press Vol. II, Part B, pp. 325–374; See Also Niyogi Commission , Vol. I, pp. 46–47.
25. File No. 233-P(S)/36, For & Pol. Dept. (Pol. Branch), NAI (henceforth refered to as Meek 1936, since his report forms the bulk of the file). Col. A.S. Meek was agent to the Governor General, Eastern States Agency, which was established in 1933, covering the Chattisgarh feudatory States, Bengal, Bihar and Orissa states.
26. Ibid.
27. The account of 1922-23 is taken from R/I/1/1417File No.883, p. (See) Part-II, disturbance in the Jashpur state and assumption of the management of the state by government. India Office Library and Recent Record Room, London (IOL).

28. Ramdhyani, *Report on Land Tenures,* Op. cit. p. 35.
29. J. Connolloy, Secretary to the Advisory Board of the GEL Church Ranchi to political agent, 13 January 1923, B. Meuleman, Archbishop of Calcutta to Ley, 14 January 1923, both in file no. 883, p (see) Part II IOL.
30. File no. 883, p (see) Part II IOL.
31. Meek 1936, p. 331.
32. W.G. Archer, *Christianity and Bihar,* November 1935, typewritten mss. In W.G.Archer papers mss eur/f 236/1, IOL.
33. Meek 1936 pp. 336-337 see also fortnightly report for the Eastern States Agency (ESA), 1st half of November 1945, Acc. No. 352, Crown Representative Records. (CR.R) NAI.
34. Fortnightly report of ESA 1st half of July 1945 dated 20 July 1945 Acc. no. 352 CRR NAI.
35. Fortnightly report of Inspector General of Police and Police Advisor, ESA for the First Half of February 1940. In File No. 11(23)-P (S)/s 40 Of 1940 Acc. No. 354, CRR NAI.
36. Meek 1936, pp. 326-328.
37. File no. 268-p. 1929, For & Pol NAI (proposed legislation by the Gwalior Darbar of a law regarding change in religion).
38. Forthnightly report of the ESA 1st half of July 1942, Acc. No. 352 CRR NAI.
39. Undated type script titled "Bhumijan Seva Mandal" in Elwin correspondence Bhula Bhai Desai papers, Nehru Memorial Museum and Library New Delhi. See also Nandini Sundar (forthcoming) 'Verrier Elwin And The Missionary Debate In Central India' in Tanka Subba, ed., *Verrier Elwin and the Tribal Question,* New Delhi: Orient Longman.
40. Fortnightly report of the ESA Acc. no. 352–357, CRR NAI.
41. Fortnightly report 2nd half of March 1938, ESA Acc. no. 352 also fortnightly report from 1938-1945 Acc. 352-357, CRR, NAI.
42. Fortnightly report ESA , 2nd half June 1942, Acc. no. 354, CRR, NAI.
43. Fortnightly report of ESA , 1st half of April 1945 Acc. No. 356 CRR NAI see also Agapit Tirkey, 2002, Jharkhand Movement : A Study of its dynamics, New Delhi: AICFAIP, p. 57.
44. The Adivasi Mahasabha had got some help from the Muslim League K.S. Singh, 1982, *Tribal Movements in India,* New Delhi: Manohar, pp. 4-5, Niyogi Commission Vol.1, pp. 9-15.
45. Surna Narain Saxena 1993, *Friends or Foes of Adivasis & Dalits?* Delhi: Publicity and Publications Bureau, Akhil Bhartiya Vanvasi Kalyan Ashram, p. 1.

46. K.D. Sapre, Shri Balasaheb Deshpande,1999, *Jeevan Aur Karya*, Jabalpur : Van Sahitya Academy, p. 24.
47. Ibid, p. 25.
48. Bruce Graham, 1999, *Hindu Nationalism and Indian Politics* Cambridge : Cambridge University Press, pp. 19-20, 24-25.
49. Christophe Jaffrelot, 1996, *The Hindu Nationalist Movement and Indian Politics*, New Delhi: Viking.
50. Niyogi Commission Vol. 1, p. 9.
51. Niyogi Commission Vol. 1, p. 13, pp. 49-51.
52. The Catholics, especially in Jashpur complained that Catholic candidates for government posts were asked to give up their religion, that they were not enrolled as home guards their contributions to the Gandhi Memorial Fund were not accepted, etc. (Niyogi Comm. Vol. 1, p. 15-16)
53. Sapre Shri Balasaheb, Op. cit, p. 32.
54. Niyogi Commission Vol. II, A, p. 189.
55. Niyogi Commission Vol. I, pp. 18-19.
56. Niyogi Commission Vol II, A p. 222.
57. Niyogi Commission Vol. I, pp. 28-29.
58. 236 out of a total 480 foreigners working in Missions were American. Niyogi Commission Vol. 1 : 104.
59. Niyogi Commission, Vol. 1, p. 102.
60. Niyogi Commission, Vol. 1, pp. 95-131.
61. Niyogi Commission, Vol. 1, p. 132.
62. Niyogi Commission, Vol. 1, p. 155.
63. Niyogi Commission, Vol. 1, p. 158.
64. Balasaheb Deshpande, 1990, *Sanstha, Shasan Aur Karyakarta Delhi* ABKVA, pp. 8-9.
65. See M.S. Golwalkar,1939, *We Or Our Nationhood Defined* Nagpur: Bharat Publications, p. 62.
66. Sapre Shri Balasaheb, Ibid, p.11.
67. Ibid.
68. Ibid p. 16.
69. Sapre Shri Balasaheb, Op. cit. pp. 20-22.
70. Niyogi Commission, Vol. II, a.p. 225.
71. Niyogi Commission, Vol. II, a.p. 226.
72. Reprinted in Niyogi Commission, Vol. 1, p. 9.
73. Niyogi Commission, vol. I, p. 14.
74. Fieldnotes October 2001. After Naik's visit the VKA has been given funds to run the Pahari Korwa Project for the 'uplift of the Pahari Korwas, K.P. Singh proudly said the Korwas stay in the ashram whenever they come to Jashpur for a court case—which is quite often because they get into trouble with the forest dept.

for cutting wood, or not supplying chickens, etc. yet there is no attempt by the VKA to challenge the authority of the forest dept. It is also not clear how much of the money for Korwas or for their hostels is spent on these activities and how much on other propaganda activities for the Sangh.

75. Niyogi Commission, Vol. II, a.p. 199.
76. Niyogi Commission, Vol. II, a.p. 213.
77. Niyogi Commission, Vol. II, a.p. 199.
78. Niyogi Commission, Vol. II, a.p. 218.
79. That this happened is also evident from Sapre's Own Account Shri Balasaheb p. 33.
80. Sapre, Shri Balasaheb, p. 25.
81. The *Kalyan Ashram* continues to have a mutually supportive if calculating relationship with the former Jashpur ruling family enhanced by Dilip Singh Ju Deo's involvement in conversion ceremonies.
82. Sapre, Shri Balasaheb p. 28.
83. It was later termed the *Akhil Bhartiya Vanvasi Kalyan Ashram,* under which state branches may have different names like the *Vanvasi Kalyan Parishad* in Gujarat and Rajasthan.
84. Ibid, pp. 27-28.
85. Deshpande, *Sanstha Shasan* Op.cit p. 4.
86. Ibid, p. 6.
87. The decline in the *Adimjati Sevak Sangh* is blamed on the fact that they took 100% govt. funding and therefore could not establish a hold on society. Deshpande Sanstha Op.cit. p. 5.
88. A fundraising event for the VKA's North-east girls' hostel in Raipur collected Rs. 51,000/- in one afternoon. The audience seemed to consist mainly of Marwaris and Maharashtrian Brahamins. Fieldnotes, January 2002.
89. South Asia Citizens Web (SACW) and Sabrang Communications. *A Foreign Exchange of Hate.* Published by SACW and Sabrang Communications 2002.
90. Press release of the Campaign to Stop Funding Hate March 5, 2003.
91. See also D.K. Singh "Lost Tribes" *Communalism Combat* 11(102) October 2004, pp. 8–18 on the financial and legal help provided by the BJP Rajasthan Govt. to the *Vanvasi Kalyan Parishad.*
92. See also Akshaya Mukul, 'RSS holds key to "Tribal Treasury" *Times of India,* 27.09.2003.
93. Fieldnotes *Vanvasi Mela* 11–14 February 2001.
94. Fieldnotes October 2001. See also *The Hindu,* February 28, 2003.

95. Surya Narayan Saxena ed. Friends or foes of Adivasi & Dalits? (Delhi ABVKA, 1993), p. 20.
96. Fieldnotes October 2001, January 2002.
97. Fieldnotes, October 2001, Akhil Bhartiya Vanvasi Kalyan Ashram, statewise activities at a glance as on 23.09.2001.
98. ABVKA Ibid.
99. Surya Narayan Saxena, Vanvasi Kalyan Ashram kya aur kyon? (Delhi ABVKA, 1994) p. 11.
100. Avadh Bihari was then the Joint All-India Organising Secretary of the VKA. Ramesh Upadhyay is an old RSS worker stationed at the Ashram in Jashpur while Rati was an old sympathiser also living in the Ashram.
101. Raman Kirpal, 1999, 'Ghar Vaapasi–the great RSS Farce,' *Indian Express*, February 12.
102. According to Ramesh Upadhyay, "when people decide to reconvert, Swamiji goes in procession for 3-4 km to the *mandap* in the village accompanied by dancers and paltans of *pahari korwas* with bows and arrows. Converts—husband/wife—are given a saree and dhoti and after prayer, Judeo washes their feet. This is seen as a great honour and helps their assimilation into society."
103. For studies of the role of schools in Christian conversion, see Padel, Sacrifice, Brendan P. Carmody S.J., 'Conversion and Jesuit Schooling in Zambia', Leinden E.J. Brill, Carol Davens, 'If we get the girls, we get the race'.'Missionary Education of Native American Girls', *Journal of World History*, Vol. 3, no. 2, 1992.
104. Balasaheb Deshpande, *Sanstha, Shasan*, Op cit. p. 17.
105. *Akhil Bhartiya Vanvasi Kalyan Ashram, Keval Vyaktigat Upyog Ke Liye* (Mumbai ABVKA, ND), also Sapre, 1991, *Prasann Damodar Hamare Vanvasi Aur Kalyan Ashram*,Lucknow: *Lokhit Prakashan*.
106. The rest of this section is based on fieldnotes, October 2001.
107. The VKA handbook prescribes how the hostel should look—it should be named after a famous vanvasi man or woman, individual rooms should also be named after great people, there should be a cultural map of India and pictures of gods and goddesses or great men.
108. Some of them continue to read the *Hanuman chalisa* even when they go home to their villages, although others also said that the pressures of work keep them from any kind of prayer at home.
109. The RSS penetration of the North-east is beyond the scope of this paper.

4

Proselytisation of Tribal Society: A Political Agenda

Dharmendra Kumar and Moirangthem Prakash

It is disturbing. But there it is. The constituency of communalism is expanding day by day, at an alarming speed. In this process it has traversed the hitherto unchartered territories of society. One such territory is tribal society. In this process, various sections of tribal society, which earlier did not believe in dominant Hindu religious practices in the form of metaphysics, rituals, and ethics, are being proselytised to Hinduism. These proselytised tribal Hindus have not only played a significant role in parliamentary politics[1] but have also shown similar forms of religious hatred and intolerance towards other religious communities. Amita Baviskar, while discussing Gujarat riots notes:

> There were two novel features that made these communal riots a departure from previous incidents: one, violence was not confined to urban areas but also occurred in the countryside; and two, adivasis[2] participated in the attacks against Muslims. Muslim traders, whose families had been settled for generations in the villages and small towns across the region, had to run for their lives when adivasis wielding swords and sickles, shouting Hindu slogans, stormed into their houses.[3]

'Until the 1980s, they were Nakma, Budiya or Naru. Now, about two decades later, their children are Shivaram, Nathulal and Giridhar,' reports D.K. Singh in the context of growing influence of Hinduism among tribals. This is not to say that Hinduism has been introduced to tribals for the first time, but the nature and magnitude of this current phase is certainly different. Now, tribal masses are showing not only a strong adherence to Hindu symbols and mythologies but also an increased level of intolerance towards other communities.

The *adivasi* or Scheduled Tribe is a hotly debated concept in Indian social anthropological discourse. The term emerged during colonial rule, when official anthropologists, Indian Civil Service officers, distinguished it from Hindus and characterised them as 'animists'. On the other hand, Indian nationalist sociologists such as G.S. Ghurye questioned this characterisation as part of the British policy of 'divide and rule' and called them 'backward Hindus' or a group of Hindus who were not properly integrated into Hindu mainstream.[4] This implied that the path of development of tribals essentially passes through Hinduism. At the same time, there were scholars who, considering the cultural exchanges between Hindus and tribals identified some serious problems in defining the term adivasi.[5]

But, despite all these definitional problems *adivasi* objectively exists as a distinct sociological reality having distinguishing characteristics such as self-sufficiency, egalitarianism, communitarianism,[6] isolation and so on.[7] Not only that, subjectively adivasis also interpret their identity as a separate group. No matter how much fraternity is extended to them by Hindu proselytisers in the current atmosphere of communal divide, they are often pejoratively called *mamas*, and *adhivasis* (half-inhabitants). Again, despite all kinds of cultural exchanges, an adivasi individual always feels him/herself shy, bewildered and alienated in non-adivasi surroundings. But, despite all these subjective and objective distinguishing features one can easily observe an emergence of tribal Hindu identity. Why? Why have they started accepting Hindu socio-religious practises in the recent past?

The purpose of this essay is to understand this growing influence of Hindu socio-religious practices over tribal masses or the growing level of proselytisation of tribal society to Hindu society. An effort has been made to analyze this process with reference to the Jhabua district of Madhya Pradesh.

But, before coming to this analysis, it is relevant to discuss the specificities of this current form of proselytisation. The present form of proselytisaion, which we have referred to as Hinduisation[8], is different from the traditional meaning of proselytisation. Two specific features of this process of Hinduisation of tribal masses can be identified. In the first place, the process of proselytisation under question (the Hinduisation of tribal masses) is not of a traditional kind. In the traditional form of proselytisation, the motive behind the process of changing the religious beliefs and practices was predominantly the expansion of a particular sect or a religion. In contrast, in this current form the motive is not simply religious but also political. Here a tribal as a subject of proselytisation is not only aimed at to convert as a follower of particular religious beliefs but also an active supporter of a particular kind of political ideology concretised in the forms of specific roles in parliamentary and fascist politics.

Second, this process of proselytisation is not known by its agents as conversion into a new religion. It is asserted that tribals are basically Hindus. They don't have to convert to a new religion. All that they have to do is to recognise their true or original self. For this purpose, their references are shown in traditional Hindu scriptures. It is argued that if they (tribal masses) have started following socio-religious practices different from the mainstream Hinduism, they can easily correct themselves by adopting them (mainstream Hinduism). Not only that, if they have started following an alien religion such as Christianity through the process of conversion they can easily return to their own (!) Hindu religion. The practices involved in this process are called *Gharwapasi* (home-coming) and *shuddhi* (purification). Several programmes for such kinds of *gharwapasis* have been organised in the tribal populated districts of Madhya Pradesh. Hence the conversion of tribals who follow completely different socio-cultural and religious traits, into the followers of Hindu socio-cultural and religious traits is not called proselytisation.

In this essay, in contrast to these assertions, the process of Hinduisation, be it *shuddhi* or *gharwapasi*, has been considered the process of proselytisation. This process is both spontaneous and organised. In fact, the organised activities of agents of this proselytisation are supported by spontaneous leanings of tribal masses. In this study, it has been argued that this spontaneity is constituted by specific historical processes, particularly after the introduction of a specific form of modernity by the colonial regime. This form of modernity got further consolidated by the policies of the post-Independence state. This created a historical environment for organised campaign by religious, particularly Hindu organisations. It has been also argued that these organised campaigns are mediated by the material relations, particularly the relations of migrant labourers with their employers and the nature of employment.

Thus proselytisation of tribals to Hinduism is both a spontaneous and organised process. This essay aims to understand both of these processes. In order to discuss these processes this essay has been divided into three parts. The first part is a theoretical analysis of the process of proselytisation of tribal society by non-tribal society or the acceptance of the socio-cultural practices and religious traits of non-tribals by tribals; the second is a discussion of the development of specific historical environment; while the last is an analysis of conditions and processes of organised campaign.

I

In this part of the essay, we shall analyse the spontaneous acceptance or denial of the religious and socio-cultural practices of non-tribal society by the tribal society. It has been argued that this level of acceptance and denial depends upon the nature and purpose of interactions between these societies. In fact, two different societies enter into a specific form of relationship in the course of their material intercourses. The section which follows is an analysis of these interactions at the theoretical level.

Acceptance and Denial

But, why does a particular social formation (in the present context tribal social formation) embrace or deny the socio-cultural and religious features of an 'other' society? What determines the nature of these acceptances and denials? And how long do these socio-cultural and religious transformations continue? Scholars have responded to these questions in a varied manner. Three kinds of responses can be distinguished in this regard, cultural concordance approach, dominant culture approach, and hermeneutic approach.

Cultural concordance approach

This approach focuses upon the cultural compatibility between interacting social formations. According to this approach a society accepts only those socio-cultural traits of the other society, which are compatible with the dominant features of its indigenous culture. Thus this approach assumes that every culture has some permanent or unchanging features. Shaohua Hu, while explaining the non-acceptance of the Western liberal democracy in Chinese society, maintains that Western culture is completely different from the traditional Chinese Confucian culture.[9] To him, because of these elements, Chinese Confucian culture obstructs the democratisation of Chinese society.[10] The problem with this approach is that it presumes a particular society as culturally static. This follows that some elements of culture are autonomous. In fact cultural forms are representations of socio-economic conditions. Socio-cultural practices take shape and are structured into particular cultural forms by specific material conditions. Therefore, cultural practices may acquire new forms in changing material matrices. Thus new matrices of cultural interaction are created.

Dominant culture approach

This approach establishes a direct correlation between the dominant power and the dominant culture. This approach is called the power reductionist approach. According to this theory, people emulate and accept the socio-cultural traits of dominant society. Joseph Levenson, in his *Confucian China and its Modern Fate: The Problem of Intellectual Continuity* while analysing the modern Chinese intellectual life, maintains that the dominant society disrupts the socio-cultural life of the subjugated society and the ideas of the former becomes the cultural language of the latter. At the same time, if the interaction between these two societies is not domination based, the interaction between two cultures leads to enrichment of the cultural vocabulary of each other.[11]

Samuel P. Huntington, in his celebrated work *The Clash of Civilizations and the Remaking of World Order* has also put forward a similar thesis. To him, when a society becomes dominant its culture becomes attractive. Also, the dominant society uses its power to impose its culture on other societies. Thus the spread of Western culture throughout the world is due to the upsurge of Western power in modern times. On the other hand, the rejection of Western culture is engendered by the decline of the West's relative power brought about by non-Western societies' accumulation of power through modernisation.[12]

A similar kind of thesis can be found in the writings of some Marxist thinkers such as Gramsci, Althusser and Poulantzas. These writings are termed as dominant ideology thesis by Nicholas Abercrombie, Stephen Hill, and Bryan S. Turner. The ideas of these Marxist thinkers were based on Karl Marx's statement, 'The ideas of the ruling class are in every epoch the ruling ideas, i.e. the class which is the ruling material force of society, is at the same time its ruling intellectual force. The class which has the means of material production at its disposal, has control at the same time over the means of mental production, so that thereby, generally speaking, the ideas of those who lack the means of mental production are subject to it.'[13] According to these writers the dominant ideologies subjugate consciousness of the dominated masses and thus form a kind of hegemony of ruling class. Althusser has elaborated upon this process through his theory of interpellation or the recruitment of a subject by an ideology.

The problem with both of these liberal and Marxist theories is that there appears some kind of omnipotence of the ideology of the dominant society. The subject of the ideology appears a passive receiver and his/her recruitment appears as final. One can find a number of instances when the subordinated cultures refused the diktat of the dominant society at socio-cultural level. There may be a variety of reasons for this refusal. Ho Ill Lee has analysed this refusal on the basis of cultural resources. It depends upon 'First, with what cultural resources do members of a recipient society respond to foreign culture? Second, are the cultural resources subject to change? Third, how do cultural resources and alien culture affect each other? Finally, what is the end result of this interaction?' But, apart from the nature of the cultural resources, it also depends upon the level of interaction or correspondence on the one hand and the level of resistance and struggle against the dominant society on the other.

The Hermeneutic approach

Although the hermeneutic approach deals with interpretation of a text, and, is not directly associated with the problem of acceptance and denial of socio-cultural features of an alien society, its theoretical analysis may be applicable in the present context.[14] For this purpose the socio-cultural traits of alien society can be considered as a text which is interpreted by the people of indigenous society. In this regard the debate between Hans J. Gadamer and Jurgen Habermas, which continued almost for a decade, is worth mentioning. The debate started with the critique of Gadamer's book *On the Logic of the Social Sciences* by Habermas. Gadamer responded to Habermas in his book *Philosophical Hermeneutics.*

According to Gadamer, before an acceptance or denial of a particular meaning an individual establishes a process of dialogue with the text or historical and cultural artefacts.[15] Gadamer, in a true Heideggerian fashion argues that an individual enters into the dialogue with a specific cultural and historical tradition.[16] These traditions are ontologically prior to interpreter and form specific prejudices, which in turn determine the horizons of interpreters. According to Gadamer, "the horizon is the range of vision that includes everything that can be seen from a particular vantage point".[17] At the same time, texts or historical and cultural artefacts also have their own horizons. In the course of interpretations, these horizons collide with each other. In this process of dialogue, an individual encounters both familiar and unfamiliar situations. After a long process of questioning by both interpreter and text, an individual accepts some of the unfamiliar features of the text and thereby revises his/her prejudices. Gadamer calls this process a fusion of horizons. According to Gadamer, an individual interprets the socio-cultural traits of another society and accepts those traits which he finds meaningful in accordance with his/her tradition. Thus in this process both of the interacting horizons influence each other. As a result, acceptances and denials are mutual. In this way, Gadamer places the interacting communities on an equal footing.

But, what would be the nature of this 'fusion of horizon'? This is precisely the point where Habermas lays charges against Gadamer. Habermas claims that the problem with Gadamerian hermeneutics is that it assumes that every dialogue between a subject and an object, or between two subjects, is a genuine and authentic dialogue. He points out that in stressing the community of language and tradition and its consensus, Gadamer fails to take into account that language can be deceiving and distorting as well as disclosing. The tradition, which one adheres to from the past, can be ideological, playing a significant role in legitimising and thus masking the oppression and exploitation. Thus, in the process of dialogue, distortion of language takes place and this distortion does not come from the usage of the language but from relation to labour and power—that remains unrecognisable by members of the community.[18] Hence there is systematic distortion of understanding, not simply an accidental misunderstanding. This understanding and the relationship between interacting communities determine the acceptance and denials of socio-cultural features of each other.

Thus interpretations of two interacting communities about the nature of each other's socio-cultural and religious practices are based on the nature of relationship or the purpose of interaction of two communities. Habermas rightly contends that this relationship leaves a clear imprint over the acceptance and denial of language and socio-cultural traits of the other community. In this process, the relationship of dominance gets represented. If we apply it to our example of migrant tribals labourers' attraction towards Hindu religion, it can be seen that Hindu religion appears to them as the source of affluence on the one hand and solutions for their problems, on the other (we will return to it in the next part of essay).

Second, at the macro level, the consequences of these interactions are determined by the level of correspondence between two interacting communities. In the case of interaction between tribal society and modern society, the level of correspondence is very high. This is evident in the light of decreasing sources of livelihood due to deforestation on the one hand and the integrating nature of modern society as tribal masses become sources of labourers and consumers, on the other.

Last, these interpretations and the process of acceptance of the socio-cultural resources are also determined by organised efforts. The impact of these organised efforts depends upon the material relationship between interacting communities. In the context of proselytisation of tribal society, we will discuss these efforts with reference to the Jhabua region of Madhya Pradesh. But, one should always give a word of caution, that these spontaneous and organised processes are never final. It is always the space of struggle.

II

In the previous section, we discussed that the acceptances and denials of socio-cultural and religious traits of one community by the other are the product of specific forms of relationship emerging out of the material intercourses between interacting communities. These relationships provide grounds on which organised efforts to influence the other communities take shape. In this part, we shall discuss the emergence of this ground for the proselytisation of tribal masses to Hinduism.

The argument is that the process of proselytisation of tribal masses into Hinduism is closely related with the dynamics of material processes in tribal life. The material processes which influence the lives of tribal masses of this region, are created by introduction of modernity to this region. Modernity, in this region has been transmuted through the policies of the colonial and post-colonial regime. In fact, the increasing needs of modern capitalist society in the form of raw-materials sources and larger space on the one hand, and the workers in the form of dispossessed and displaced tribal masses on the other, has resulted in constant intervention of modern society into the tribal society. As a result, this area has observed a process of massive deforestation. The adversities caused by deforestation on the one hand and attractions promoted by institutions of modern society such as state and market on the other have forced tribal masses to migrate to centres of modern society.[19] This migration of labour has created a relationship between tribal and non-tribal society, which mediates the process of socio-cultural interaction between tribal and non-tribal society. This interaction is one of the main regulating factors of proselytisation of tribal society into Hinduism.

Apart from this, the process of proselytisation of tribal masses has been accentuated by the socio-cultural movements, which are also the product of material conditions of tribal society. Two movements should be mentioned in this regard, one the social reform movements, such as anti-liquor movements and the second, the introduction of new cults, such as Devi and Mata cults. Here it should be pointed out that these movements were not directly related with the issue of proselytisation; their spiritual base provided the space which was later appropriated by agents of proselytisation.

Tribal-Non-Tribal interaction: Different Phases

The interaction between tribal and non-tribal social formations has a long history. Interactions have taken place at both the individual and societal level. The individuals of non-tribal social formations have visited the tribal social formations as traders, petty shopkeepers, explorers, administrators, diplomats, researchers, travellers, etc. while at the societal level interactions have taken place in the course of wars for expanding feudal suzerainties on the one hand, and in search of labourers and the migration of labourers to non-tribal society, on the other. Here we will concentrate only on societal interactions.

Before coming to the discussion of the nature of interactions and acceptance and denial of socio-cultural and religious traits of non-tribal Hindu society by tribal society, it is necessary to understand the very process of interaction between two different kinds of social formations. In this regard, it should be noted that this process had different characteristics in different stages of history, depending upon the purposes of interaction. During the medieval period, the non-tribal society, i.e. the feudal society interacted with tribal societies with the purpose of expansion of their feudal empire. One can also find differences in different forms of feudal empires such as Mughal, Maratha, and Rajputs in India. But what was common in all these empires was that they were interested mainly in imposing their dominance concretised in the form of gifts and taxes. At the same time, the formation of the feudal system was highly decentralised. The task of collection of taxes was left either to their representatives in tribal societies or lower-level officials of the feudal social empires. Due to this form of interaction the level of interaction or correspondence between tribal and no-tribal society was very low. Most of the members of tribal society did not know anything about their feudal rulers. As a result, the level of cultural dominance of non-tribal society was very low and only the upper section of the feudal society tried to emulate the socio-cultural and religious traits of non-tribals. In fact this section always visualised its future in feudal social formations. Thus, in the pre-capitalist social formation, due to the low level of correspondence between interacting societies, diffusion at the socio-cultural and religious level was too low.

On the other hand, in the capitalist phase interaction between these societies achieved a higher level of correspondence. Tribal society ekes out its living from forests. Their survival had become dependent on forest produce. There was more or less a kind of symbiosis between these two. But, due to the process of rapid deforestation on the one hand and penetration of modern society through its institution such as surveys, schools, markets and others on the other, this symbiosis has been broken. These two processes have forced them to become dependent over on capitalist society. Hence they are now forced to eke out their living by selling their labour power.

This is concretised in the form of agrarian migrant labourers and contract labourers.

This transformation of tribal masses into free workers has not been completely accomplished. Nor has it ended their forest dwelling. They still experience a pull towards their own society. Not only that, most of the time, their movements towards the modern society are largely prompted by their cultural needs such as repayment of their loans and bride price and others. Due to this cultural specificity as well as their relatively late arrival in the labour market deprives them of the minimum honour which a non-tribal worker gets. They are largely employed as ad hoc and contract labourers in building construction.

Capitalism always wants to integrate the larger part of human society into its fold. This integration of human society serves as the increasing source of labour which capitalism needs in the wake of its constant expansion. In addition, this new addendum always provides a greater base of consumers. Thus, inclusion of tribal society is an essential part of the integrating process of capitalism. The point to be underlined is that this integrating process on the one hand, and the need of the tribal masses to migrate towards the labour market on the other, has led to the greater level of interaction or correspondence between tribal society and modern society. Now the interaction is no more concentrated in the upper section of society. It has permeated to almost all the strata of tribal society. The section which follows would be an analysis of this evolution in the context of the Jhabua region of Madhya Pradesh.

Jhabua is located at the confluence of four Indian states, Madhya Pradesh, Gujarat, Maharashtra and Rajasthan. It is a tribal dominated district, mainly inhabited by the Bhil, Bhilala and Patiliya tribes.[20] Jhabua is one of the most backward regions of Madhya Pradesh. The area is characterised by the features of high mortality rate, low per capita income, low literacy rate, and high unemployment rate, etc. The tribals of this region are primarily engaged in agrarian activities. Since agriculture is mainly dependent on the monsoon, most of the time in a year the fields remain unused leading to under-employment. In

Jhabua and adjoining districts, more than 90 per cent villagers remain unemployed nearly eight months in a year. Consequent droughts and untimely rains add fuel to the deteriorating economic conditions of the tribals. Even looting and robbery, due to their limited options, are being reported in these areas.[21]

The Jhabua district was carved out after the merger of Jhabua, Alirajpur, Jobat, Kathiwara and Mathwara princely states of Madhya Bharat. Along with this, Petalawad Pargana of Holkar state and Kannwada village of Dhar state were also included in this district. Although Jhabua district is named after a tribal leader of the Labana clan, Jhabbu Naik Jhabua state was founded by Kesho Das of Jodhpur in 1584, who had defeated Jhabbu Naik. It is said that Kesho Das was backed by Mughal Emperor Jehangir. However, formal inclusion to the Mughal Empire took place in 1618 and Kesho Das's *jagirs* were attached. Further, Shahjehan restored these territories to Maha Singh, a nephew of Kesho Das.

Thus Jhabua experienced the conjugal feudal dominance of Rajputs and Mughal. In the early 18th century, during the reign of Kushal Singh of this dynasty, this feudal dominance of Mughals and Rajputs was challenged by another kind of feudal rulers the Marathas of Holkar state. The Marathas forced Rajput rulers to pay the taxes levied as *Tanka* and *Chauth*. In this way Jhabua region enjoyed a third kind of feudal regime, that of the Marathas.

During all these feudal rules, the level of correspondence between alien community and the tribal society was concentrated only to the upper echelon of society. This is why the socio-cultural traits and habits of the ruling community could influence only the upper section of society. In fact, this section of society envisaged its future in association with feudal rulers and set its values accordingly. The point to be argued is that socio-cultural traits of the dominant society could not permeate to the lower or general layers of society.

Interaction with modern society

Modernity was introduced to the tribal society through the policies of the colonial state. It was introduced in the process of administrative integration, exploitation of natural resources for colonial purposes and integration of tribal society into market economy on the one hand and politico-legal framework, on the other. Here it should also be pointed out that although the focus of the policies changed significantly in the post-colonial state, one can observe a paradigmatic continuity in relation to tribal societies. It can be seen that policies regarding exploitation of natural resources and integration of tribal society with market and civil society remained unchanged.

Administrative Integration

Administrative integration during the colonial period was organised through the processes of survey and settlement. These processes significantly altered the relationship of tribal masses with land. Land was defined as private property. The new settlement introduced was more centralised and revenue was enhanced. But, what made the real difference was the introduction of the *malguzaari* system, based on intermediaries. This replaced the old system of tax payment based on assessment and levied by village councils. The ruthlessness of the new system can be gauged by the fact that land revenue increased from 25 per cent to 65 per cent of the total produce.[22] At the same time, this system of tax collection altered the social composition of this region. It was because most of the agents of tax collection were from *Baniya* (trader) caste. 'This led to the increasing infiltration of these traders into interior areas, using dishonest practices to defraud the *adivasis* of their produce. Thus the surpluses that the *adivasis* used to have to tide them over the occasional years of bad monsoons were available no more and famines became the order of the day'.[23] More injuries were added by the insistence of tax payment, irrespective of crop failure and the ruthless collection by *sahukars* and moneylenders, on the other. As a consequence, surpluses were siphoned to tax collecting intermediaries and *adivasis* became pauperised and indebted. In addition, Britishers, in order to increase the land revenue, 'brought in Kanbi Patidar and Jat farmers from Gujarat and Rajasthan respectively and settled them on the Bhil lands in the plains so as to both increase the earnings from land revenue and commercial agriculture and also to tame the militant Bhils'.[24]

This form of settlement of non-adivasis made a significant impact over social relationship. 'While some of the Bhils withdrew into the hills most others were converted into serfs or bonded labourers of these non-adivasi farmers'.[25] 'Most of the fertile black cotton soil areas of the Malwa plateau and the Nimar plains are in the control of non-adivasi farmers with the Bhils reduced to being landless labourers or marginal farmers with low levels of economic and human development'.[26] Eventually, this form of settlement led to concentration of social, economic and political power in the hands of a non-adivasi community in this region. The non-adivasi community largely live in towns and are known as *bajariyas*. The non-adivasi community also influences adivasis through money lending and linking them other outer markets through weekly *haats*. In addition, they have a significant influence over their cultural life. We shall discuss this impact under the section organised campaign.

Deforestation

What has significantly influenced the lives of tribal masses are forest-related policies and processes of deforestation. Forest-related policies restricted the use of forests by forest dwellers by declaring jungles as state's property while deforestation ruptured the symbiosis between forest and tribals. The colonial regime, in order to meet the needs of Royal navy and expansion of railway, started massive deforestation. The illegal forest cutting also contributed substantially to this process. This process of ruthless and rapacious deforestation has not only de-sheltered the tribal masses but has also given birth to environmental problems such as lower precipitation and soil erosion and thereby poor water retaining capacity, and thus tribals are forced to eke out their living from the options provided by modernity, by becoming labourers.

As mentioned earlier, modernity was introduced through the transmutation of the colonial regime, its impact can be observed on its policies regarding forests. In this context it can be seen that the colonial regime not only rapaciously exploited forest resources through commercial forestry, it introduced rules which restricted the people's right over jungles. This dual policy was the beginning of dispossession of tribal masses from their natural habitats. This started with the formation of syndicate in 1796 by Mr. Mackonchie of the Medical Service for the extraction of teak wood in the Malabar region to meet the demands of shipbuilding and military purposes. Following the shortage of oak trees in England, in 1806, Captain Watson was appointed as the first conservator of Forests in India to extract teak wood for the Royal navy. He sealed the indigenous trade and denied peasants' rights. This further led to rapacious exploitation of forests without thought of any sort of regeneration.

Later, the colonial regime started formulating systematic policies for the conservation of forests for colonial purposes. In 1855, Governor General Lord Dalhousie issued a memorandum on forest conservation called the 'charter of Indian forests'. This suggested conservation of teakwood as state property and strictly regulated its use. In 1856, Dietrich Brandis, a German botanist, was appointed as the first Inspector General of Forests. The first Act for the regulation of forest was passed in 1865 that empowered government to declare any forest as state's property. Further, in Indian Forest Act of 1878, government introduced classification as reserve forest, protected forest and village forest. In this way, forest as common property was transformed into state property. In 1894, this statisation of common property took a new turn and forest policy emphasised state control over forest resources and state's right to exploit forests for the augmentation of state revenue. It also empowered the colonial state to dispossess private owners of land against nominal compensation in public interest. This exploitatian increased with the laying of rail lines, which began in Western India in the 1850s. The extraction of timber reached altogether new levels, requiring deep inroads into the densely forested adivasi territory and as elsewhere in India the domain of the Bhils too was encroached upon.[27]

In the post-colonial period, the focus on commercial forestry of colonial state continued and rights of forest-dwellers over forest were denied. In the report of National Commission on Agriculture, of which forest was a part, was advocated commercialisation of forests with complete disregard for the sustenance of adivasi and other forest dwelling communities. It asserted that 'production of industrial wood has to be the *raison d' etre* for the existence of forest'.[28] It was argued that free supply of forest produce to the rural population and their rights and privileges have brought destruction to the forests and so it is necessary to reverse the process. The rural people have not contributed much towards the maintenance or regeneration of the forests. Having over-exploited the resources, they cannot in all fairness expect that somebody else will take the trouble of providing them with forest produce free of charge.[29]

Thus the needs of both colonial and post-colonial states of forest products resulted in massive deforestation. According to Atkinson's *Gazetteer*, the forests were denuded of good trees in all places. The destruction of trees of all species appears to have continued steadily and reached its climax between 1855 and 1861 when the demands of the Railway authorities induced numerous speculators to enter into contracts for sleepers, and these men were allowed, unchecked, to cut down old trees far in excess of what they could possibly export, so that for some years after the regular forest operations commenced, the department was chiefly busy cutting up and bringing to the depot the timber left behind by the contractors. In addition, tribal society has also been pushed to the margin because of the restrictions issued by government policies on the use of forest produce.

Integration into the market economy

The process of integration of tribals into the market economy started with inclusion of adivasis as labourers. However, this process was started during British rule when tribals had started working as agricultural labourers in the fields of non-adivasi landlords. It gained new momentum when adivasis started migrating to the neighbouring cities of Gujarat. 'Bhils of Jhabua and Ratlam districts that even during the busy kharif season there is always a rush of people travelling either way by the Vadodara–Kota passenger train that runs on the Delhi Mumbai trunk railroute passing through these districts. Consequently this train has come to be called "mama gari" by all and sundry!'[30] This had a serious impact over social and cultural lives.

In fact, the policies of colonial and post-colonial state resulted in the development of a specific geography of this region, i.e. geography without forest. Deforestation coupled with restriction on the use of forest ruptured the symbiosis between forest and tribal society. Tribal society had to adopt new modes of existence. This followed agriculture as the sole source of living. But the low fertility and erratic rainfall proved insufficient to feed the entire tribal society. Besides, tribal society also needed some source of income to meet their cultural demands such as 'bride price'. This resulted in indebtedness to traditional moneylenders (*sahukars*), which in turn forced tribal masses to migrate to cities of Gujarat and Maharashtra. David Mosse writes :

> Migration provides cash income to supplement agriculture and allow savings and investments (in wells, pumps or good marriages), and sometimes upward mobility as gang leaders and 'recruiters'. It allows investment in social networks, increases social prestige and creditworthiness. For a majority, however, labour migration is linked to long-term indebtedness and fails to generate net cash returns and perpetuates below-subsistence livelihoods.[31]

Initially, migration of tribal youths was directed towards the agrarian sector, particularly towards paddy fields, but with the development of urban-industrial corridor and conurbation extending from Ahmedabad to Bombay now Mumbai, the direction of migration shifted towards these centres. The scale of this migration was very high. According to an estimate of neighbouring tribal district of Gujarat 'around 65 per cent of households (up to 95 per cent in some villages) and 48 per cent of the adult population are involved in seasonal migration'.[32] According to David Mosse, 'over 10–15,000 adivasis migrate to each of the major cities (Surat, Ahmedabad etc.) each year'.[33]

This process of migration substantially influenced the lives and society of this region. Accordingly, its impact can also be observed on the socio-cultural and religious sphere. One of these impacts has been the acceptance of Hindu rituals and symbols by the tribal masses. In order to understand this impact it is necessary to understand the pattern of migration.

In this context, it should be noted that although tribal youths migrated to different centres, their migration was guided primarily by the economic and cultural needs of their society. It included the need of cash for repayments of loans incurred in the process of cultivation and in course of performing certain religious and cultural rituals. This implies that despite their excursions in search of jobs they maintained strong bonds with their villages. That is to say, they did not shift to cities once forever. They kept on shuttling between cities and their villages. This resulted in constant import of ideas of outer society through narration of their experiences.

In order to understand this process of import of ideas, it is necessary to understand the nature of employment of tribal migrants. In this context, it should be noted that non-tribal society never treated tribal workers on a par with non-tribal workers. Because of their impoverishment and lack of assertiveness on the one hand and lower position in the caste hierarchy (even lower than the lower caste Hindus) on the other hand, tribal workers could not get regular jobs. To quote Jan Breman:

> The most significant change from the viewpoint of my research was the complete replacement of locals by migrant workers. The specialised machine operators all belong to higher castes and enjoy formal conditions of employment. This does not, however, apply to the approximately 150 migrants who, as seasonal workers, have set up camp on the open plain at the foot of quarry a collection of huts made of reed mats.[34]

They were mostly employed in the informal sector as domestic labourers, as workers in road building, as workers in stone quarries, as brick-makers, at construction sites as loaders and unloaders of raw materials or manufactured produce, and so on. The building industry—the principal sector of employment for Bhil migrants—involved, Breman estimates, at least 60,000 labourers in Surat. Transport is another part of this informal sector, attracting migrants. This includes headloaders, loaders of trucks, handcart operators, and (a very few) drivers. Some of these migrants work in industrial plants, but not as regular and skilled employees. They are employed through contractors to work at construction sites and maintenance work.

Thus they are considered as unskilled workers employed through contractors. The supply of labour is ensured through village-level middlemen called *mukkadams*. Needless to say, their working conditions are extremely wretched, completely unprotected or without any access to labour laws. 'Most adivasi migrants sleep in the open or bivouac under makeshift structures. Staying in urban spaces, migrants face harassment, abuse, theft, forcible eviction by the police, or the demolition of their dwellings by urban authorities. The abuse of adivasi migrants is closely related to their lack of identity or dwelling in urban places. Here they stand out as marginal, transitional people. They are subject to prejudice, stigmatised, 'criminalised' and falsely accused of theft or looting, and commonly detained and beaten by the police. 'The adivasi migrants also move to these cities with their families. The weaker section of these families women and children also face the brunt of hardship. Migrant women describe fear at night and fitful sleep in exposed places. For the most part, children at worksites have no care or shelter — 'they spend their days crying'. 'A dispossessed rootless adivasi feels bewildered and lost in cities. It should be noted that mere migration does not ensure any job guarantee. In one study 91 per cent of labourers at the local labour markets in Ahmedabad were *unemployed* for 10–20 days in a month,[35] and the picture in Baroda is similar (only 7 per cent found work for 5 days a week).[36]

The pressure to get a job and save something to send to his/her village forces him/her to work in completely adverse conditions. The need of job makes him/her dependent over *mukkadums* and contractors. This dependence is increased because of certain needs, such as advance for shop credits to be deduced from their payments and security from criminals and police and so on. Since most of these migrants are illiterate and docile, they do not get the amount that they are promised for. As David Mosse put it,

> Even when paid in full, migrant wages fall well below the legal minimum (especially piece-rate jobs), but payment is often late or withheld, especially towards 'the end of the season when the balance of power has firmly shifted from employee (coaxed with advances) to the employer, and when migrants are under pressure to return home for the cultivation season'.[37]

Among these harsh conditions of life and work, an adivasi migrant feels bewildered and lost. In these conditions, he/she does not perceive his/her job-givers simply as purchasers of labour. He/she observes him as a master who obliges him by providing a job. Thus their relationship becomes one of a patron–client relationship.[38] He/she also gets some relaxation and sometimes some food during his/her masters' religious ceremonies. As a result, he/she consciously and unconsciously gets attracted towards his/her masters' religious beliefs.

He/she sees his/her masters' life and affluence with an awe and reverence. This is clearly evident in the relationship between Hindu *seths* (businessmen) of Gujarat and the migrant tribal labourer. Employers' economic dominance gets translated into other spheres of life, like culture, spiritualism, fashion, etc. Villagers start offering puja to the pictures of Hindu gods and goddesses; particularly Lakshmi, by putting lights and *agarbatti* (incense) sticks in imitation of their employers . Changes can be observed in their food habits too. This also attracts him/her towards his/her master's religious beliefs and rituals. Not only that, they carry these beliefs with them to their villages. Gujarati festivals like *Gharva, Navarathri*, etc. are also being celebrated and slowly dominating their traditional tribal festivals. In this way most of the time, Hindu beliefs are imported to tribal villages.

Political leaders have also indirectly forced these workers to cast their vote in favour of the BJP, failing which they might not get employment in Gujarat. So, it was an indirect allurement for the dispossessed workers. At an election rally at Alirajpur, as villagers express, great politicians like Narendra Modi asked the voters to vote for the BJP, the only party that can possibly develop MP as Gujarat, which will relieve the sufferings of migrants. He even threatened the villagers that he would not allow them to work in Gujarat if they did not vote in favour of BJP. It is to be noted that the party swept all the five Assembly seats in the last State Assembly Election.

This import of Hindu faiths is also influenced by an atmosphere created by social reform movements in this region. The section that follows is an analysis of the creation of this soft background by such movements.

Socio-Religious Movements and Soft Hindutva

Non-tribal society has made religious inroads in the tribal areas through some socio-religious movements. Although these movements were centred on the goal of eradication of certain social problems, particularly against liquor consumption, they carried a religious fervour with them. These movements created a soft leaning towards Hinduism. Thus they encouraged a background for proselytisation of tribal society to Hinduism. At the same time, they also provided a space for organised campaign by Hindutva forces. Among the various social reform movements, we can discuss the movement started by Baleshwar Dayal, popularly known as *Mama* among the tribals, and a much-revered socialist leader in the tribal belt. He played great role in the political awakening of tribal masses of this area after national independence. He mobilised Bhil tribes to rise against exploitations of *sahukars* and landlords, encouraged them to give up drinking and discouraged superstition, polygamy and giving money to the bride's family, which was different from the mainstream Hindu practices.

The Hindutva brigade co-opted Mama Baleshwar Dayal's movements and his popularity by suddenly becoming ardent admirers of Mama Baleshwar, who had opposed all sectarian philosophies throughout his life. They attribute their own ideas to this tribal icon. They are now making blatant attempts to cash in on his popularity among the tribals, claiming that he was opposed to the conversion activities of the Christian missionaries, which is absolutely wrong.[39] In Thandla, from where Baleshwar Dayal was MLA , Janata Dal (U) leader Sharad

Yaday reminded the adivasis of Mama Baleshwar Dayal's contribution and asked them to vote for the BJP. Here, it should be pointed out that two things were picked up by Hindu mobilisers, who are nowadays known as Bhagats; one, the bride price and two drinking habit of tribals. These two practices provide entry point for Hindu mobilisers.

An another movement which has played a significant role in recent past is the *mata* movement. The movement started in the early 1990s in Pavgarh in Gujarat and passing through Meghnagar and Alirajpur, spread in nearby Dhar District. The Mata movement also emphasised Hindu values, the cessation of adivasi rites of worship, animal sacrifice, liquor usage, bride price, abduction and elopement and so on.[10] David Hardiman describes similar movements that occurred in South Gujarat during the 1920s among adivasis.

Thus the imported Hindu beliefs by migrant labourers to a crisis-ridden tribal society on the one hand, and soft leaning created by socio-religious movements on the other created a favourable ground on which proselytisation of tribal society into Hindu society accelerated by the efforts of organised campaigns by Hindutva forces in the recent past. This process coincided with the emergence of organised and belligerent Hinduism in the last two and a half decades. This process has consolidated after two major incidents, one the demolition of Babri Masjid and two Gujarat riots after Godhara train burning incidents. In the next part of the essay we shall discuss the nature of these organised campaigns with reference to the process of proselytisation in the Jhabua region.

III

The Organised Campaign

In the previous section, we discussed that the encounter of tribal society with the specific form of modernity during the colonial regime and a paradigmatic continuity of this form in the post-colonial period by the post-colonial state created a specific form of social relationship. This social relationship, in which a geographically de-sheltered and socially and economically deprived adivasi was at the receiving end, created conditions for the introduction of alien religious practices. This introduction was made easier by the socio-cultural movements which were also the product of the socio-economic conditions of an alienated de-sheltered tribal society. But the process of proselytisation would have been incomplete without the organised campaigns by the Hindutva forces. In this context the RSS and its outfits, which are commonly known as the Sangh Parivar, have played a significant role in recent history. The section that follows is a discussion of a recent organised campaign by these outfits. This analysis is based on our field study of this region.

The mode of proselytisation by the Hindutva forces has been different from the modes of other religions like Christianity and Islam. In other religions, a proselyte is baptised into a particular religion through processes like evangelism. Here, tribals are not called followers of some different religion. An adivasi is considered an integral part of the larger Hindu society, who follows some different religious rituals. Thus, advocates of Hinduism ask the tribal masses to recognise their real self, that is Hinduism. Thus advocates of Hindutva have adopted an inclusivist approach based on multispiritualism.

Aggressive Expressions

The effort to establish Hindutva in the tribal areas is apparently succeeding. The tribals of the nearby villages of Alirazpur tehsil of Jhabua district are almost Hinduised. They proudly call themselves Hindus. The dominant Hindu religious practices such as idol worship and celebration of popular Hindu festivals have been enthusiastically started. But what is most alarming is the emergence of aggressive Hinduism. Today Jhabua bristles with aggressive Hindu symbolsm, such as trishuls. Small shrines and saffron banners are visible everywhere. Houses are decorated with saffron flags and 'Om' symbols are inscribed on the doors and vehicles. Slogans like *Har Har Mahadev* and *Jai Ma Kali* are shouted.[41]

In this context one can also observe acceleration in the temple-building process. There are more than 30 Hindu temples in Alirazpur Bazar itself. Most of them have been constructed in the past three-four years and many are in the process. Also, the sites of construction of new temples are cautiously selected as public places, at the heart of the markets, along the roadsides, or at any other place where others can see them easily. Besides, a large number of temples is being constructed just next to places of worship of other religions. In November, at Aamkhud, Hindus extended Diwali celebration for many days only to interrupt the Id of Muslims that was just two days after Diwali.[42] A hidden assertion of aggressive and intolerant Hinduism can easily be deciphered in these symbolisations.

Apart from these aggressive expressions, the process of proselytisation is carried out by several organised processes. These processes have been mobilising funds, organising of public welfare programmes, setting up educational institutions, organising specific religious conferences and campaigns against other religions.

Fund Mobilisation

The campaigns for Hinduisation involve huge funding. Funds are generated through both domestic and foreign funding. One of the main foreign funding organisation has been IDRF (India Development and Relief Fund). The IDRF was set up as a tax-exempt, non-profit organisation in 1989. Its official, self-stated purpose is to raise money for organisations in India "assisting in rural development, tribal welfare, and urban poor." However, a report *A Foreign Exchange of Hate* co-published by the *South Asia Citizens Web* (SACW) based in France, and *Sabrang Communications,* Mumbai, India, documents in rich detail the fundamental connections between the IDRF and the *Sangh Parivar.*[43] A similar report has also been furnished about Sewa International, a UK-based organisation. It claims that most of the £2 million raised by Sewa International for the Gujarat earthquake victims was spent on RSS schools.[44]

Public Welfare Programmes

Most of the time, the organised campaigns are camouflaged as welfare programmes. Imitating Christian missionaries, the

Sangh Parivar is also rendering many welfare services only with the purpose of the Hinduisation of tribals. The Parivar runs Vanvasis Kalyan Parisads (hostels for tribal youths) in many parts of Jhabua. In these hostels stay tribal students who are studying in schools and colleges and they are provided basic training of RSS, like yoga, physical exercises how to use *lathis* (sticks), singing bhajans, and offering puja. One such Ashram is in Alirajpur, *Shri Vallabh Vanvasi Kalyan Parmarthik Sewa Ashram*. On one edge of the signboard, is a picture of Ram with bow and arrows and on the other, an adivasi in the same pose.

Vanvasi Kalyan Parishad, the affiliate of Parivar, launched its project to set up *talavs* (ponds), check dams and stop dams in 131 tribal villages. Each village that launched the project must install first a Shivling, the main motive behind the gimmick of welfare measures. The 131 Shivlings have already been moved from Indore to Jhabua and installed on Shivratri, 8 March 2004, when the project got underway. But the Sangh Parivar saw this only as a starting point. Eventually, it wanted to extend the programme to some 2,500 tribal villages in the Jhabua Dhar belt, said Harsh Chauhan, the Parishad's state president. Nor will the process of reaching out to the tribals stop at installing Shivlings. On 4 February, 20 youths from each village were invited to a camp where they took a pledge to contribute to the success of the project. "The tribal boys were asked to do *shram daan* (manual labour) for two months while money would be raised in the cities," says Laxman Goud, BJP MLA from Indore.

Educational Institutions

Another major process in the mission of Hinduisation is the setting up of educational educations. The RSS has been massively expanding its educational and schools network across India from about the mid-1990s. Akhil Bharatiya Shiksha Sansthan, usually known as Vidya Bharati, was founded in 1997 and is the main, but not the only, RSS educational network. The cluster of RSS educational activities includes the one-teacher schools (*ekal vidyalayas*) run by the VHP, Vidya Bharati, Sewa Bharati and the Vanvasi Kalyan Ashram. RSS schools are typically called:

- Saraswati Vidya Mandirs (RSS schools, which can also include residential schools)
- Saraswati Shishu Mandirs (RSS primary schools)
- Shishu Vatikas (pre-primary indoctrination)
- Sanskar Kendras (ideological indoctrination centres and activities, often one teacher schools operating in rural, tribal or slum areas)
- Ekal Vidyalayas (one-teacher schools) or Ekalavyas.
- Vivekananda Kendras/Vidyalayas[45]

Detailing the development of these organisation Vishnu Kumar reports:

> In Jhabua and Dhar Districts, Tribal comprise about 85% of the total population, from where more than 2 lakhs of them participated in the Hindu Sangam. Sewa Bharati started its activity at about 5 years back with a single OTS (One Teacher, One School). The seed, thus planted, has grown into a full big tree, extending its branches into 350 OTS, typing, sewing, embroidery and computer training and health centres into other scores of activities, such as Bhajan Mandlies, Mahila Small Savings Schemes and so on.[46]

He further writes that

> Behind the success of Hindu Sangam is the devotion and hard work of 350 Ekal Vidyalayas, and 250 whole-time workers of Sewa Bharati. They travelled continuously to practically every village for 3 months and visited about 3 lakh 25 thousand families and established a place of worship by putting a photo of Bajrangbali (Shri Hanumanji). They also taught them how to worship and also made them learn and sing Bhajans. In this Yagya of awakening, another 3,500 workers also participated for one week and helped in garlanding 28 lakhs tribals with lockets of Hanumanji.[47]

Ekal Vidyalayas run by the Friends of Tribal Society (FTS) in collaboration with the Vishwa Hindu Parishad have been operating in the tribal belts of the country. Students respond to roll call as "Jai Shri Ram" in the classroom. The schools distinctly display posters/statues of Hindu god and goddess. Majority of schools do not enroll students from Christian and Muslim communities and students are well adept in chanting Hindu religious songs, but there are no songs from other religions, neither were children from religious communities like Muslims on the rolls.[48]

The Sangh aims at 100,000 Ekal schools in Tribal India by 2011, and has tied up with Zee TV to collect funds. The RSS supported Ekal Vidyalaya movement, widely held to be heavily financed by NRIs (Non-Resident Indians) from the US as it spreads a network of institutions in tribal India, has been on the Internet, soliciting funds worldwide. It wants to expand from its current 14,000 schools to one lakh (1,00,000) schools in the next five years or so.[49]

Religious Conferences

Apart from these camouflaged efforts, religious conferences are organised to woo the tribal masses. These religious conventions not only create a mass leaning it also give them a sense of festivity.

Hindu Mahasangam, Jhabua 2002

On 18th January 2002, a massive Hindu Mahasangam was organised where Vishwa Hindu Parishad (VHP) leaders such as Pravin Togadia and Sadhvi Ritambara addressed a rally of 2.5 lakh people. For this, they launched a focused campaign of "Door-to-door, man-to-man, heart-to-heart" mobilisation in Jhabua. In preparation of the *sangam*, around 300 activists of *Sewa Bharati*, from three months prior to the event, visited the whole villages. They arranged for pictures of Hindu gods, particularly Hanuman, for every house. They taught the villagers how to offer puja and sing bhajans. To make it a grand success, 4,000 activists of the Sangh Parivar lived with every tribal family for about seven days. They put up saffron flags in every house and got a Hanuman locket for every individual.[50]

Hindu Samelan, Alirajpur, 2004

In continuation of its campaign for Hinduisation, the Hindu Jagran Manch, Alirajpur, Seva Bharati, Vishwa Hindu Parishad, and RSS organised a Hindu Sangam (confluence) on 23 February 2004[51] at Alirajpur, where more than 40 thousand villagers took part in the occasion. The stated purpose of the Hindu Sangam was to 'stop the activities of missionaries' (read forceful conversions by allurement) and to bring back the converted Christian tribals to the Hindu fold (*gharwapasi*). It was particularly organised to re-enforce the Hindutva ideology to the tribal villagers after the Aamkhud and Alirajpur incidents following the death of a girl inside the church compound at Jhabua at the beginning of the year.[52]

Campaigns against other Religions

The conversion or the proselytisation of tribals to Hinduism is accompanied by a campaign of hate and bigotry towards other religions. In the case of Jhabua, this campaign is directed mainly towards Christian missionaries. This is more evident in a recent report of state-sponsored Narendra Prasad Committee. The committee, which probed the rape and murder of Sujata at a missionary school on January 11, 2004 and consequent attacks on Christian minorities in different parts of Jhabua, submitted its report on May 21, 2005. The report blamed the missionaries and government machinery for the huge conversion of tribals around Jhabua. The panel also suggested that the simmering tension between Christians and tribals in the area was the result of this large number of conversions.

These strategies target unemployed tribal youths. As we have discussed in the previous section of this paper, organised strategies appeal to the estranged migrant labour force. The report blamed the missionaries and government machinery for the huge conversion of tribals around Jhabua. The panel also suggested that the simmering tension between Christians and tribals in the area was the result of this large number of conversions.

Conclusion

To conclude, it can be said that the process of proselytisation of tribal soceity into the Hindu soceity is on. This process is not just the expansion of the Hindu religion. It is also an enterprise of recruitment of new masses into the fold of fascist politics. Fascist politics in India is mediated by the electoral politics.

Therefore, proselytisation of tribal masses is also aimed at reaping benefits in parliamentary politics. There is no doubt that this form of proselytisation is the product of organised campaigns by Hindu proselytisers, but the roots of this process lie in the specific historical and geographical development of this region. This historical geographical development has produced and reproduced a specific kind of material relationship which provided grounds for the proselytisation of tribal masses. In this development the interaction between tribal and non-tribal society has played a significant role.

REFERENCES

1. The realisation by Madhya Pradesh Chief Minister Digvijay Singh, "I knew we had definitely lost the elections when the Jhabua results came in" shows the level of confidence in tribal society of Congress I which lost all five seats of Jhabua to BJP.
2. The term 'adivasi' meaning the original inhabitant is used for the people who are classified as Scheduled Tribes in the Indian Constitution.
3. Amita Baviskar, "Indian Indigeneities:Adivasi Engagements with Hindu Nationalism in India"an un-published Paper written for the conference on *'Indigenous Experience Today'*. Wenner-Gren Foundation, March 19–24, 2005.
   On This topic see also "Tribals made cannon fodder in Gujarat's communal war", by Chandrakant Naidu, *Hindustan Times*, May 6, 2002.
4. Sumit Guha also establishes a link between the notion of tribe and the structure of colonial power. Guha, Sumit. 1999. *Environment and Ethnicity in India, 1200-1991.* Cambridge: Cambridge University Press.
5. Andre Beteille, 1986. "The Concept of Tribe with Special Reference to India." *European Journal of Sociology,* XXVII.
6. Tribal society has many communitarian traditions such as *Dhas,* in which one member of every family of the village contributes without any charge in major works such as erecting mud walls, making cottages, works during harvesting season, and so on.
   Not only that, it was the tradition that 'surpluses accumulated beyond a certain limit be spent on communal merrymaking and feasting'. As quoted in Rahul, 2003, *"Sahukars Rule The Roost—Status of Informal Rural Financial Markets in Adivasi*

Dominated Regions of Western Madhya Pradesh, (Paper for ICSSR, Unpublished), www.panchayats.org/downloads/Sahukars%20Rule%20the%20Roost.PDF

7. 'Adityendra Rao disputed this in Tribal Social Stratification, in which he dealt so comprehensively with the differences between tribal religion and Hinduism. "The concepts of Karma and Dharma are foreign to the Bhils. They are this worldly. For them there is no existence of heaven and hell... The notions of 'good' and 'evil' are not religious in essence..." said Rao, a lecturer in sociology at the Government College, Nathdwara, Rajasthan. Bhils do not enter Hindu temples nor do they have any images or idols in their houses. They do not employ Brahmin priests for any of their ceremonies, such as births, marriages, and deaths, but employ their own Bhopas and Jogis who are Bhils. They believe that they become spirits after death, but they do not believe in rebirth into human or animal form. Even today the animist Bhils are fond of eating beef and do not show any special regard for the cow'.
   As quoted in D.K Singh, 1984, "Lost Tribes", *Communalism Combat*, October.
8. Some of my friends have expressed their reservations on the use of the term Hinduisation. To them it should have been Hindutvaisation. The term Hindutvaisation refers to the analysis of Hindu by Savarkar as one whose 'punyabhoomi' (holy land) and 'matribhumi' (motherland) both is India. Thus Hindutva, in this sense refers to the process associated with Sangh Parivar. We don't have any problem with such characterization of the term Hindutva. But what is problematic is the hidden implication of this differentiation that they don't have any problem with Hinduism. The question arises: is there any interconnection between Hinduism and Hindutvaism? The answer to this question warrants a separate discussion. Therefore we are using these terms interchangeably.
9. Hu, Shaohua, 1997. "Confucianism and Western Democracy," *Journal of Contemporary China*, Vol. 6, No. 15, pp. 347–363.
10. Ibid, pp. 359–363.
11. Joseph R Levenson. 1958. *Confucian China and its Modern Fate: The Problem of Intellectual Continuity.* Berkeley: University of California Press.
12. Samuel P Huntington, 1996. *The Clash of Civilizations and the Remaking of World Order*. New York: Touchstone.
13. Karl Marx, and F. Engels, 1976. *"The German Ideology"*, Moscow: Progress Publishers.

14. Schleiermacher strongly advocated to transforming hermeneutics into a universal method. To him, if truth is the object of any interpretation then interpretation must be universalised. The dream for a universal hermeneutics can be attained, Schleiermacher believes, in two ways: through Grammatical and Contextual Interpretation and Psychological or Divinatory Reconstruction.
15. For a discussion of Gadamer-Habermas debate and analysis of their positions please see, R.J. Anderson, Hughes, J,A. and Sharrock, W.W., 1986, *"Philosophy And Human Sciences"*, London: Croom Helm.
16. Gadamer, Hans-Georg. 1989. *Truth and Method*. (Second, Revised Edition, translated by Joel Weinsheimer and Donald G. Marshall.) New York: Crossroad. See especially Part-II when he criticises the romantic and historical school of hermeneutics.
17. Ibid, p. 302.
18. Anderson et. al., op.cit.
19. This is the process through which capitalist society tries to enclose the tribal society in the process of accumulation. This process has been discussed as the movements of primitive accumulation. According to this approach, primitive accumulation is the process of separation of a group of people from their means of production and livelihood. Thus, for this approach this process is not over or an accomplished fact. See "The New Enclosures" *Midnight Collective* appeared at www.commoner.org.uk.com, September 2001.
    Here, it must be pointed out that this critique of the interventions by the modern capitalistic society into the tribal society does not aim at romantic idealisation of tribal society as an ideal society. All that we want to emphasise is that the modern capitalist society has given a particular meaning to their hardships and has co-opted them into its framework by introducing its culture and ideology and thereby integrating them to the capitalist fold.
20. The districts of western Madhya Pradesh including Jhabua are primarily inhabited by Bhil, Bhilala, Barela, Pateliya and many other groups who have been included under the Bhil population by the Census Organisation of India. See Jayanta Sarkar, 1986, *'Social Mobility In Tribal Madhya Pradesh'*, Delhi: B.R. Publishing Corporation.
21. See Nishikant Chouhan, 2004, *'Majheb ke Nam Par', Jhabua me Hindu Sangam,* Madhya Pradesh Bharat Gyan Bigyan Samiti, Bhopal.

22. Mishra, DP, (ed), 1956, *The History of the Freedom Movement in Madhya Pradesh*, Nagpur. As quoted in Rahul op.cit.
23. Rahul, op. cit., CE, 1908, *Central India Gazetteer Series : Western States* (Malwa), Vol. V, British India Press.
24. Ibid.
25. C.E. Luard, 1908, *Central India Gazetteer Series: Western States (Malwa)* Vol.V, Mumbai: British India Press.
26. Rahul, op.cit.
27. Y.V.S. Nath, 1960, *Bhils of Ratanmal: An Analysis of the Social Structure of a Western Indian Community*, Vadodara: M S University, as quoted in Rahul op. cit.
28. *National Commission of Agriculture Report* (pp. 32-33).
29. Ibid, p. 25.
30. Rahul, op. cit.
31. David Mosse, S. Gupta, M. Mehta, V. Shah and J. Rees, 2002, Brokered livelihoods: debt, labour migration and development in tribal western India. *Journal of Development Studies*, 38 (5), pp. 59–88.
32. Ibid.
33. Ibid.
34. Breman, p. 76.
35. DISHA 2002 : 27.
36. TRU 1998 : 7.
37. Ibid.
38. As villagers expressed during our field visit, November 2004.
39. D.K. Singh, 2004, *Lost Tribes, Communalism Combat*, October 2004.
40. For details seeAmita, Baviskar, 1994, "Negotiating with Hinduism: Adivasi and the Mata", *Lokayan Bulletin*.
41. *'Har Har Mahadev'* and *'Jai Ma Kali'* are typical war slogans.
42. A Hindu activist proudly narrated this event.
43. http://stopfundinghate.org/sacw/part3.html
44. Awaaz - South Asia Watch, a foundation comprising British Indian academics and lawyers.
45. See www.awazsaw.org
46. www.hvk.org/articles/0102/98.html
47. Ibid.
48. Ibid.
49. *Communalism Watch*, June 15, 2005.
50. As villagers inform; see also *The Frontline* March 26, 2004 on Sangh's effort in Saffronising the tribal heartland.
51. *'The Indian Express'*, February 28, 2004.
52. *Choutha Sansar*, February 24, 2004.

5

Ordeals and Upheaval: A Critique of Hindu Proselytisation in Manipur

Thingnam Kishan Singh

I

As the majestic Himalayas gradually loop and descend in size and altitude towards the Southeast Asian frontier, interspersed with green valleys and blue hills, before immersing in the waters of the sea lies the land of Manipur washed with the Barak basin on the west and the Chindwin River on the east. History bears testimony to the travails of a civilisation of the people of this land running through a course of two thousand years. Known as *Kathe* to the Burmese, *Meklee* to the Ahoms, *Mooglie* to the Cacharies, *Cassey* to the Shans, the people of this ancient Asiatic land presently called Manipur have experienced numerous upheavals as a result of encounters with different cultures and powers. Situated along the Southern Silk Route, Manipur has historically been described as a meeting point of different peoples and cultures from the East, the South and the Southeast Asian region.[1] Manipur is located between latitude 23°50′ and 25°30′ North and longitude 93°10′ and 94°30′ East, and consists of about 7,000 square miles of hill territory, and of 1,000 square miles of level country forming a broad valley. The constant interactions resulting from trading activities between different peoples and the struggles for political domination among the various ethnic groups and migrating tribes have resulted in the intermingling of different cultures.

Constant interaction and assimilation of several ethnic groups in the valley resulted in the emergence of the Meeteis as the dominant group by the first century A.D. The recorded history of Manipur dates back to 33 A.D. with the ascent of Nongda Lairen Pakhangba of the Ningthouja clan to the throne at Kangla, which remained the seat of power till the British colonial conquest in 1891.[2] The royal chronicle *Cheitharol Kumbaba* records the uninterrupted reign of the clan. It also recorded cultural encounters of the Meeteis with the *Ava* (Burmese), the *Pong* (Shan), the *Khaki* (South China), the *Tai Ahom* or *Tekhao* (Assamese) and *Takhel* (Tripura). The Cheitharol Kumbaba has three phases covering the long span of the history of this ancient Asiatic kingdom—the first phase covers the period of Nongda Lairen Pakhangba's ascension to 1484 A.D. (the reign of Kyamba), the second phase covers the period between 1484 A.D. and 1780 A.D. (the reign of Bhagyachandra) and the third phase covers the period between 1780 A.D. to the middle of the 20th century.[3] Another chronicle, known as the *Ningthourol Lambuba* provides a much more detailed account, inspite of its lack of chronological documentation. The long-drawn historical process witnessed the evolution and emergence of a common faith, a philosophy, a cosmology, a system of complex cultural practices, a language, a script and a written code of conduct. It is pertinent to note that the first written codified laws were promulgated during the period of King Loiyamba, who reigned from 1074 to 1112 A.D. Known as the *Loiyumba Sinlen,* it assumed the basis and form of a constitution through which the administration of the kingdom was carried out till the British conquest in 1891. Modifications and changes from time to time, to engage the emerging realities were incorporated in the historical life-span of the *Loiyumba Sinlen.* The present name of the land, Manipur, is of relatively recent origin, dating from the 18th century only.[4] It came with the advent of Hinduism. *Sanamahi Laikan,* a historical account, mentions that the name Manipur was first officially introduced in the early 18th century during the reign of the Hindu convert King Garibniwaz (1709–1748).[5] It is clear that the name 'Manipur' does not appear in any of the pre-Hindu literatures, more specifically in the chronicles of the Kingdom.[6] Prior to the advent of this name, Kangleipak, Poireipak and Meitrabak were used.[7] Its geographical location—sandwiched between South Asia and Southeast Asia—played an important role in shaping history and cultural development.[8] The Meetei faith, prior to the advent of Hinduism in Manipur presented a distinct complex set of beliefs with its own cosmology, rites and festivals. Fused with a legacy of mythology and legends, the religion of the Meeties had marked similarities with the indigenous faiths of the surrounding hill tribes.[9] An exposition of this faith underlines the association with nature, which exists in all its abundance in this part of the world. The deities worshipped can broadly be classified into three categories that come under the term *Umang Lai*. Literally translated, it means 'forest god', but the etymological sense has a wide difference from actual practice as the *Umang Lai* is not limited or confined to 'forest deities'.[10] As seen from practice, it refers to four different forms of worship:

(a) Ancestral deities transposed with human existence at some point of time in the past. These are linked with the mythical associations of defied ancestors.
(b) Important deities associated with a clan or tribe.
(c) Domestic deities that are worshipped inside the house. These are also 'possessions' of particular clans of families.
(d) Tutelary deities or guardian spirits associated with particular places or areas considered sacred. Hills, in particular, are considered sacred to the Meeteis, with several important pilgrimage sites like the Thangjing hill in Moirang, Nongmaiching Hill, Mount Koubru, Mount Kounu, Cheirouching Hill, Kondong Leirembi, etc.

Traditional Meetei religion is based on beliefs rooted in a cosmology evolved over the years in the pre-historic stages. This cosmology conceptualised a notion of cosmic evolution that has been part of the ancient Meetei tradition preserved through subsequent generations. It was subsequently recorded in historical time as society and culture developed. The cosmological frameworks are recorded in *Leithak Leikharon*,

Pudil, Shakok Lamlen, Thiren Layat, Pakhangba Phambal and other works in the indigenous Meetei script. Many other manuscripts in the Meetei script also give accounts of the cosmological traditions that speak of a beginning where there was only an empty darkness. At this point, the supreme god, known by different names, like *Taipangpanba Mapu* (lord of the Universe), *Taibirel Sidaba* (immortal soul), *Atiya Sidaba* (immortal lord of space), went on to create the Universe, gods and living beings.[11]

II

With the passage of time and the development and consolidation of the kingdom, encounters and contacts with other cultures and people became an inevitable feature. However, the ancient religion of the Meeteis still continued to hold a dominant sway over the lives of the people in the valley and ancient animistic tribal religions had an overarching presence amongst the hill tribes.[12] The 17th and 18th centuries witnessed the emergence of immense proselytising activities in the Indian subcontinent. Historians have assessed the origins of these proselytising waves in terms of increasing persecution of Hindu missionaries during Aurangazeb's reign.[13] As a result of this persecution, the Hindu missionaries had to look eastward as the region beyond Bengal remained outside the domain of Aurangazeb's power. The predominantly difficult geographical terrain of this region prevented any major power from the west from extending influence. History bears testimony to the repeated attempts by the Mughals to invade Ahom (present Assam), only to face successive failures. The series of conflicts between the mighty Mughals and the determined and fiercely independent Ahoms perhaps formed the basis of increasing Hindu proselytising missions. Ahom opposition to the Mughals provided fertile ground for the hectic activities of the persecuted Hindu missionaries, who found enthusiastic support among the Ahom ruling class. The Ahom court of Assam, the Kachari kingdom and Tripura gradually fell under the influence of these Hindu missionaries. It has been pointed out that by the 17th century, these neighbouring kingdoms in the west of Manipur were already under the influence of Vainshnavite Hinduism.

These kingdoms and their successive rulers gave active support to the Brahmins who migrated to Manipur on proselytising missions.[14] These missionaries contributed significantly to the introduction and growth of Hinduism in Manipur. *Bamon Khunthok*, an account of Brahmin migrancy to Manipur, accurately describes a steady flow of Brahmin missionaries from different parts of India into the Manipur valley. The strong legacy of traditional Meetei faith never perceived these Brahmin missionaries as a substantial threat and, on most occasions, was viewed with amusement. As they were never taken seriously, the ruling monarchs presumably allowed them to settle. In fact, most of these Brahmins were allotted clan names and absorbed into the Meetei fold.[15] On most occasions, they were allowed to marry Meetei women. They primarily came without family or women. It has been recorded that these Brahmin immigrants were made to marry women of the *Kei* class. These women were labourers who had to provide and pound rice for the royal family.[16] Thereby, the status of the Brahmins was greatly lowered. It is a clear indication of the fact that they were not given a respectable status in society, nor was their faith or doctrines accepted readily by the people.

The scene gradually began to change with the accession of Charairongba to the throne of Manipur in 1697. His short reign from 1697 to 1706 sowed the seeds for what would become a catastrophic upheaval shortly afterwards. Charairongba became the first Meetei king who converted to Vaishnavite Hinduism. Mentioned in the chronicle as the first Meetei king who formally took the sacred Hindu thread with rites and rituals, he did not make any attempt to establish Hinduism as the official religion in the kingdom.[17] The chronicle maintains clearly that Charairongba, inspite of his conversion to Hinduism, could never break away from the traditional Meetei religion and its practices. Traditional Meetei religion and culture flourished as there was no prohibition on consumption of meat and wine during his reign. Hinduism was yet to make a decisive impact on the traditional Meetei religion. Moreover, the people still saw the new faith and its missionaries with amusement rather than a substantial threat to their culture and identity. It was with Charairongba's death and his son Pamheiba's accession to the throne that eventually turned the tables.

III

The chronicle *Chitharol Kumbaba* records that Pamheiba ascended the throne of Manipur in August 1709 after a gap of 40 days after his father's death. The eldest of the five sons born to the four wives of King Charairongba–Pamheiba was 20 years of age when he took over the reins of administration of the kingdom. His reign of forty years witnessed dramatic increase in the military and political strength of Manipur, which no doubt has been perceived to precipitate a series of crises that eventually led to Manipur's loss of sovereignty and independence.[18] Relations with neighbouring kingdom of Ava (Burma), which started deteriorating during Charairongba's reign saw further degeneration with Pamheiba as he made a series of incursions. With rapid strides in military prowess, he soon became a terror for the Burmese. Huge quantity of literature—historical religious and creative—supplemented by modern archaeological findings like coins and stone inscriptions, and numerous references in the contemporary chronicles of Burma[19] bear testimony of the political and military prowess and achievements of Garibaniwaz, who emerged as the most prominent ruler in the eastern frontier of India and Burma. In fact, no other king in this frontier region and Burma had anything in comparison with Garibaniwaz's military conquest in early 18th century.[20]

Various Hindu sects made attempts to influence the king's court after Charairongba's time. In 1715, 39 *Bairagis* reached the capital of Manipur to intensity the proselytisation process. The *Cheitharol Kumbaba* records that Garibaniwaz took the sacred thread of Vaisnhavite Hinduism from a preceptor called Guru Gopal Das in October 1717. *Sanamahi Laikan* corroborates this fact. Prior to the king's initiation to Hinduism, there were no restrictions on the cultural practices, the rituals and festivals associated with traditional Meetei religion. Eating of meat, including beef and consumption of liquor, was widespread as earlier. However, October 1717 marked a paradigm shift in terms of proselytisation and spread of Hinduism, with the despotic monarch declaring it the official religion of the kingdom. Official sanction witnessed massive patronage to the Brahmin missionaries, the construction of several Hindu shrines and temples and the persecution of those who opposed conversion to Hinduism. Amongst the shrines and temples constructed in the zeal of religions fervour, mention can be made of the images of Hindu God Krishna and Goddess Kali placed in a tank in 1726 in Kangla as part of the consecration ceremony. These images were found at the foot of the consecration post in the exact position described in the chronicle *Ningthourol Lambuba* in 1906 by a British colonial officer.[21] *Cheitharol Kumbaba* mentions the departure of the king's perceptor Guru Gopal Das in 1720. With Gopal Das's return to Bengal, another perceptor by the name of Shanta Das Goswami from Nara Singh Tilla of Sylhet in Bengal, took his place and induced Garibaniwaz to execute a series of programmes meant to erase and obliterate the traditional Meetei religion. Shanta Das was a Brahmin missionary who belonged to the Ramanandi sect of Hinduism in eastern India. Constantly harassed by Aurangazeb's religious policies, these missionaries were compelled to leave their homeland in search for new pastures for missionary activities.[22] Brahmins, pilgrims and ascetics entered Manipur in larger members to push forward the proselytisation process further,[23] beyond the massive influx of proselytising missionaries cultural contacts with neighbouring Ahom, which had already been Hinduised increased manifold.

Shanta Das's entry marks a significant turning point in the proselytisation process. A rigorous thrust towards the use of state power and machineries as instruments to further the propagation of the new faith could be seen henceforth. The despotic and feudal structure was dexterously exploited to present the alien faith in a grand and aesthetically attractive manner to the common people. Existing power configuration where the monarch wielded exclusive state power worked effectively as a political force, coercing the common masses to submit to the despot's dictat. Blatant use or abuse of state power could be seen in a series of edicts issued by the king, who took on the Sanskritised title 'Maharaja'. These edicts were aimed at the traditional culture and lifestyles of the people. The underlying motive was to change the culture and lifestyle of the masses. Edicts proclaimed included prohibition of consumption of meat and liquor, the rearing of poultry and animals like pigs, and burial of the dead. Strict punitive measures were meted out against those who went against Hindu dietary laws. Those who were caught eating beef or any other meat faced severe punishment that even included capital punishment. People who reared livestock other than cows were declared unclean. They were subsequently outcast from society fined and banished to the far-flung peripheral regions. These outcasts, who reared poultry and pigs, ate meat and consumed liquor, were called *lois*. It is pertinent to note that they still inhabit the fringes and continue with the same lifestyle even today. Many researchers have been able to gain significant insights into the original culture and religious belief of the Meeteis by studying them.

Frantic and desperate measures aimed at obliterating traditional Meetei faith included not only persecution of those who opposed conversion but blatant attempts to destroy and efface the shrines of the traditional deities or *Umang lais*. An instance is the destruction of nine *Umang lais* and their shrines by an official dictat in 1723. Calculative moves by the King's new preceptor, Shanta Das resulted in widespread vandalism and destruction of the *Umang lais*. In 1726, the *Cheitharol Kumbaba* mentions further large-scale destruction of sacred *Umang lai* shrines. Razed to the ground, the ashes were buried in the newly-built Hanuman temple near the Palace. In 1724, the King ordered the opening of the tombs of former kings and members of the royal family. He exhumed the bones of his ancestors and cremated them on the banks of the Chindwin River, popularly known as Ningthee River to the Manipuris. The ashes were scattered in the river in vindication of the newly acquired Hindu faith. Considered a sacrilege by the Meeteis, the opening of the tombs agitated the people intensely. However, the despotic ruler spared nothing to repress the swelling dissent. The *Cheitharol Kumbaba* records that cremation was introduced and made mandatory from that year. Another frantic measure was the burning of books in Meetei script by Shanta Das and his Brahmin followers. Manuscripts and texts in the indigenous script were confiscated and burnt in full public view in ceremony dubbed *'Puya Meithaba'* or *'Puya Burning'*. Altogether, a total of 123 books in manuscripts were burnt on this occasion.[24] Use of the indigenous script was banned with dire consequences for those who attempted to resist. It was to be replaced by the Bengali script.

Shanta Das went to the extent of composing an entirely different chronicle in Bengali known as *Vijay Pancholi,* which was a deliberate attempt to efface the history of the people. It projected the land as the Manipur of the Hindu epic *Mahabharata* and traced the lineage and genealogy of the first king of Manipur to Chandrabhanu whose daughter Chitrangada was married to Arjuna, the Pandava archer. Babrubahana was the son born of this wedlock. His son Yavistha was then identified with Nongda Lairen Pakhangba who first ascended the throne in Kangla in 33 A.D. Imported art forms, like the *Natya Sankirtan* actively encouraged by the royal power gained popularity. Corruption in language became the order of the day as the elite and aristocratic class got increasing exposure to Indo-Aryan languages like Sanskrit and Bengali. With the restrictions on the practice of the indigenous faith and the widespread patronage to the newly imported alien faith, a sudden influence of literature in the Indo-Aryan languages, especially Sanskrit and Bengali, was felt by the people.[25]

The proselytisation campaign made attempts to transform the whole social and political system of Manipur into a Hindu State and society.[26] Shanta Das drew up a scheme of transplanting the indigenous Meetei social structure with Hindu structures. The Meetei social structure was based on a federation of clans or tribes known as Yeks or Salais. *Cheitharol Kumbaba* records the preparation of genealogies of the Meeteis in order to supplant them with Shanta Das's Hindu *gotra* system in 1731. The King and all the converted Meeteis were proclaimed *kshatriyas* and transplantation of the *gotras* assumed significance:

Yek/Salai	*Gotra*
Ningthouja	*Shandilya*
Angom	*Kaushika*
Chenglei	*Bhardhwaja*
Luwang	*Kashyap*
Khuman	*Madhugalya*
Moirang	*Aitereya*
Khaba-Nganba	*Gautam*

Festivals associated with the traditional Meetei religion were either banned or transformed and modified by giving Hindu names and forms. An important festival known as the *Heigru Hidongba* celebrated with an annual boat race was rechristened *Jal Yatra*. *Ayang Yoiren Iruppa*, an annual bathing ceremony in the month of *Wakching* (December/January) was transformed into *Snan Yatra* at Lilong Sahanpat. The annual archery festival called *Waira Tenkap* festival in the month of *Phairen* (February/ January) was transformed into a *Kirtan* of the Hindu god Rama. *Kongba Leithong Phatpa*, an oracular ceremony in the Manipuri New Year month of *Sajibu* (April) was converted to *Vishnu Sankranti*. *Rath Jatra* soon replaced *Ahom Khongching* festival in *Ingel* (June). The traditional festival associated with offerings to ancestors in the month of *Langban* (September/October) was replaced by *Tarpan* or offering to *pritulok*. *Wakambung Chingnung Nongombi* festival was replaced by *Dasana Kwaktanba* of *Durga Puja* or *Dusserah*. *Chanou Hui Chintu*, a festival associated with the new harvest was replaced by *Goverdhon Puja*. Hindu proselytisation brought about an upheaval resulting in dramatic changes in the hitherto self-contained world of the Meeteis and the hill tribes of Manipur. Prior to the conversion to Hinduism, the Meetei society was totally alien to the concept and practice of caste system. It was fundamentally a casteless society. One of the tragic implications for the people of this ancient land was to face the ramifications of casteism as the Meeteis including members of the royal lineage were declared *Kshatriyas*. The Brahmins who enjoyed exclusive patronage remained a separate caste outside the Meetei society. Gradually, the consolidation of this caste system led to the seclusion of the non-Hindu Meetei *Lois* and the hill tribes and the Shan Buddhists in the Kabaw valley, which was then a part of Manipur. Casteless society based on traditional Meetei faith had seen cordial relations between the valley people and the hill tribes. With the widening gap between the valley and the hill people due to steady polarisation on grounds of seclusion and ocstracisation practised by the Hindu converts zealously, intermingling and intermarriage declined rapidly. For the first time, rules of commensality, concept of pollution and dietary differences began to be used to exacerbate this widening gap. Increasing practice of casteism led to a widening gap between the people in the valley and the hills. This widening gap consequently weakened Manipur in the face of conflicts perpetrated by forces from outside.

Another effect, though shortlived, was the valorisation of the heinous practice of *Sati*. Although it was confined to the upper-class affluent members of society, it nonetheless witnessed systematic glorification in an effort to percolate down to the level of the common masses. The zeal and fervour of the newly imported alien faith made its adherents project a glorified image of *Sati* as wives of princes, Brahmins and noblemen started immolating themselves in the funeral pyres of their dead husbands. *Cheitharol Kumbaba* mentions many instances of *Sati* in Manipur with a note that these were voluntary acts. The first instance was in 1726 A.D. when the two wives of Prince Murari immolated themselves in the funeral pyre of the dead prince. Other instances are Sapam Khwairakpam's wife committing *Sati* in 1733, Wahengbam Nongthouba's two wives in 1735 and Keirungba Thanogai's two wives in 1737. It really needs to be looked deeper as the element of voluntariness associated with these instances might be a deliberate propaganda on the part of the elite in their attempt to glorify this heinous practice. A detailed study and critique of the period may throw a different light on the matter.

The zeal and fervour of the king, the Brahmins and the new converts, who in the beginning were mostly from the feudal class, have been analysed by historians in terms of religious fanaticism.[27] As seen from the instances mentioned above, there was a discernible streak of fanaticism involved. The King and the feudal class who followed him, had to face stiff opposition in their attempt to push forward the proselytisation process by relegating the traditional Meetei faith. It has been pointed out that the King forced members of the court to accept the new religion as an early measure.[28] Most of them were compelled to follow the King, as they were apprehensive of losing their status and position. Having thus garnered support of the feudal class, the King used state power as an instrument to perpetrate the process of conversion which was never voluntary.[29] Widespread dissent amongst the people who strongly resisted the conversion was a serious threat to the King and his legitimacy as a ruler. As mentioned earlier, sections of the populace who made strong objections were displaced through banishment as *Lois* in the remote areas. Garibaniwaz then proceeded to carry out a series of raids against Burma. He comes out as a valiant and successful military campaigner against the Burmese, for whom he became a terror. The chronicle *Ningthourol Lambuba* records a number of incursions into Burma where Garibaniwaz indulged in large-scale loot and plunder including destruction of a number of Buddhist pagodas at the behest of his religious mentor, Shanta Das.

The factors behind these campaigns have been a crucial point of several studies. Certain historians have attributed a revenge motive to these campaigns on account of the ill treatment given to Garibaniwaz's sister, Chakpa Nakhao Ngambi, who was married to the Burmese King. After the birth of a son, the Burmese king apparently slighted her. In his dying moments, Charairongba is believed to have urged his son Garibaniwaz to avenge this humiliation.[30] Western scholars, like Pemberton, through Burmese historical accounts, have attributed these attacks to the fanatical religious belief behind Hinduism which made Garibaniwaz think that he would gain merit and acceptability amongst the people by bathing in the Irrawady.[31] However, a critical analysis of the prevailing circumstances, in the wake of the conversion process, point towards the need to evolve a strategy of diverting the attention of the people. In the presence of widespread dissent and opposition to the imposition of Hinduism, there was a need to mitigate the emerging conflict between the people and the ruling class. The compelling need to mitigate this emerging conflict between adherents of the Meetei faith and the newly converted ruling elite led Garibaniwaz and his Brahmin perceptor Shanta Das evolve a diversionary strategy by undertaking these military campaigns against Burma. These campaigns served the twin purpose of diverting the people's attention from the conversion issue and unifying the people at the same time in the face of a series of battles against a rival foreign power. The conspicuous presence of Shanta Das in all the campaigns gave credibility to the newly imparted alien faith as Garibaniwaz emerged highly successful against the Burmese. On the other hand, Shanta Das tried desperately to convert the Burmese into his religion amidst these invasions. Inspite of repeated attempts he never succeeded in bringing Hinduism into Burma.

The uneasy tussle between Hinduism and the traditional Meetei religion persisted even as Garibaniwaz emerged successful in converting a majority of the people in the valley. Resistance and opposition to Hinduism erupted in an unprecedented fashion with the assassination of Garibniwaz and Shanta Das in 1748, by a person none other than the King's own son, Chit Sai. As he grew old, Garibaniwaz retired as a *sanyasi*, abdicating the throne in favour of Chit Sai, a son from his third marriage. Chit Sai tried to expunge Hinduism from Manipur but he did not live long. Much as the new religion gained ground, court intrigue and conspiracies associated with the ruling class, who had by now become a staunch supporter of Hinduism, were against Chit Sai's attempts to restore the traditional Meetei faith. His act of committing particide was used meticulously to fan hatred and opposition against him. A powerful alliance of feudal lords and some members of the royal family succeeded in dethroning him and sending him into exile. His exile marked the steady consolidation of Hinduism in Manipur. Apart from historical importance of this clash between the indigenous Meetei faith and the alien Hindu faith, the nature of its impact on the collective experience of the people and its culture needs careful scrutiny. It was essentially an encounter between two pre-modern, traditional worldviews. An uneasy synthesis gradually emerged, which led Western scholars like T.C. Hodson comment that Hinduism exist in Manipur solely in its esoteric form without its subtle metaphysical doctrine.[31] It is perhaps natural to attribute the modern generation's quest for identity with the persisting tussle between Hinduism and the traditional Meetei faith.

Emerging debates in the arena of cultural studies underscore duality as a distinct feature of the existing Meetei cultural identity. This duality is moulded by the continuous interplay of two forces, the forces of Hinduisation on the one hand and the indigenisation on the other.[32] Located at the level of discourse, the two different ontological experiences are woven together in a site simmering with tension arising out of a deep-seated contestation. Articulating in different languages or practices, the two paradoxically represent a riven terrain in contemporary Manipuri society. It has been succinctly argued that the Hindu discourse articulates in a language placing itself in the 'great tradition' of the mainstream Indian Sanskritic culture while the traditional Meetei discourse reinforces rootedness in the pre-Hinduised state, drawing its strength from oral history, written chronicles, native categories of thought and popular belief.

REFERENCES

1. Kabui Gangumei, 1991, *History of Manipur.Vol.I. Pre-Colonial Period,* New Delhi: National Publishers.
2. Ibohal Singh Wahengbam, 1986, *The History of Manipur: Early Period,* Imphal : Manipur Commercial Co.
3. Gangumei, Ibid., 34.
4. Manihar Singh Chongtham, 1996, *A History of Manipuri Literature,* New Delhi: *Sahitya Akademi.*
5. Bogeshwor Oinam,1972, *Sanamahi Laikan,* Imphal:Manipuri Sahitya Parishad.
6. W. Yumjao "Report on Archaeological Studies in Manipur", *Bulletin No.1.Imphal.* 1935.
7. Gangumei Kabui, Ibid.
8. Gangumei Kabui, Ibid.

9. T.C. Hodson. 1913, "The Religion of Manipur" *Folk-lore, 24:518-123*. London.
10. S. Nalini Parrat, *The Religion of Manipur: Beliefs, Rituals and Historical Development* (Calcutta:Firma KLM).
11. Ibohal Singh, Wahengbam, Ibid.
12. Gangumei Kabui, Ibid. 251.
13. Gangumei Kabui, Ibid. 251.
14. Gangumei Kabui, Ibid. 251.
15. S. Nalini Parrat, Ibid.133.
16. W. McCulloch, "An Account of the Valley of Munnipore and of the Hill Tribes". *Selections from the Records of the Government of India, No. XXVIII.*
17. S. Nalini Parrat, Ibid.135.
18. S. Nalini Parrat, Ibid.
19. R.B. Pemberton, 1998, *Report on the Eastern Frontier of India.* (first published 1835, London, Indian reprint, New Delhi: Low Price Publications).
20. Gangumei Kabui, Ibid, 239.
21. J. Shakespear, "The Religion of Manipur" *Folk-lore 24:409-55.1913*. London.
22. Gangumei Kabui, Ibid. 252.
23. S. Nalini Parrat, Ibid. 146.
24. N. Khelchandra, 1969, *Ariba Manipuri Sahitya Itihas*, Imphal: Ningthoujam.
25. Chongtham Manihar Singh, Ibid.
26. Gangumei Kabui, Ibid., 256.
27. Gangumei Kabui, Ibid and S. Nalini Parrat, Ibid.
28. Gangumei Kabui,Ibid., 259.
29. Gangumei Kabui, Ibid., 259.
30. Chongtham Manihar Singh. Ibid.
31. T.C. Hodson, 2001, *The Meitheis* (first published 1908,London. Indian reprint. New Delhi: Low Price Publications, p. 96.
32. Rekha Konsam, *2005,* "Lai Haraoba: Discursive Practices and Cultural Contestations". *Eastern Quarterly.* Vol. 3 Issue III. Oct-Dec. pp. 206-214.

6

Conversion in Chhattisgarh: Myths and Facts

Rajendra K. Sail

At the Root of the Controversy

After the creation of the Chhattisgarh State in November 2000, the Bhartiya Janata Party (BJP) has been using the issue of Conversion by Christians in Chhattisgarh as one of the planks for political campaign, basically to gain political control over the State. However, conversion as a political issue was an obvious choice for BJP, primarily because of the then Congress(I) Chief Minister, Shri Ajit Pramod Kumar Jogi, who was himself a Christian.[1]

The BJP and the Sangh Parivar, hold fascist beliefs in thriving on rumours. Mr. Gobbles, the Information Minister in Adolf Hitler's Nazi Germany had stated, "a lie repeated ten times turns into truth". The Sangh Parivar spread the rumour that "*Sonia Gandhi has appointed Ajit Jogi as the Chief Minister of Chhattisgarh at the behest of Pope John Paul II*". One heard of the same rumour being repeated from Raipur to Delhi, cutting across class and creed lines!

Obviously, such arguments do not fit the frame of common sense or political science—falsehoods are not spread on rationality. But, it does fit into the propaganda machine of Sangh Parivar. In such frameworks, it becomes easier to link up conversion by Churches in Chhattisgarh with Pope's call for Conversion in India during his 3rd visit to India in 1999.[2] Thus, the ultimate objective of transforming Chhattisgarh into 'Christigarh' (meaning a land belonging to Christ)!

The BJP and its coalition partners in the then NDA (National Democratic Alliance) government of the Indian state were pursuing the Globalisation Agenda ('India shining' and 'feel good factor' were the main election bogeys of BJP in the Parliamentary Elections of 2004). However, in Chhattisgarh State Assembly Elections held in 2003, the BJP had declared "*Dhan Aur Dharmantaran*" (Paddy & Conversion) as the election issue. It was quite in line with the BJP's policy of cashing on the communally surcharged atmosphere, especially in the wake of the Gujarat's so-called success story in State Assembly Elections held in 2002. In Chhattisgarh, its obvious target was the Church and its various activities, especially related to evangelisation (with an ingredient of proselytisation), in short, conversion. The history of conversion needs to be traced in the current context of rise in communal attacks on the Churches and Christians in Chhattisgarh.

On 16th April 1954, the Congress Government of Madhya Pradesh, headed by Pandit Ravi Shanker Shukla, set up 'The Christian Missionary Activities Enquiry Committee' lead by Sri Bhawani Shanker Niyogi, retired Chief Justice. The Niyogi Committee Report was highly critical of conversion activities, particularly the conversion of tribals and activities of foreign missionaries. The Madhya Pradesh *Dharma Swatantrya Adhiniyam*, 1968 (that is still in force in Madhya Pradesh) provides sufficient ground for actions against conversion attempts by the Church in Chhattisgarh (as part of Madhya Pradesh)! It totally bans forcible conversion, and those violating its provision are punished with one year's imprisonment or a fine of Rs. 5000 or both. However, in the case of conversion of a minor, woman, tribal or dalit, the imprisonment is for two years, and fine up to Rs. 10,000.

The much-publicised *Grah Vapasi* ("Operation Home Coming") mostly spearheaded by the then Cabinet Minister of State for Environment & Forest and a Member of Rajya Sabha, Sri Daleep Singh Judeo.[3] It is an attempt to' bring back' tribals (and dalits) into the Hindu fold, who were converted to

Christianity. The functions include washing the feet of tribal people by Shri Daleep Singh Judeo, who is a former Raja of Jashpur State. These acts did not result in large-scale 'return' to Hindu fold. Instead, often the people re-converted to Hinduism publicly claimed that they had not been earlier converted to Christianity!

Serious sociological questions have also been raised in the wake of *Grah Vapasi*. Tribals are not Hindus, but follow religions like 'Sarna', etc. and were categorised as animists. An issue that remains unresolved is the position of tribals in the Hindu caste hierarchy after 'home coming'. Those brought back to the Hindu fold were mostly tribals and dalits who continue to be subjugated, not even allowed to enter temples. Thus, it did not result in creating the basic relationship of "Roti aur Beti" (meaning sharing of bread and daughter in marriage). It has not had any impact, in spite of media hype!

The Sangh Parivar's oft-repeated refrain is about unprecedented rise in Christian population in Chhattisgarh due to large-scale conversion, especially among the tribals and dalits. Such a refrain has become more frequent and louder after the Bhartiya Janata Party came to power in 2003. However, the Sangh Parivar and/or the BJP leaders have never substantiated such a serious statement with facts and figures. Their publications have only rhetoric regarding conversion, but no facts. Moreover, not many cases been filed under the Madhya Pradesh Dharam Swatantra Adhiniyam, 1968. A few stray cases that were filed have not necessarily met with success in convicting the 'converter' or 'converts'.

Whether in power, after gaining control of the State machinery in 2003 or as opposition, during Congress (I) rule, the BJP failed to challenge the official version regarding conversion in Chhattisgarh in the State Assembly on 5th March 2003. It gives credence to the belief that the bogey of large-scale conversion by Christians is for certain political mileage. During the debate in the Vidhan Sabha, Sri Shivratan of BJP claimed that since the Congress (I) government led by Sri Jogi came to power in the state, the conversion to Christianity increased by ten times. Again, there were no facts and figures either official or collected through own sources. What was managed was a walkout by BJP members!

In reply to questions, the Home Minister of Chhattisgarh Government, Sri Nand Kumar Patel put forward the following facts in the Vidhan Sabha:

TABLE 6.1

Total Conversion:	424
Conversions from Hinduism to Christianity:	268
Conversions from Christianity to Hinduism:	138
From Muslim to Christianity:	001
From Hinduism to Sikhism:	001
From Hinduism to Muslim:	013

District-wise distribution was also provided: 220 in Dantewada, 22 in Beejapur, 113 in Mahasamund, 19 in Raigarh, 20 in Rajnandgaon, 6 in Durg, 9 in Bilaspur and 3 in Sarguja. It was also stated that all these persons had voluntarily converted to another religion.

The demographic figures from the Census of India reports would expose the fallacy of BJP's claims. In examining the figures for the period 1951 and 1991 (figures for religious composition of 2001 are not yet available), it is seen that the Christian Population in Madhya Pradesh (and Chhattisgarh) is less than the national average:

TABLE 6.2

Madhya Pradesh	*1951*	*1961*	*1971*	*1981*	*1991*
Hindus	95.00%	93.99%	93.68%	92.96%	92.99%
Muslims	04.03%	04.07%	04.36%	04.80%	04.96%
Christians	00.31%	00.58%	00.69%	00.67%	00.64%

The above table shows that the Christian population in Madhya Pradesh has never been more than one per cent of the total population in independent India. Even in absolute numbers, it reached the figure of only 4,26,600 in 1991, which was only 0.64 per cent of the total population. Out of a total of 45 districts in Madhya Pradesh, only three districts recorded a percentage population of Christians above one per cent of the total population. These are Raigarh 9.92%, Sarguja 2.31% and Jhabua 1.32% in 1991. Thus, it becomes difficult to deduce the necessity of the Madhya Pradesh Dharma Swaytantra Adhiniyam, 1968.

While the national average of Christian population in 1991 was 2.32 per cent, in Chhattisgarh it was 1.71 per cent. In 1981, it was 1.80 per cent against the national average of 2.43 per cent. Even in absolute numbers, the Christian population in Chhattisgarh is merely 3 lakhs out of a total population of 1.76 crores in 1991.

TABLE 6.3

Chhattisgarh	*1951*	*1961*	*1971*	*1981*	*1991*
Hindus	97.81%	96.67%	96.14%	95.13%	95.47%
Muslims	1.25%	1.21%	1.40%	1.65%	1.70%
Christians	0.59%	1.46%	1.80%	1.80%	1.71%

Fig. 6.1 : Religious composition of Indian Union: 1951–1991
(For the total enumerated population, in thousands)
(In Absolute Numbers)

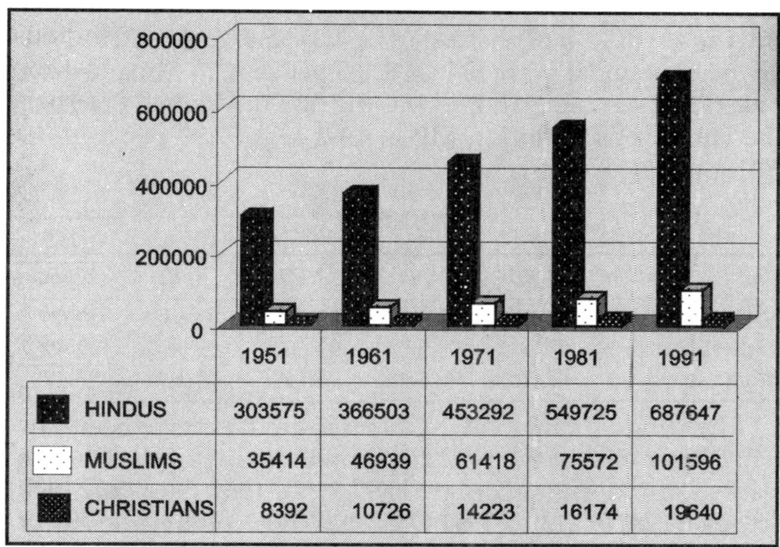

	1951	1961	1971	1981	1991
HINDUS	303575	366503	453292	549725	687647
MUSLIMS	35414	46939	61418	75572	101596
CHRISTIANS	8392	10726	14223	16174	19640

The Hindu population in Chhattisgarh has been above the national average, by about ten to fifteen per cent. In 1991, the

Fig. 6.2: Religious composition of Madhya Pradesh: 1951–1991

(In Absolute Numbers)

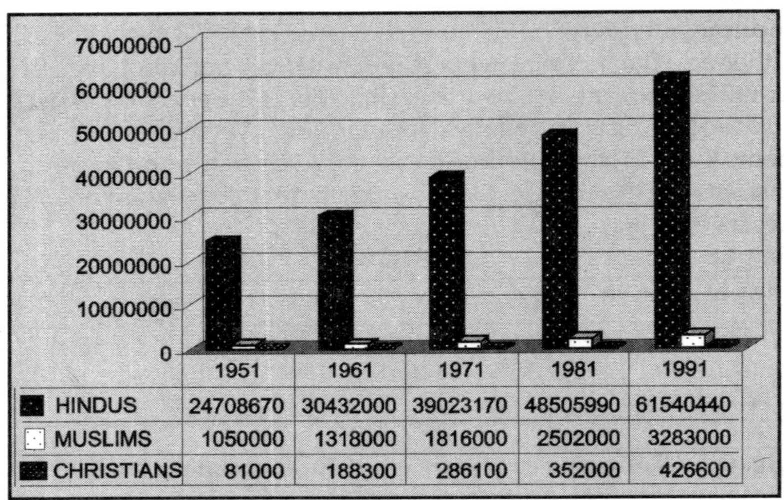

	1951	1961	1971	1981	1991
HINDUS	24708670	30432000	39023170	48505990	61540440
MUSLIMS	1050000	1318000	1816000	2502000	3283000
CHRISTIANS	81000	188300	286100	352000	426600

Hindu population was 82 per cent of the total population in India as a whole, in Chhattisgarh it was 95.47 per cent; in 1981 when the national average was 82.63 per cent, in Chhattisgarh it was 95.12 per cent. And, so was the case in Madhya Pradesh! The Hindu population in MP in 1991 was 92.99 per cent; in 1981 it was 92.96 per cent.

TABLE 6.4

Hindu Population	*1951*	*1961*	*1971*	*1981*	*1991*
India	84.98%	83.51%	82.73%	82.63%	82.00%
Madhya Pradesh	95.00%	93.99%	93.68%	92.96%	92.99%
Chhattisgarh	97.81%	96.67%	96.14%	95.13%	95.47%

The Hindu population in Chhattisgarh has never been less than 95 per cent of the total population in any of the Census years after independence: 1951 (97.81%), 1961 (96.67%), 1971 (96.14%), 1981 (95.13%), 1991 (95.47%). Thus, the statement that "Christian population in Chhattisgarh (and in Madhya Pradesh) is rising with alarming proportions that Hindus would vanish one day" does not hold any water. Even in absolute numbers, the Hindu population in Chhattisgarh has increased from 72, 93,530 in 1951 to 1, 68,17,294 in 1991. The decadal growth recorded by the Hindu Population in Chhattisgarh has been either on a par with or higher than the national average (except in 1971-1981), as is evident from the Table 6.5.

A deeper analysis of the Census Reports would also bring home the point that the Christian population in five out of seven districts of Chhattisgarh has never been more than one per cent. Let us examine percentage figures for Christian population in Raipur: 1991 (0.47%), 1981 (0.60%), 1971 (0.59%), 1961 (0.57%), 1951 (0.93%), 1941 (0.54%).

TABLE 6.5 : Decadal Growth of Hindu Population in Chhattisgarh (In percentage)

	1951–61	*1961–71*	*1971–81*	*1981–91*
In India (Total)	21.64%	24.80%	24.66%	23.86 %
In Chhattisgarh (Hindu Population)	21.33%	26.42%	19.79%	25.46%

A popular rhetoric that "Hindu population is fast dwindling, and one day (by 2055), it would become less than the Christians & Muslims" is seen to be baseless from the data in Table 6.6.

TABLE 6.6 : Population of Chhattisgarh (Hindus, Christians & Muslims)

	1951	*1961*	*1971*	*1981*	*1991*
Christians	44,695	1,33,901	2,09,694	2,53,858	3,02,637
Muslims	93,234	1,11,356	1,63,124	2,32,603	2,99,673
Hindus	72,93,530	88,49,715	1,11,88,659	1,34,03,897	1,68,17,294

During the forty years (1951–1991), the population of Hindus has recorded a growth of 126.51 per cent and of Christians 134.03 per cent. In absolute numbers, Hindu population increased in forty years by 38,40,72,000, and Christian population by 1,12,48,000.

Out of a total of 452 districts in India in 1991, the Hindu population was above fifty per cent in 398 districts. It was only in 21 districts that the Christian population was above fifty per cent; and Muslim population was more than fifty per cent merely in merely 8 districts.

Out of the 21 districts in which Christian population recorded more than fifty per cent population in 1991, twenty are in North-East States (Manipur-4, Meghalaya-5, Moziram-3, Nagaland-8), and the remaining one is Andaman-Nicobar Islands. Of the 8 districts in which Muslim population was more than fifty per cent, 4 are in Assam, one each in Bihar, Kerala, Lakshadweep and West Bengal. In the same manner, it may be noted that either out of 66 districts in which the Hindu population was less than fifty per cent, or 21 districts in which the Christian population was more than fifty per cent, none of these districts are in Chhattisgarh and/or Madhya Pradesh.

DECADAL GROWTH OF CHRISTIAN POPULATION IN CHHATTISGARH

While the average Decadal Growth (in percentages) in India, Madhya Pradesh (and in Chhattisgarh) between 1951 and 1991 has been to the tune of 20 to 25 per cent, the percentage decadal growth among Christians in Chhattisgarh has been unusually high between the decades 1951–1961 (199.58%) and 1961–1971 (56.60%). In absolute numbers also, the decadal growth among Christians in Chhattisgarh during these two decades has been: 89,206 during 1951–1961, and 75,793 during 1961–1971.

However, during the next two decades, the decadal growth of Christian Population in Chhattisgarh drastically reduced. In fact, during 1971–1981 it was 44,164 (21.06%), much below the percentage decadal growth in India (24.66%) and in Madhya Pradesh (27.2%). And, in 1981-91 it became 48,779 (19.21%), which was much less than the percentage decadal growth recorded in India (23.86%)and Madhya Pradesh (24.3%).

The unprecedented decadal growth both in absolute numbers and percentage during the two decades 1951–1971 possibly explains the mass conversions to Christianity in Chhattisgarh. A further analysis of the data related to decadal growth in each district of Chhattisgarh brings home the point that the mass conversions to Christianity took place basically among tribals in the districts of Sarguja and Raigarh, former princely states that had earlier restricted the entries of Christian missionaries through legislation (Please note that the Raigarh State Conversion Act was passed in 1936), which required that a person seeking conversion needed to obtain a certificate of conversion from the authorities and disallowed preaching for the purpose of conversion. Followed by it, the Sarguja State Apostasy Act was also passed in 1945.

TABLE 6.7 : Christian Population in Chhattisgarh
(Decadal Growth)

District	*1951-61*	*1961-71*	*1971-81*	*1981-91*	*1991-2001*
Raigarh	76,486 (551.32%)	41,841 (46.30%)	12,546 (9.49%)	26,177 (18.08%)	NA
Sarguja	8,240 (1511.92%)	16,158 (183.92%)	13,267 (53.19%)	9,900 (25.90%)	NA
Bastar	717 (17.53%)	1,920 (39.95%)	4,346 (64.62%)	2,960 (26.73%)	NA

TABLE 6.8 : Total Population in Chhattisgarh (District Wise)

District	*1951-61*	*1961-71*	*1971-81*	*1981-91*
Surguja	214,697 26.12%	289,701 27.94%	327,504 24 69%	428,687 25.92%
Raigarh	121,706 13.24%	237,479 22.81%	224,492 17.56%	219,094 14.58%
Bilaspur	342,156 20.37%	419,169 20.73%	512,404 20.99%	840,200 28.45%
Durg	403,480 27.23%	576,665 30.59%	–571,717 –23.22%	506,950 26.82%
Rajnandgaon			1,167,501 100%	272,450 23.33%
Raipur	361,996 22.07%	611,529 30.55%	465,945 17.83%	828,566 26.91%
Bastar	253,755 27.77%	348,455 29.85%	325,909 21.50%	429,449 23.32%
Total:	16,97,790 22.76%	24,82,998 27.12%	24,52,038 21.07%	35,25,396 25.02%

Note: The minus growth in Durg district during the decade 1971–1981 has been recorded due to the bifurcation of the district and creation of Rajnandgaon district in 1973.

An inference could thus be drawn that after the Constitution of India was inaugurated in 1950, and with the amalgamation of the princely states in the Union of India, these laws were withdrawn and Christian missionary activities (including conversion) increased in these two districts. And, the people of these two former princely states (mostly tribals) were drawn into the Christian Church and educational institutions.

However, it is worth noting that even in these two districts, the decadal growth stabilised in the next two decades (1971–91), and almost came on a par with the national and state figures in terms of percentage decadal growth.

It could also be stated that in absolute numbers, the decadal growth in these two districts did not record any unprecedented growth in Christian population except in Raigarh district for two decades, 1951–61 (76,486) and 1961–1971 (41,841). For the remaining decades and districts, the decadal growth in absolute numbers is very insignificant. For instance, for Sarguja these were: 8,240 (1951–61); 16,158 (1961–71); 13,217 (1971–81); 9,900 (1981–91). And, for Raigarh these were: 12,546 (1971–81); 26,177 (1981–91).

As compared to these two predominantly tribal districts, Bastar stands out as an exception. The decadal growth, cannot explain the allegation against Christian missionaries targeted the tribal population. Bastar has not only been one of the biggest districts of India with a tribal population of 67.7 per cent, but has been also a centre for studies in anthropology. The well-known anthropologist, Verrier Elvin, who was also a Christian Priest of the Anglican Church of England, worked in Bastar for many years studying the lives, customs and cultures of tribals in Bastar. Why were mass conversions to Christianity not carried out in pre-dominantly tribal district of Bastar, and in other tribal belts of Chhattisgarh to the exclusion of Raigarh and Sarguja is a question for further studies.

There probably is need for an explanation for the unprecedented decadal growth in percentage among the Christian population in the district of Durg. The reason seems to be the influx of working class population from various parts

TABLE 6.9 : DECADEL GROWTH
(Hindu Population in Madhya Pradesh/Chhattisgarh)

District	*1951-61*	*1961-71*	*1971-81*	*1981-91*
Madhya Pradesh				
Sarguja	198825	261257	276456	417163
	24.54%	25.89%	21.76%	26.97%
Raigarh	42360	192956	146387	246702
	4.70%	20.46%	12.89%	19.24%
Bilaspur	340662	401512	483650	797385
	20.76%	20.27%	20.30%	27.82%
Durg	353673	549684	-570217	479428
	24.22%	30.30%	-24.12%	26.73%
Rajnandgaon				249535
				22.14%
Raipur	369428	593136	438041	804717
	23.43%	30.48%	17.25%	27.03%
Bastar	251237	340399	314042	418467
	27.76%	29.44%	20.98%	23.11%
Decadal Growth	**1556185**	**2338944**	**2215238**	**3413397**
(Percentage)	**21.33%**	**26.42%**	**19.79%**	**25.46%**

Note: The minus growth in Durg district during the decade of 1971-1981 has been recorded due to the bifurcation of the district and creation of Rajnandgaon district in 1973.

of the country due to industrialisation resulting in the establishment of Bhilai Steel Plant (a public sector undertaking established in 1956–57 in collaboration with the then USSR), and other ancillary industries. That is why after recording an unprecedented decadal growth in percentage during the first two decades (1951–1971), it drastically dipped below national and state average (Madhya Pradesh, including that of Chhattisgarh). And, so appears to be the case with Bilaspur, which became the centre for the South Eastern Railways, and also various industrial activities including the power plant and collieries, etc.

There was an unusual decline in the Christian population in the district of Raipur, which became the capital of Chhattisgarh. Its population went down from 15,188 in 1951 to 11,459 in 1961, i.e. registering the minus decadal growth (–3729).

TABLE 6.10 : Christian Population in Urban-Industrial Districts
(Decadal Growth)

District	*1951-61*	*1961-71*	*1971-81*	*1981-91*	*1991-2001*
Durg	6,049 (303.20%)	8,497 (105.63%)	3,236 (19.56%)	852 (4.30%)	NA
Bilaspur	1,443 (16.02%)	3,451 (33.07%)	5,493 (39.51%)	8,463 (43.63%)	NA

The main reason for this decline in the Christian population in Raipur was due to the migration of Christians from Raipur district in the wake of communal tension in 1957. It may be recalled that due to some misunderstanding, the Gass Memorial Centre (a Christian Institution built up on the patterns of Young Men's Christian Association - YMCA) near Jaistambh Chawk at Raipur was burnt by the mob agitating against the "alleged insult of a Hindu deity" by the GMC authorities. During this agitation on 27th August 1957, police opened fire to control the mob, which had set up the GMC on fire, and many people (including the Director and senior staff) were trapped in the basement, where they had taken shelter to save themselves from the fury of the agitating mob. A student named Krishna Kumar was killed in the police firing. The present KK Road is named after him.

This was also the period (1954-57) when the then Madhya Pradesh Government had set up the Christian Missionary Activities Enquiry Committee (Niyogi Committee). Thus, as a combined result of both the burning of the GMC and the Niyogi Enquiry in the missionary activities and conversion, the Christian population of Raipur had fled to other neighbouring districts of Chhattisgarh. Christian population in 1961 went down by 3,729 in absolute numbers from the previous census year, 1951.

It is of significance that Raipur district never registered an unprecedented decadal growth among Christian population, except during the decade of 1961-71 (34.26%), when the Christian families that had fled in the wake of communal tension in the earlier decade, returned to their homes. It recorded a

TABLE 6.11 : DECADAL GROWTH
Christian Population in Madhya Pradesh/Chhattisgarh

District	*1951-61*	*1961-71*	*1971-81*	*1981-91*
Madhya Pradesh				
Sarguja	8240	16158	13267	9900
	1511.93%	183.93%	53.19%	25.91%
Raigarh	76486	41841	12546	26177
	551.33%	46.31%	9.49%	18.08%
Bilaspur	1443	3451	5493	8463
	16.02%	33.03%	39.52%	43.64%
Durg	6049	8497	3236	852
	303.21%	105.63%	19.56%	4.31%
Rajnandgaon			2187	669
			100%	30.59%
Raipur	-3729	3926	3089	-242
	-24.55%	34.26%	20.08%	-1.31%
Bastar	717	1920	4346	2960
	17.54%	39.96%	64.62%	26.74%
Total	89,206	75,793	44,164	48,779
(%)	199.58%	56.60%	21.06%	19.21%

negative rate of decadal growth both in numbers and percentage in 1981–1991, i.e. (–) 242 and (–) 1.30 per cent.

TABLE 6.12 : Christian Population in Raipur District (Decadal Growth)

District	*1951-61*	*1961-71*	*1971-81*	*1981-91*	*1991-2001*
Raipur	-3729 (-24.55%)	3,926 (34.26%)	3,089 (20.07%)	-242 (-1.30%)	NA

There has not been any abnormal growth in the Christian population in Chhattisgarh and Madhya Pradesh in the recent past, i.e. almost three decades. On the contrary, the way in which there has been a gradual and regular decline in the percentage of Christian population in Chhattisgarh and in India, establishes that conversion does not appear to be the agenda of the Christian Church today. The Sangh Parivar and its political wing, the

Bhartiya Janata Party are targeting the Christian Church as part of their overall objective of creating the 'Hindu Rashtra' based on fascist ideology.

Historical Background

It would be worth noting here that Madhya Pradesh (MP) has always been a stronghold of proponents of 'Hindu Rashtra'. It was part of the Central Provinces & Berar (CP & Berar), with its headquarters at Nagpur, birthplace of the Hindu Mahasabha, founded in 1923, and later of the Rashtriya Swayamsevak Sangh (RSS), founded in 1925 by Keshav Baliram Hedgewar. Nagpur was the capital of MP till it became part of Maharashtra in November 1956 after the reorganisation of the states in independent India.

According to Vinayak Damodar Savarkar (the first exponent of the doctrine of Hindutva), those who regard this land as their 'father-land' and 'holy-land' are the only ones who are Hindus and, thereby, the people to whom this land belongs. In his book, *Hindutva: Who is Hindu* (1923), that became the basic political, he maintains that this land belongs to Hindus and so, by implication, Muslims with Holy Land in Mecca and Christians with Holy Land in Jerusalem cannot have equal status with Hindus. M.S. Golwalkar later made this concept explicit by granting them the status of second-class citizens in the 'Hindu Rashtra'. In his book, *We or our Nationhood Defined*, Golwalkar describes three enemies of the Hindu Rashtra: (a) Muslims; (b) Christians; and (c) Communists (in that order, of course!). This is summed up in the Sangh Parivar's slogan: "*Pahle Kasai, phir Isai, phir CPI*" (meaning, 'first hit Muslims, then Christians, and finally the Communist Party of India'!).

It may also be of interest to note that the exponents of the 'Hindu Rasthra' neither use nor believe in 'mother-land', but 'father-land' for two basic reasons. One, the Manuvadis (followers of Manu) do not believe in woman's independent self, as she is born subservient to man—the 'swamy'. Two, the 'alien' invaders and armies came to Hindu Land without their women and, subsequently, married the local women. Thus, it would be safer to use the term 'father-land' rather than 'mother-land'. This coincides with Hitler's description of Nazi's Germany as 'father-land'!

The proponents of Hindutva made increasing attempts prior to Independence to prohibit conversion in various parts of India. The focus of missionary activities was the tribals and dalits, the deprived and marginalised of the Hindu society. Although it is a fact that Christianity came to India in 52 A.D., it also came as a package of colonialism. However, it also brought with it liberal values like equality, liberty and fraternity, etc., through education, ultimately leading to social upliftment of the rejected and neglected masses. Thus, conversion in the earlier period of Christianity resulted in providing an entirely new identity to the outcastes, and enabled them to assert their self-hood.

As a result of the passing of the *lex loci*, the "Regulation Law" in 1832 and the amendment to it in 1850 known as the "Caste Disabilities Removal Act" or the "Freedom of Religion Act", the disadvantages caused by change of religion had been largely removed in British India. However, this did not apply in the princely states, where Hindu or Muslim law was practised and, in the period before Independence, various restrictions concerning conversion were held in these states.

A reason why the princely states were openly active in opposing the missionary activities was related to their desire of maintaining the status-quo, the control over their subjects, who were, through missionary activities (like schools, hospitals, etc.) getting aware about their rights and freedom, and moving into the mass movements led by the freedom fighters. Thus, a number of princely states were not only opposed to the missionary activities but the freedom movement led by Gandhiji, who had adopted unique and novel ways to ensure that vast masses of peasantry and other downtrodden segments of society—women, harijans and adivasis—became part of it. A large number of princely states were hesitant to merge with the Indian Union after Independence. After Independence, the heads of the princely states, along with Zamindars, moved mostly towards Hindutva through parties like Jan Sangh, which later became Bhartiya Janata Party.

After the assassination of Mahatma Gandhi by Nathuram Godse on 30th January 1948, the RSS was banned. The RSS eventually launched its political party—Jan Sangh—during early 1950s. Initially it was led by S P Mookerjee, and later emerged as the Bhartiya Janta Party (BJP). Jan Sangh launched an "Anti-Foreign Missionary Week" in November 1954.

It may be worth noting that in Madhya Pradesh (including Chhattisgarh), the Raigarh princely state had brought into force the Raigarh State Conversion Act in 1936, followed by the Surguja State Apostasy Act in 1945. Both these districts are presently at the hub of the conversion controversy, and the 'Home Coming' is being led by one of the former Rajas of Jashpur State. The Central Provinces and Berar Public Safety Act was also introduced in 1947, which stated that any conversion had to be validated before a District Magistrate. However, this clause was deleted because of strong opposition from Christians.

The princely states were vehemently opposed to missionary activities; yet, they were not shy of inviting Englishmen (almost all of them Christians), to run institutions for elitist education for their siblings. The Rajkumar College at Raipur is one such example in Chhattisgarh. It was founded in 1882 at Jabalpur with just five students, who were heirs to the princely states of the Madras Province and the Eastern State Assembly—now Bihar (Jharkhand), Orissa and Chhattisgarh. Founded by Andrew Fraser, the then Chief Commissioner of C.P & Berar, admission was restricted to the sons and relatives of the ruling chiefs and zamindars of the Eastern states. It was shifted to Raipur in 1894.

A residential school provided several aspects of education in English medium from history and horse riding to Western ways of life, the Rajkumar College came to be recognised as the Oxford of Chhattisgarh. The motto reads: 'A raja is honoured in his own country, a learned man throughout the world' and the School magazine is titled 'Mukut' (crown). The contradictions in practices of princely states could be explained only in terms of their desire to maintain social and political dominance.

The Constitution of India came into full force in January 1950. Thereafter, some of the princely states were amalgamated into Madhya Pradesh. As a result, the 'anti-conversion' laws of these states became invalid. The Christian missionaries began their work among the tribals, including social service and proselytising. However, the former Maharajas continued to resist the entrance of the missionaries, and considered it as an attack on the autonomy of their former states.

The socio-cultural factor that resulted in resistance to missionary activities by the 'elite' of the Hindu society in Madhya Pradesh was the fact that it had a significant tribal population (18 per cent in 1950), which went up to 23.22 per cent in 1994. Chhattisgarh also has a considerable large proportion of tribals and dalits i.e. 10.52 per cent of Scheduled Tribes, and 35.41 per cent of Scheduled Castes.

Yet another political factor that led to increased demand by the dominant classes for curtailing the freedom of the Christian missionaries was the uprising of tribals demanding a separate state for themselves called Jharkhand. It covered the adjoining districts of Raigarh (in MP), Ranchi (in Bihar) and Sundergarh (in Orissa), which witnessed a high growth in Christian population. As mentioned earlier, the Christians form less than one per cent of the population in the entire region, and their absolute numbers amount to just about 3 lakhs. But, Christians form about 14.5 per cent of the population of these three districts.

The high rate of conversion among the tribals in this area was looked on with suspicion especially due to the political demand for Jharkhand. However, it must be understood that any form of people's movement for asserting their political and cultural identity, and self-hood (sometimes, the right to self-determination) has always been opposed by the dominant classes/castes in India. It is another matter that in the later years, the demand for a separate state for Jharkhand, Chhattisgarh and Uttarakhand was politically encashed by the Bhartiya Janata Party (BJP), as it conceded to the popular demand by 2000.

Thus, the fact that the resistance to missionary activities in Madhya Pradesh (including Chhattisgarh) was not only because of the increase in Christian population in the area but mainly due to the state's socio-political background.

Fig 6.3 : Religious composition of Chhattisgarh: 1951–1991

(In Absolute Numbers)

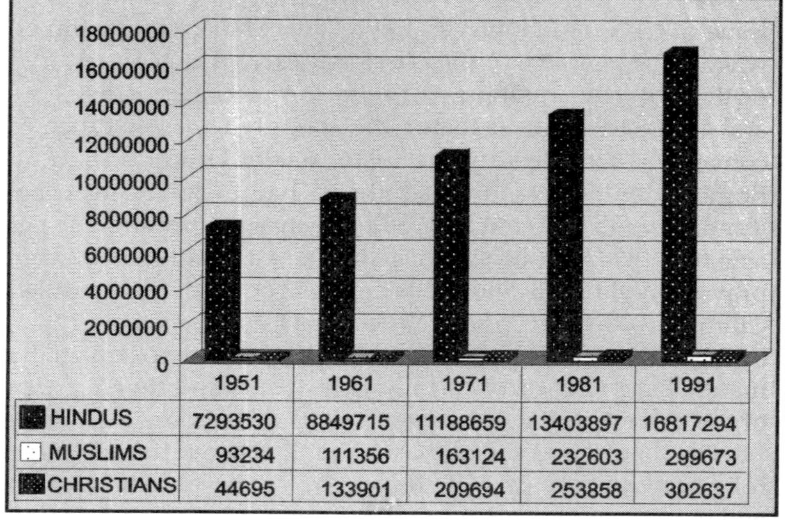

	1951	1961	1971	1981	1991
HINDUS	7293530	8849715	11188659	13403897	16817294
MUSLIMS	93234	111356	163124	232603	299673
CHRISTIANS	44695	133901	209694	253858	302637

CONSTITUENT ASSEMBLY DEBATE ON "CONVERSION"

The debates and discussions in the Constituent Assembly were primarily focused on the inclusion of the freedom to "propagate" as one of the fundamental rights. The contradiction between Hindu and Christian views on conversion became clear in the course of this debate. While Christians based their argument that conversion was a basic tenet of the faith and the individual's right to freedom, Hindus argued that conversion was against Hindu dharma. The objections to conversion were concretised in three ways: one, by the introduction of Hindu 'personal laws', which were disadvantageous for caste Hindus who converted to another religion; two, by the limitation of the social benefits of converts from Scheduled Caste backgrounds; and three, by the passing of the 'freedom of religion' acts.

The Constituent Assembly started functioning on 9th December 1946 with the objective of formulating the Indian Constitution. The first meeting of the Assembly was held on 24 January 1947, to set up an Advisory Committee. The Advisory Committee, in turn, had set up five sub-committees including the Fundamental Rights Sub-Committee and the Minorities Sub-Committee.

The Fundamental Rights Sub-Committee dealt with the issue of Conversion. Its Chairman was Sri J B Kripalani, who was also the Congress President. Several drafts were submitted on the subject of religion, but the draft articles by Sri K M Munshi and Dr B R Ambedkar basically dealt with the question of conversion. Sri Munshi, being the former Home Minister of Bombay, emphasised that 'duties' were inseparable from 'fundamental rights' and that the law of the Union should be able to prevent the misuse of rights. He included in his draft a preventive measure on conversion, 'The Right to Religious and Cultural Freedom': 'Conversion from one religion to another brought about by coercion, undue influence or the offering of material inducement is prohibited and is punishable by the law of the Union'.

Dr. Ambedkar saw the main purpose of the section on religious freedom as 'the right of every subject to life, liberty and pursuit of happiness and to free speech and free exercise of religion'. His draft section on 'Fundamental Rights of Citizens' stated: "The State shall guarantee to every Indian citizen liberty of conscience and the free exercise of his religion including the right to profess, to preach and to convert within limits compatible with public order and morality". He further argued that there should be no compulsion to participate in any religious act. Sri Munshi expressed concern about protecting the rights of those who would be exposed to conversion activity. On the other hand, Dr. Ambedkar stressed that conversion was the right of each individual to exercise his or her freewill.

The Fundamental Rights Sub-Committee on 24th March decided to take up Munshi's draft and examine it in relationship to other drafts. After a long discussion, the report was submitted to the Advisory Committee on 16th April 1947. This included Clause 16 on religious freedom and Clauses 21 and 22 regarding the prohibitions on conversion, which were basically the same as in Munshi's original draft.

The Minorities Sub-Committee met on 17th April for the first time, and went through these recommendations by the

Fundamental Rights Sub-committee for the purpose of protecting minority rights. In this meeting, M. Ruthnaswamy proposed that certain religions were 'proselytizing religions' in their doctrine, so propagation of their faith should be permitted as a fundamental right. The Sub-Committee sent its report and recommendations to the Fundamental Rights Sub-Committee on 19th April.

The Report of the Minorities Sub-Committee consisted of two main recommendations. First, the phrase ' the right freely to profess, practice and propagate religion' was inserted in Clause 16 in place of 'freedom of religious worship and to freedom to profess religion'. And second, they proposed amendment to Clause 21 with restrictions on conversion. The conversion of minors was prohibited, except in the case of following the decision of their parents to change religion, and any conversion of an adult had to be recognised by a Magistrate. Thus, in a way both points of view were balanced in these clauses: the Christian view on the right to propagation, and the Hindu desire at prevention of conversion.

The Advisory Committee then examined both the draft and the amendments. Regarding Clause 16, there were both strong objections and support to the word 'propagate'. But after voting, the word 'propagate' was accepted.

The clauses on fundamental rights finally sent by the Advisory Committee to the Constituent Assembly on 23rd April 1947 included the following:

"(13) All persons are equally entitled to freedom of conscience, and the right freely to profess, practice and propagate religion subject to public order, morality or health, and to the other provisions of their chapter.

(17) Conversion from one religion to another brought about by coercion or undue influence shall not be recognized by law."

The Constituent Assembly report was prepared and presented to the Drafting Committee (headed by Dr. Ambedkar) on 27th October 1947. It went through it clause by clause and submitted their revised draft Constitution to the President of the Constituent Assembly on 21st February 1948. The clause allowing the right of conversion was as follows:

"Article 19 (1) Subject to public order, morality and health and to the other provisions of this Part, all person are equally entitled to freedom of conscience and the right freely to profess, practice and propagate religion".

The draft Constitution was published so that the people and organisations of India had an opportunity to express their views before it was adopted by the Constituent Assembly. Once again on 3rd December 1948 there was a debate on the word 'propagate'.

During this debate, Sri TT Krishnamachari, argued convincingly for the need and significance of accommodating the concerns of the minorities unless they clearly restricted the rights of others. He argued that the right to propagate was meant for all citizens. He mentioned about the members of Arya Samaj, who had started the 'Operation home coming', i.e. bringing back converts to Hinduism. According to him, as long as the right to propagate was subject to public order, morality and health, as was already stated in the article, it should be granted. He said that we must be humble enough to openly acknowledge that Untouchables were accepting Christianity more for social reasons, and purely religious motive was not behind their conversion. Under this Constitution, all were equal and this equal right should be given equally to anyone to 'propagate his religion, and to convert people' if a person should be convinced that this was his 'duty towards his God and his community'.

Sri KM Munshi insisted that the fears of a few were ill founded that conversion in independent India could cause a political instability as was noticed during the freedom struggles. Such a possibility did not exist in Independent India. He realised that this issue would have to be solved by compromise and he expressed his sympathy with Christians:

"....It was on this word that the Indian Christian community laid the greatest emphasis, not because they want to convert people aggressively, but because the word 'propagate' was a fundamental part of their tenet.... So long as religion is religion, conversion by free exercise of the conscience has to be recognized."

Sri Munshi's speech made all the difference, although still there were attempts to delete the word 'propagate' or to add provisos to it. In the ensuing votes on each amendment, the Constituent Assembly opted to retain the word 'propagate', and the article was included in the Constitution as Article 25 in the section on 'The Right to Freedom of Religion'. The Assembly finally adopted it on 26th November 1949.

The United Nations Assembly approved the Universal Declaration of Human Rights on 10th December 1948, the time when the Constituent Assembly in India was shaping the Constitution. The former extended influences on the debate on religious freedom as a fundamental human right in India. Article 18 of the Universal Declaration of Human Rights stated "the right to freedom of thought, conscience and religion" which includes the freedom of 'everyone' 'to change his religion or belief' and 'to manifest his religion or belief'.

Dr. Ambedkar had taken a liberal position vis-à-vis religious freedom, because he, along with thousands and thousands of outcastes in India, was seriously considering conversion as 'social uplift', 'caste mobility' or 'social protest'. And, ultimately, Dr. Ambedkar led hundreds and thousands of dalits, including his own community (Mahars) to accept Buddhism. They came to be recognised as "neo-Buddhists", and are even today considered to be at the forefront of the socio-political movement of struggle for Dalit dignity and self-hood.

Even though the conversion by untouchables (dalits) to Buddhism has taken place in substantial numbers, the Buddhist population in India in 1991 was merely 0.8 per cent of the total population in India. By comparison, the Buddhist population and the spread of Buddhism in the South East and Far East countries of Asia have been remarkable—Tibet (97 %), Myanmar (89%), Thailand (94.4%), Sri Lanka (74%), Bhutan (75%), Malaysia (28%), South Korea (47%), Japan (20%) in 1991.

An obvious question arises on the rise of Buddhism in countries far and near to India than in India itself, where Buddha was born, and where Emperor Ashoka had used the state machinery for its spread. Buddhism believes in equality and peace and non-violence, all are basic tenets of Indian culture and human society. This could be a subject matter for another study.

During the debate on Reservation Policy for the Scheduled Castes and Scheduled Tribes, Dr. Ambedkar argued, "the untouchables are not Hindus, but a separate element". He argued "The whole tradition of the Hindus is to recognize the untouchable as a separate element and insist upon it as a fact... For Caste is another name for separation and untouchability typifies the extremist form of separation of community from community." He comes out strongly in favour of reservation policy by stating that: "If there is a real separation between the Hindus and Untouchables and if there is the danger of discrimination being practiced by the Hindus against the Untouchables then the Untouchables must receive political recognition and must be given political safeguards to protect themselves against the tyranny of the Hindus. The possibility of a better future cannot be used as an argument to prevent the Untouchables from securing the means of protecting themselves against the tyranny of the present".

The coincidence of Nagpur is of great interest where the Rashtriya Swamsevak Sangh was established in 1925, and which also became the centre for the dalit mukti movement led by Dr. Ambedkar.

The Constituent Assembly debates on the "religious freedom" must be seen also in the context of movements among the socially outcast.

APPENDIX

TABLE 1 : Religious Composition of Indian Union: 1951–1991
(For the total enumerated population, in thousands)

Year	*Hindus*	*Sikhs*	*Jains*	*Buddhists*	*Muslims*	*Christians*	*Others*	*Total*
1951	303,575	6,219	1,618	181	35,414	8,392	1,848	**357,247**
	84.98%	1.74%	0.45%	0.05%	9.91%	2.35%	0.52%	**100%**
1961	366,503	7,845	2,027	3,250	46,939	10,726	1,607	**438,897**
	83.51%	1.79%	0.46%	0.74%	10.69%	2.44%	0.37%	**100%**
1971	453,292	10,379	2,605	3,812	61,418	14,223	2,221	**547,950**
	82.73%	1.89%	0.48%	0.70%	11.21%	2.60%	0.41%	**100%**
1981	549,725	13,078	3,193	4,720	75,572	16,174	2,827	**665,289**
	82.63%	1.97%	0.48%	0.71%	11.36%	2.43%	0.42%	**100%**
1991	687,647	16,260	3,353	6,388	101,596	19,640	3,685	**838,569**
	82.00%	1.94%	0.40%	0.76%	12.12%	2.34%	0.44%	**100%**

TABLE 2 : Religious Composition of Madhya Pradesh: 1951–1991

Year	*Hindus*	*Sikhs*	*Jains*	*Buddhists*	*Muslims*	*Christians*	*Others*	*Total*
1951	2,47,08,670	39,910	1,81,300	2,290	10,50,000	81,000	8,830	**2,60,72,000**
	95%	0.15%	0.70%	0.009%	4.03%	0.31%	0.03%	**100%**
1961	3,04,32,000	65,720	2,47,900	1,13,400	13,18,000	1,88,300	12,980	**3,23,78,300**
	93.99%	0.20%	0.77%	0.35%	4.07%	0.58%	0.04%	**100%**
1971	3,90,23,170	98,970	3,45,200	83,820	18,16,000	2,86,100	840	**4,16,54,100**
	93.68%	0.24%	0.83%	0.20%	4.36%	0.69%	0.002%	**100%**
1981	4,85,05,990	1,43,000	4,45,000	75,310	25,02,000	3,52,000	1,55,700	**5,21,79,000**
	92.96%	0.27%	0.85%	0.14%	4.8%	0.67%	0.30%	**100%**
1991	6,15,40,440	1,61,100	4,90,300	2,16,700	32,83,000	4,26,600	62,460	**6,61,80,600**
	92.99%	0.24%	0.74%	0.33%	4.96%	0.64%	0.09%	**100%**

TABLE 3 : Religious Composition of Chhattisgarh (Madhya Pradesh): 1951–1991

Year	*Total Population*	*Hindus*	*Muslims*	*Christians*	*Sikhs*	*Buddhists*	*Jains*	*Others*	*Not Stated*
1951	**7,456,706**	7,293,530	93,234	44,695	8,880	1,034	9,327	6,006	
		97.81%	1.25%	0.59%	0.11%	0.01%	0.12%	0.08%	
1961	**9,154,496**	8,849,715	111,356	133,901	16,497	17,118	15,754	9,535	620
		96.67%	1.21%	1.46%	0.18%	0.18%	0.17%	0.10%	0.00%
1971	**11,637,494**	11,188,659	163,124	209,694	28,364	20,389	26,144	15	1,105
		96.14%	1.40%	1.80%	0.24%	0.17%	0.22%	0.00%	0.00%
1981	**14,089,532**	13,403,897	232,603	253,858	104,021	19,381	37,289	38,483	
		95.13%	1.65%	1.80%	0.73%	0.13%	0.26%	0.27%	
1991	**17,614,928**	16,817,294	299,673	302,637	50,605	48,651	43,213	17,370	35,485
		95.47%	1.70%	1.71%	0.28%	0.27%	0.24%	0.09%	0.20%

TABLE 4 : Hindu Population in Madhya Pradesh/ Chhattisgarh

Sl. No.	*District*	*1951*	*1961*	*1971*	*1981*	*1991*
1	Madhya Pradesh					
2	Sarguja	8,10,304	10,09,129	12,70,386	15,46,842	19,64,005
		98.57%	97.34%	95.77%	93.52%	94.30%
3	Raigarh	19,00,582	9,42,942	11,35,898	12,82,285	15,28,987
		97.94%	90.56%	88.83%	85.30%	88.78%
4	Bilaspur	1,16,40,560	19,81,222	23,82,734	28,66,384	36,63,769
		97.67%	97.99%	97.61%	97.05%	96.58%
5	Durg	14,60,387	18,14,060	23,63,744	17,93,527	22,72,955
		98.56%	96.22%	96.01%	94.89%	94.82%
6	Rajnandgaon				11,26,879	12,76,414
					96.52%	95.59%
7	Raipur	15,76,822	19,46,250	25,39,386	29,77,427	37,82,144
		96.15%	97.22%	97.16%	96.69%	96.78%
8	Bastar	9,04,875	11,56,112	14,96,511	18,10,553	22,29,020
		99.03%	99.02%	98.72%	98.30%	98.14%
	Total	1,72,93,530	88,49,715	1,11,88,659	1,34,03,897	1,68,17,294
	(In Percent)	97.81%	96.67%	96.14%	95.13%	95.47%

Raigarh was part of Bilaspur district in 1951, once again for clarity it has been clearly specified.

TABLE 5 : Christian Population in Madhya Pradesh/Chhattisgarh

Sl.	District	1941	1951	1961	1971	1981	1991
1	Madhya Pradesh	-	81,000	1,88,300	2,86,100	3,52,000	4,26,600
			0.31%	0.58%	0.69%	0.67%	0.64%
2	Sarguja	-	545	8,785	24,943	38,210	48,110
			0.07%	0.85%	1.88%	2.31%	2.31%
3	Raigarh	-	*13,873	90,359	1,32,200	1,44,746	1,70,923
			1.51%	8.68%	10.34%	9.63%	9.92%
4	Bilaspur	-	*9,006	10,449	13,900	19,393	27,856
			0.54%	0.52%	0.57%	0.66%	0.73%
5	Durg	-	1,995	8,044	16,541	19,777	20,629
			0.13%	0.43%	0.67%	1.05%	0.86%
6	Rajnandgaon	-	-	-	-	2,187	2,856
						0.19%	0.20%
7	Raipur	8,163	15,188	11,459	15,385	18,474	18,232
		0.54%	0.93%	0.57%	0.59%	0.60%	0.47%
8	Bastar	-	4,088	4,805	6,725	11,071	14,031
			0.45%	0.41%	0.44%	0.60%	0.62%
	Total-Chhattisgarh		44,695	133,901	209,694	253,858	302,637
	Sl.No. 2 to 8		0.59%	1.46%	1.80%	1.80%	1.71%
9	Bilaspur & Raigarh	-	*22,879	1,00,808	1,46,100	1,64,139	1,98,779
	(Combined)		0.88%	3.29%	3.93%	3.68%	3.60%

*Raigarh was part of Bilaspur district in 1951, once again for clarity it has been clearly specified.

TABLE 6 : Muslim Population in Chhattisgarh

Sl.	*District*	*1951*	*1961*	*1971*	*1981*	*1991*
1	Sarguja	10,600	17,252	26,766	40,556	59,041
		1.29%	1.66%	2.10%	2.61%	2.83%
2	Raigarh	-	6,365	8,792	12,422	15,441
			0.61%	0.69%	0.86%	0.90%
3	Bilaspur	29,870	25,641	37,122	47,962	60,916
		1.15%	1.27%	1.52%	1.62%	1.61%
4	Durg	14,680	26,120	40,412	42,423	54,979
		0.99%	1.39%	1.64%	2.24%	2.29%
5	Rajnandgaon	-	-	-	19,715	23,014
					1.69%	1.60%
6	Raipur	34,140	31,250	42,564	57,458	71,034
		2.08%	1.56%	1.63%	1.87%	1.82%
7	Bastar	3,944	4,728	7,468	12,067	15,248
		0.43%	0.40%	0.49%	0.65%	0.67%
	Total	**93,234**	**1,11,356**	**1,63,124**	**232,603**	**2,99,673**

TABLE 7 : Census of Chhattisgarh–1951

District/ City	*Total Population*	*Hindus*	*Muslims*	*Christians*	*Sikhs*	*Buddhists*	*Jains*	*Others*
Raipur	16,40,006	15,76,822	34,141	15,188	5,193	1013	4582	3067
		96.15%	2.08%	0.93%	0.32%	0.06%	0.28%	0.19%
Bilaspur	16,79,637	16,40,560	27,479	9,006	1,525	1	903	163
		97.67%	1.64%	0.54%	0.09%	0.00%	0.05%	0.01%
Durg	14,81,756	14,60,387	14,679	1,995	1411	3	3242	39
		98.56%	0.99%	0.13%	0.10%	0.00%	0.22%	0.00%
Bastar	9,13,746	9,04,875	3,944	4,088	84	17	410	328
		99.03%	0.43%	0.45%	0.01%	0.00%	0.04%	0.04%
Raigarh	9,19,520	9,00,582	2,389	13,873	275	N.A.	N.A.	2401
		97.94%	0.26%	1.51%	0.03%			0.26%
Sarguja	8,22,041	8,10,304	10,602	545	392	N.A.	190	8
		98.57%	1.29%	0.07%	0.05%		0.02%	0.00%
Rajnandgaon	N.A.	N.A.	N.A.	N.A.	N.A.	N.A.	N.A.	N.A.
Total	74,56,706	72,93,530	93,234	44,695	8,880	1,034	9,327	6,006
		97.81%	1.25%	0.59%	0.12%	0.01%	0.13%	0.08%

TABLE 8 : Census of Chhattisgarh - 1961

District/ City	Total Population	Hindus	Muslims	Christians	Sikhs	Buddhists	Jains	Others	Not Stated
Sarguja	1,036,738	1,009,129	17252	8,785	1,077	9	361	125	0
		97.34%	1.66%	0.85%	0.10%	0.00%	0.03%	0.01%	0.00%
Bilaspur	2,021,793	1,981,222	25641	10,449	2,535	319	1,285	342	0
		97.99%	1.27%	0.52%	0.13%	0.02%	0.06%	0.02%	0.00%
Raigarh	1,041,226	942,942	6365	90,359	617	5	330	608	0
		90.56%	0.61%	8.68%	0.06%	0.00%	0.03%	0.06%	0.00%
Durg	1,885,236	1,814,060	26120	8,044	7,653	15214	7,158	6367	620
		96.22%	1.39%	0.43%	0.41%	0.81%	0.38%	0.34%	0.03%
Raipur	2,002,002	1,946,250	31250	11,459	4,269	1247	5,501	2026	0
		97.22%	1.56%	0.57%	0.21%	0.06%	0.27%	0.10%	0.00%
Bastar	1,167,501	1,156,112	4728	4,805	346	324	1,119	67	0
		99.02%	0.40%	0.41%	0.03%	0.03%	0.10%	0.01%	0.00%
Total-	9,154,496	8,849,715	111,356	133,901	16,497	17,118	15,754	9,535	620
		96.67%	1.22%	1.46%	0.18%	0.19%	0.17%	0.10%	0.01%

Table 9 : Census of Chhattisgarh - 1971

District/ City	*Total Population*	*Hindus*	*Muslims*	*Christians*	*Sikhs*	*Buddhists*	*Jains*	*Others*	*Not Stated*
Surguja	1,326,439	1,270,386	26,766	24,943	2077	1626	641	0	0
		95.77%	2.02%	1.88%	0.16%	0.12%	0.05%	0.00%	0.00%
Bilaspur	2,440,962	2,382,734	37,122	13,900	4999	583	1,619	4	1
		97.61%	1.52%	0.57%	0.20%	0.02%	0.07%	0.00%	0.00%
Raigarh	1,278,705	1,135,898	8,792	132,200	1253	59	479	11	13
		88.83%	0.69%	10.34%	0.10%	0.00%	0.04%	0.00%	0.00%
Durg	2,461,901	2,363,744	40,412	16,541	12116	16124	12,792	0	172
		96.01%	1.64%	0.67%	0.49%	0.65%	0.52%	0.00%	0.01%
Raipur	2,613,531	2,539,386	42,564	15,385	6774	1417	8,001	0	4
		97.16%	1.63%	0.59%	0.26%	0.05%	0.31%	0.00%	0.00%
Bastar	1,515,956	1,496,511	7,468	6,725	1145	580	2,612	0	915
		98.72%	0.49%	0.44%	0.08%	0.04%	0.17%	0.00%	0.06%
Total-	11,637,494	11,188,659	163,124	209,694	28,364	20,389	26,144	15	1,105
		96.14%	1.40%	1.80%	0.24%	0.18%	0.22%	0.00%	0.01%

Table 10 : Census of Chhattisgarh—1981

District/ City	Total Population	Hindus	Muslims	Christians	Sikhs	Buddhists	Jains	Others
Sarguja	16,53,943	15,46,842	40,556	38,210	3,129	1,608	971	22,627
		93.52%	2.45%	2.31%	0.19%	0.10%	0.06%	1.37%
Bilaspur	29,53,366	28,66,384	47,962	19,393	7,106	648	2,462	9,411
		97.05%	1.62%	0.66%	0.24%	0.02%	0.08%	0.32%
Raigarh	15,03,197	12,82,285	12,422	1,44,746	61,889	88	756	1,011
		85.30%	0.83%	9.63%	4.12%	0.01%	0.05%	0.07%
Rajnandgaon	11,67,501	11,26,879	19,715	2,187	3,329	7,984	6,808	599
		96.52%	1.69%	0.19%	0.29%	0.68%	0.58%	0.05%
Durg	18,90,184	17,93,527	42,423	19,777	16,488	6,378	10,835	756
		94.89%	2.24%	1.05%	0.87%	0.34%	0.57%	0.04%
Raipur	30,79,476	29,77,427	57,458	18,474	10,201	2,190	11,474	2,252
		96.69%	1.87%	0.60%	0.33%	0.07%	0.37%	0.07%
Bastar	18,41,865	18,10,553	12,067	11,071	1,879	485	3,983	1,827
		98.30%	0.66%	0.60%	0.10%	0.03%	0.22%	0.10%
Total-	1,40,89,532	1,34,03,897	2,32,603	2,53,858	1,04,021	19,381	37,289	38,483
		95.13%	1.65%	1.80%	0.74%	0.14%	0.26%	0.27%

Table 11 : Census of Chhattisgarh–1991

Sl.	District/ City	Total Rural	Total Population	Hindus	Muslims	Christians	Sikhs	Buddhists	Jains	Others	Not Stated
1	Sarguja	Total	2,082,630	1,964,005	59,041	48,110	3,553	1,544	1,318	1,234	3,825
				94.30%	2.83%	2.31%	0.17%	0.07%	0.06%	0.06%	0.18%
2	Bilaspur	Total	3,793,566	3,663,769	60,916	27,856	8,128	4,183	2,942	12,002	13,770
				96.58%	1.61%	0.73%	0.21%	0.11%	0.08%	0.32%	0.36%
3	Raigarh	Total	1,722,291	1,528,987	15,441	170,923	1,725	240	827	275	3,873
				88.78%	0.90%	9.92%	0.10%	0.01%	0.05%	0.02%	0.22%
4	Rajnandgaon	Total	1,439,951	1,376,414	23,014	2,856	3,535	22,826	7,299	588	3,419
				95.59%	1.60%	0.20%	0.25%	1.59%	0.51%	0.04%	0.24%
5	Durg	Total	2,397,134	2,272,955	54,979	20,629	19,367	12,496	12,873	547	3,288
				94.82%	2.29%	0.86%	0.81%	0.52%	0.54%	0.02%	0.14%
6	Raipur	Total	3,908,042	3,782,144	71,034	18,232	12,062	5,266	3,228	641	5,435
				96.78%	1.82%	0.47%	0.31%	0.13%	0.34%	0.02%	0.14%
7	Bastar	Total	2,271,314	2,229,020	15,248	14,031	2,235	2,096	4,726	2,083	1,875
				98.14%	0.67%	0.62%	0.10%	0.09%	0.21%	0.09%	0.08%
	Total		17,614,928	16,817,294	299,673	302,637	50,605	48,651	43,213	17,370	35,485
	Percentage			95.47%	1.70%	1.71%	0.29%	0.27%	0.24%	0.10%	0.20%

Table 12 : Enumerated Population of Sikhs: 1951–1991

(In thousands)

	1951	*1961*	*1971*	*1981*	*1991*
Indian Union	6,219	7,845	10,379	13,078	15,260
Punjab		6,178	8,160	10,199	12,768
Haryana		517.1	631	802.2	956.8
Himachal Pradesh		54.15	44.91	52.21	52.05
Chandigarh		28.32	65.47	95.37	130.3
Rajasthan	148.2	274.2	341.2	492.8	649.2
Delhi	137.1	203.9	291.12	393.9	455.7
Jammu & Kashmir		63.07	105.9	133.7	
Uttar Pradesh	197.6	283.7	369.7	458.6	675.8
Madhya Pradesh	39.91	65.72	98.97	143	161.1
Maharashtra	41.43	57.62	101.8	107.3	161.2
Bihar	37.95	44.41	61.52	77.7	78.21
West Bengal	30.62	34.18	35.08	49.05	55.39
Gujarat	7.03	9.65	18.23	22.43	33.04
Andhra Pradesh	5.17	8.56	12.59	16.22	21.91

Table 13 : Enumerated Population of Buddhists: 1951–1991

(In thousands)

	1951	*1961*	*1971*	*1981*	*1991*
Indian Union	181	3,250	3,812	4,720	6,388
Maharashtra	2.49	2,790	3,264	3,946	5,041
Madhya Pradesh	2.29	113.4	83.32	75.31	216.7
Karnataka	1.71	9.77	14.14	42.15	73.01
Andhra Pradesh	0.23	6.75	10.04	12.93	22.15
Delhi	0.5	5.47	8.72	7.12	13.91
Gujarat	0.2	3.19	5.47	7.55	11.62
Orissa	0.97	0.45	8.46	8.03	9.15
Uttar Pradesh	3.22	12.89	39.64	54.54	221.4
Punjab		2.33	1.37	0.8	24.93
Himachal Pradesh		18.09	35.94	52.63	64.08
Jammu & Kashmir		48.36	57.96	69.71	
West Bengal	81.67	112.3	121.5	156.3	203.6
Assam		16.78	22.63		64.01
Sikkim	39.4	49.89		90.85	110.4
Arunachal Pradesh			61.4	86.48	111.4
Tripura	15.4	33.72	42.29	54.81	128.3
Mizoram		18.72	22.64	40.43	54.02

TABLE 14 : Enumerated Population of Jains: 1951–1991

(In thousands)

	1951	*1961*	*1971*	*1981*	*1991*
Indian Union	1,618	2,027	2,605	3,193	3,353
Maharashtra	337.6	485.7	703.7	939.4	965.8
Rajasthan	359.8	409.9	513.5	624.3	562.8
Gujarat	374.9	409.8	451.6	467.8	491.3
Madhya Pradesh	181.3	247.9	345.2	445	490.3
Karnataka	139.9	174.4	218.9	298	326.1
Uttar Pradesh	97.74	122.1	124.7	141.5	176.3
Delhi	20.17	29.6	50.51	73.92	94.67
Punjab		21.51	21.38	27.05	20.76
Haryana		25.84	31.17	35.48	35.3
Tamil Nadu	22.17	28.35	41.1	49.56	66.9
Andhra Pradesh	4.89	9.01	16.11	18.64	26.56
Bihar	8.17	17.6	25.19	27.61	23.05
West Bengal	19.61	26.94	32.2	38.66	34.36

(Appendix-I)

The Proceedings of the Debate on Conversion in the Constituent Assembly, 1947-49.

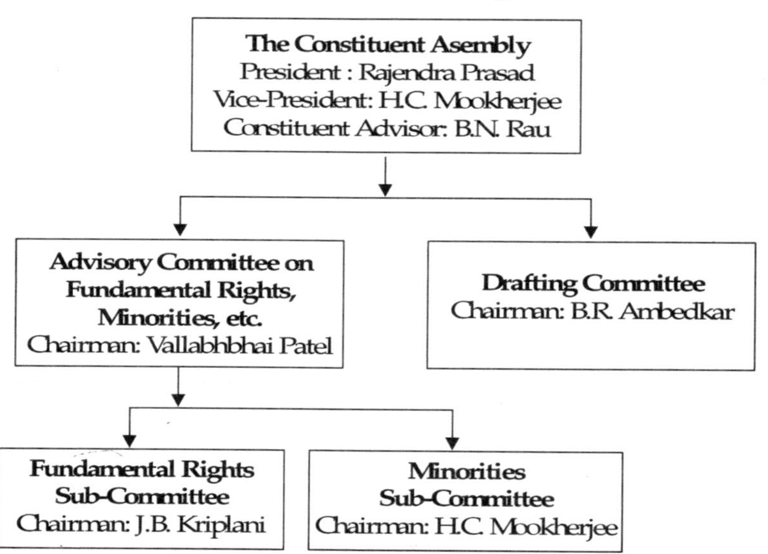

1. Draft articles by K.M. Munshi (17 March 1947):

VI (1) All citizens are equally entitled to freedom of conscience, and to the right freely to profess and practise religion in a manner compatible with public order, morality or health: Provided that the economic, financial or political activities

VI (6) No person under the age of eighteen shall be free to change his religious persuasion without the permission of his parent or guardian.

VI (7) Conversion from one religion to another brought about by coercion, undue influence or the offering of material inducement is prohibited and is punishable by the law of the Union.

2. Draft articles by B.R. Ambedkar (24 March 1947):

(14) The State shall guarantee to every Indian citizen, liberty of conscience and the free exercise of his religion including the right to profess, to preach, and to convert within limits compatible with public order and morality.

(15) No person shall be compelled to become a member of any religious association, submit to any religious instruction or perform any act of religion. Subject to the foregoing provision, parents and guardians shall be entitled to determine the religious education of children up to the age of sixteen years.

3. Report of the Sub-Committee on Fundamental Rights (16 April 1947):

(16) All persons are equally entitled to freedom of conscience, to freedom of religious worship and to freedom to profess religion, subject to public order, morality or health and to the other provisions of this chapter.

(21) No person under the age of eighteen shall be made to join or profess any religion other than the one in which he was born or be initiated into any religious order involving loss or civil status.

(22) Conversion from one religion to another brought about by coercion or undue influence shall not be recognized

by law and the exercise of such coercion or influence shall be an offence.

4. Suggestions from the Minorities Sub-Committee (19 April 1947):

(16) All persons are equally entitled to freedom of conscience and the right freely to profess, practise and propagate religion, subject to public order, morality or health and to the other provisions of this chapter.

(21) (a) No person under the age of eighteen shall be made to join or profess any religion other than the one in which he was born, except when his parents themselves have been converted and the child does not choose to adhere to his original faith; nor shall such person be initiated into any religious order involving loss of civil status.

(b) No conversion shall be recognized unless the change of faith is attested by a Magistrate after due inquiry.

5. Advisory Committee Reports on Fundamental Rights (23 April 1947):

(13) All persons are equally entitled to freedom of conscience, and the right freely to profess, practise and propagate religion, subject to public order, morality or health and to the other provisions of this chapter.

(17) Conversion from one religion to another brought about by coercion or undue influence shall not be recognized by law.

6. Amendment brought by K.M. Munshi in the Constituent Assembly (1 May 1947):

(17) Any conversion from one religion to another of any person brought about by fraud, coercion or undue influence or of a minor under the age of eighteen shall not be recognised by law.

7. Draft Constitution prepared by the Drafting Committee (21 February 1948):

Article 19: (1) Subject to public order, morality or health and to the other provisions of this Part, all persons are equally entitled to freedom of conscience, and the right freely to profess, practice and propagate religion.

8. Adopted into the Constitution of India by the Constituent Assembly (26 November 1949).

Article 25. Freedom of conscience and free profession, practice and propagation of religion.

(1) Subject to public order, morality or health and to the other provisions of this Part, all persons are equally entitled to freedom of conscience, and the right freely to profess, practice and propagate religion.

(2) Nothing in this article shall affect the operation of any existing law or prevent the State from making any law-

(a) Regulating or restricting any economic, financial, political or other secular activity which may be associated with religious practice;

(b) Providing for social welfare and reform or the throwing open of Hindu religious institutions of a public character to all classes and sections of Hindus.

Explanation I: The wearing and carrying of kirpans shall be deemed to be included in the profession of the Sikh religion.

Explanation II: In sub-clause (b) of clause (2), the reference to Hindus shall be construed as including a reference to persons professing the Sikh, Jaina or Buddhist religion, and the reference to Hindu religious institutions shall be construed accordingly.

(Appendix- II)

The Madhya Pradesh Dharma Swatantrya Adhiniyam, 1968

An Act to provide for prohibition of conversion from one religion to another by the use of force or inducement or by fraudulent means and for matters incidental thereto.

Be it enacted by the Madhya Pradesh Legislature in the Nineteenth Year of the Republic of India as follows:

Note: It is observed that large-scale conversions are taking place mostly among the Adiwasis and persons belonging to other backward classes of the State. The illiteracy and poverty of the people is exploited and promises of monetary, medical and other aid are given to allure them to renounce their religion and adopt another religion. The Bill seeks to prohibit such conversions by use of force or by allurement or by any fraudulent means.

[Vide Statement of Objects and Reasons published in Madhya Pradesh Rajpatra (Asadharan) dated 6 September 1968 page 1391.]

1. **Short title, extent and commencement:**
   1. This Act may be called the Madhya Pradesh Dharma Swatantrya Adhiniyam, 1968.
   2. It shall extend to the whole of the State of Madhya Pradesh.
   3. It shall come into force at once.
2. **Definitions:** In this Act, unless the context otherwise requires:
   (a) 'Allurement' means offer of any temptation in the form of-
   (*i*) Any gift or gratification either in cash or kind;
   (*ii*) Grant of any material benefit, either monetary or otherwise;
   (b) 'Conversion' means renouncing one religion and adopting another;
   (c) 'Force' shall include a show of force or a threat of injury of any kind including threat of divine displeasure or social excommunication;
   (d) 'Fraud' shall include misrepresentation or any other fraudulent contrivance;
   (e) 'Minor' means a person less than eighteen years of age.
3. **Prohibition of forcible conversion:** No person shall convert or attempt to convert, either directly or otherwise, any person from one religious faith to another by the use of force or by allurement or by any fraudulent means nor shall any person abet any such conversion.
4. **Punishment for contravention of the provisions of section 3:** Any person contravening the provisions

contained in section 3 shall, without prejudice to any civil liability, be punishable with imprisonment of either description, which may extend to one year or with fine, which may extend to five thousand rupees or with both; Provided that in case the offence is committed in respect of a minor, a woman or person belonging to the Scheduled Castes or Schedule Tribes, the punishment shall be imprisonment to the extent of two years and fine up to ten thousand rupees.

5. **Intimation to be given to District Magistrate with respect to conversion:**
   1. Whoever converts any person from one religious faith to another either by performing himself the ceremony necessary for such conversion as a religious priest or by taking part directly or indirectly in such ceremony shall, within such period after the ceremony as may be prescribed, send an intimation to the District Magistrate of the district in which the ceremony has taken place of the fact of such conversion in such form as may be prescribed.
   2. If any person fails within sufficient cause to comply with the provisions contained in sub-section (1), he shall be punishable with imprisonment, which may extend to one year or with fine, which may extend to one thousand rupees or with both.
6. **Offence to be cognisable:** An offence under this Act shall be cognisable and shall not be investigated by an officer below the rank of an Inspector of police.
7. **Prosecution to be made with the sanction of District Magistrate:** No prosecution for an offence under this Act shall be instituted except by, or with the previous sanction of the Magistrate of the District or such other authority, not below the rank of a Sub-Divisional Officer, as may be authorised by him in that behalf.
8. **Power to make rules:** The State Government may make rules for the purpose of carrying out the provisions of this Act.

Religious Composition of Chhattisgarh (in Percentage) : 1991

District – Sarguja

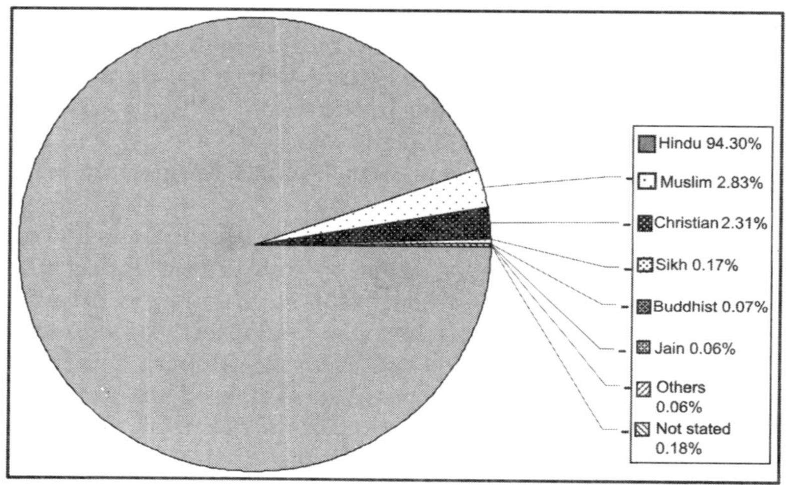

District – Bilaspur

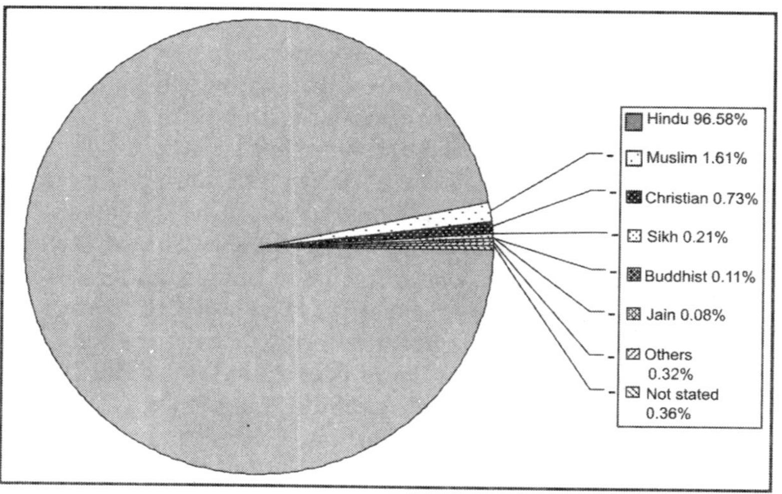

District – Raigarh

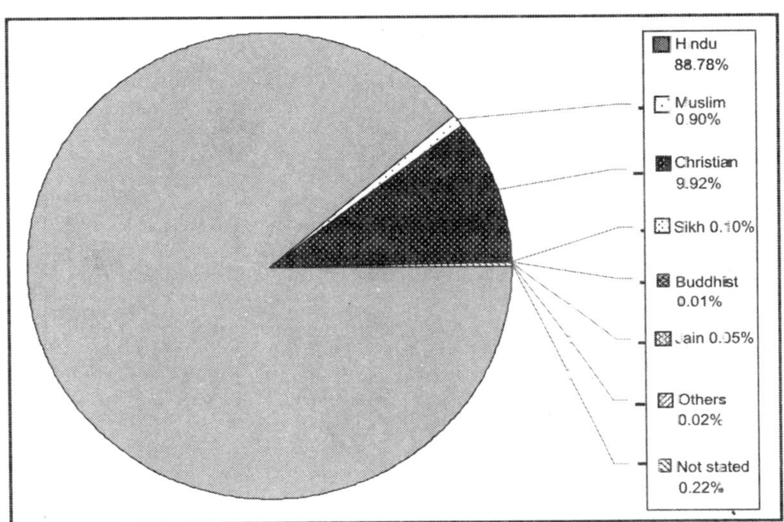

District – Rajnandgaon

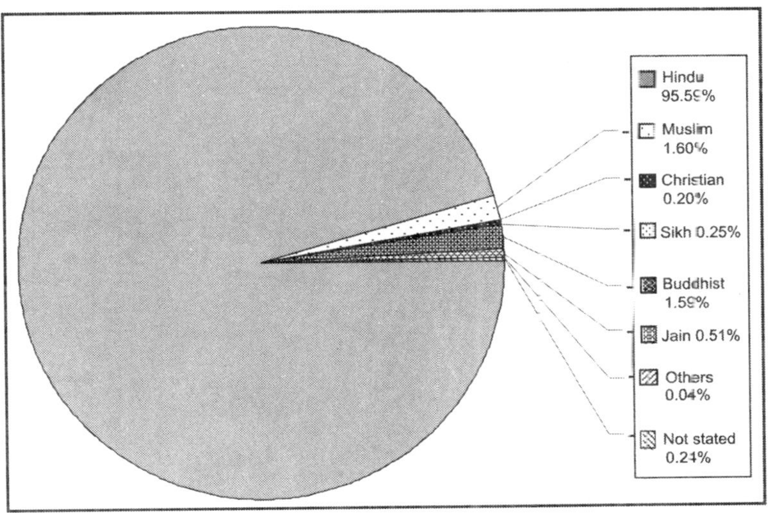

District – Durg

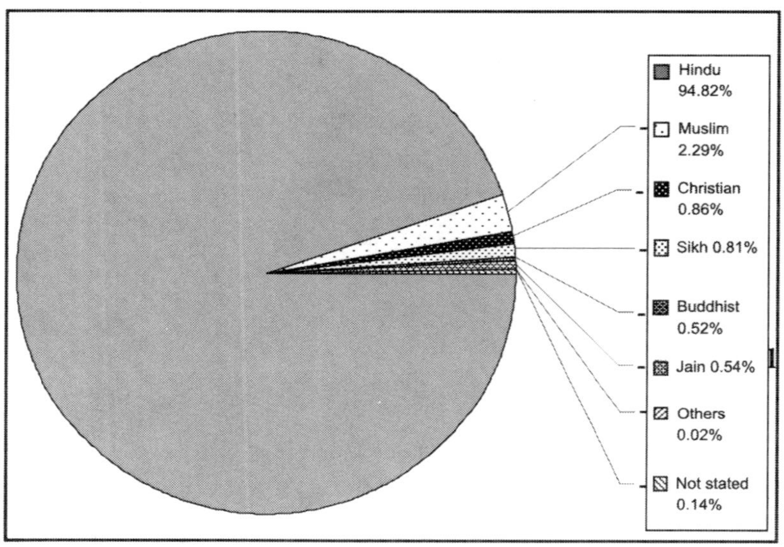

District – Raipur

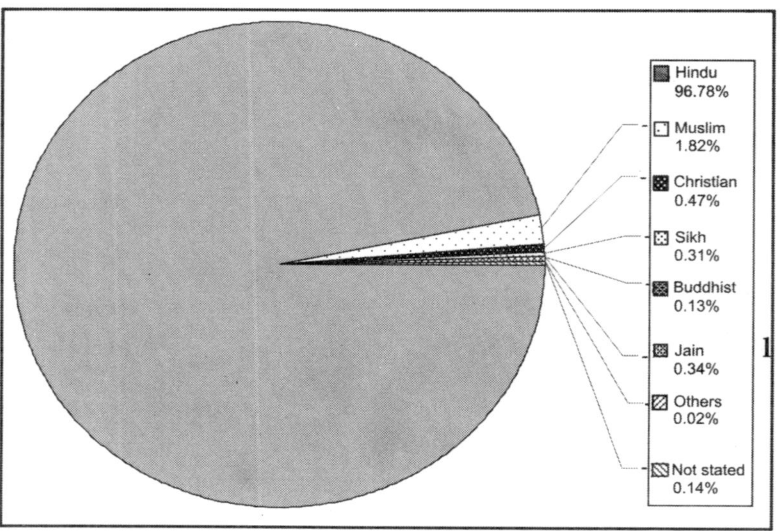

District – Bastar

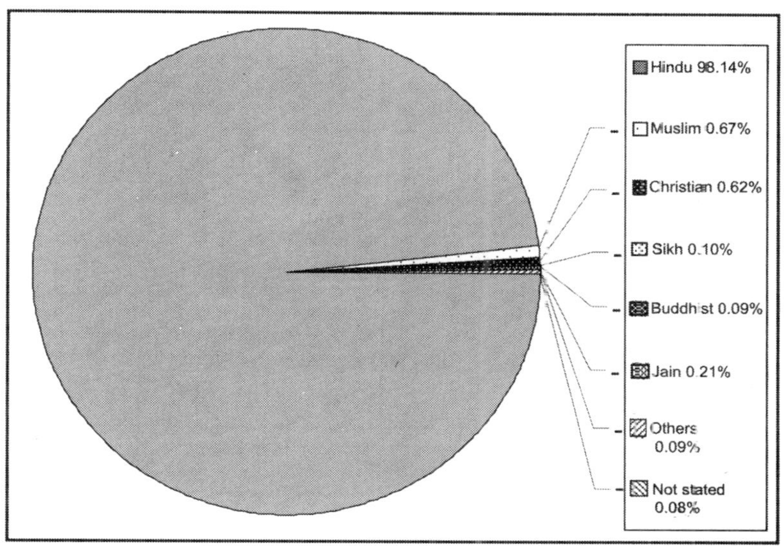

Graph Depicting Religious Composition of Chhattisgarh (in Percentage) : 1951–1991

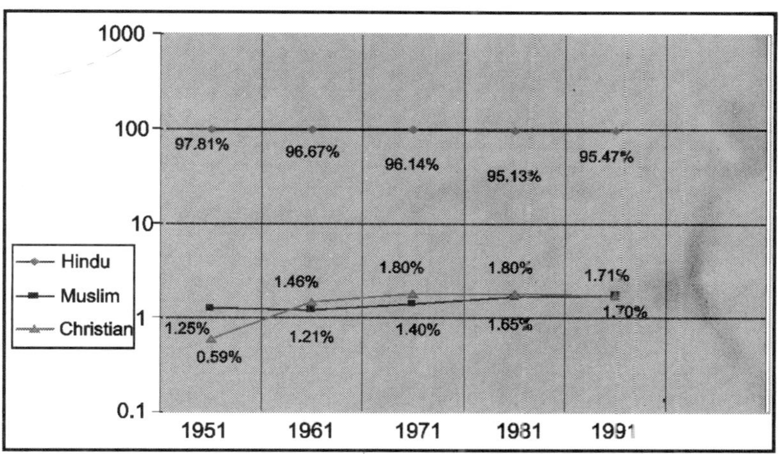

Graphic description of Decadal Growth Christian Population in Madhya Pradesh/Chhattisgarh (District wise : 1951–1991)

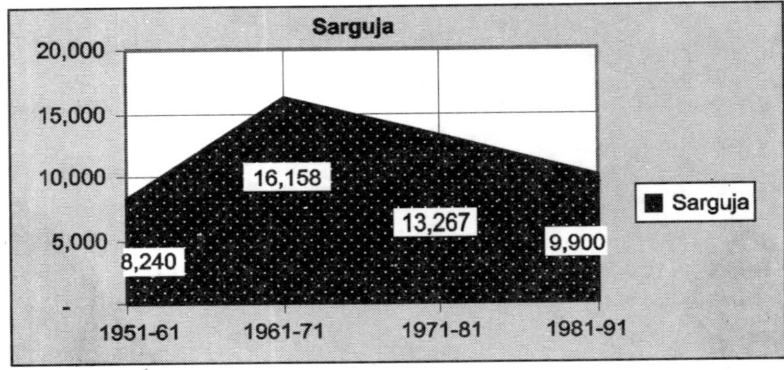

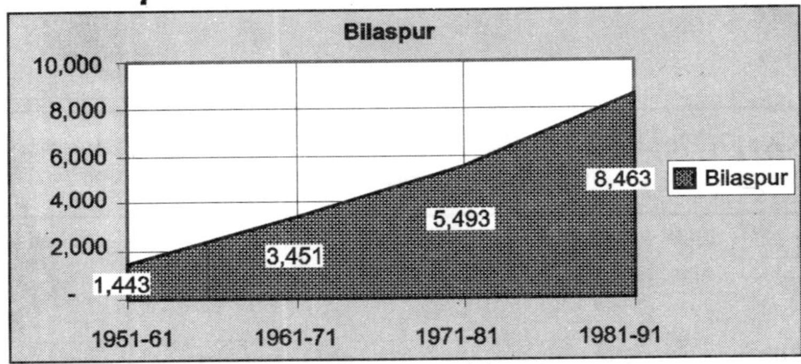

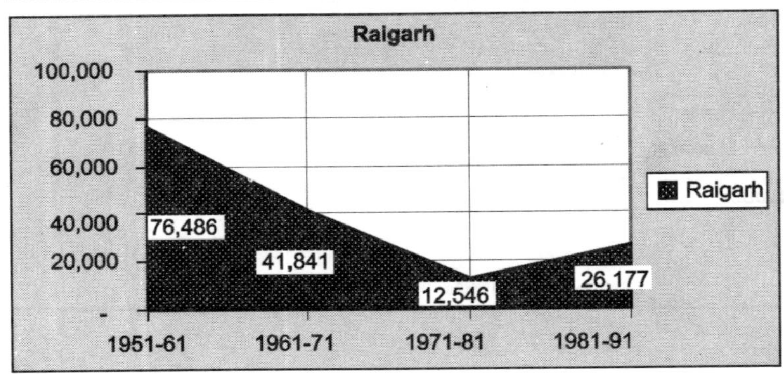

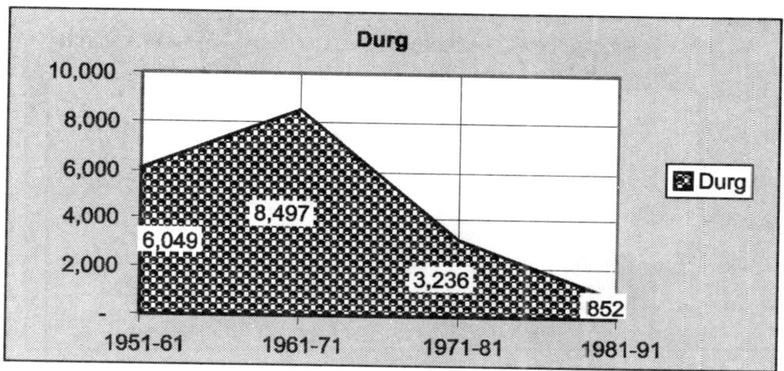
Durg
10,000
8,000
6,000
4,000
2,000
-
6,049
8,497
3,236
852
1951-61
1961-71
1971-81
1981-91
Durg

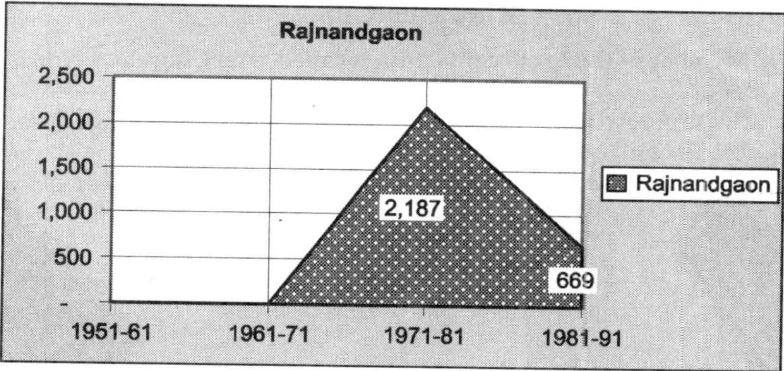
Rajnandgaon
2,500
2,000
1,500
1,000
500
-
2,187
669
1951-61
1961-71
1971-81
1981-91
Rajnandgaon

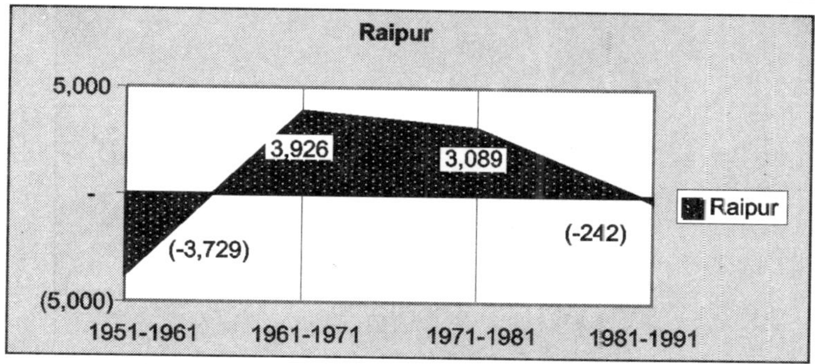
Raipur
5,000
-
(5,000)
3,926
3,089
(-3,729)
(-242)
1951-1961
1961-1971
1971-1981
1981-1991
Raipur

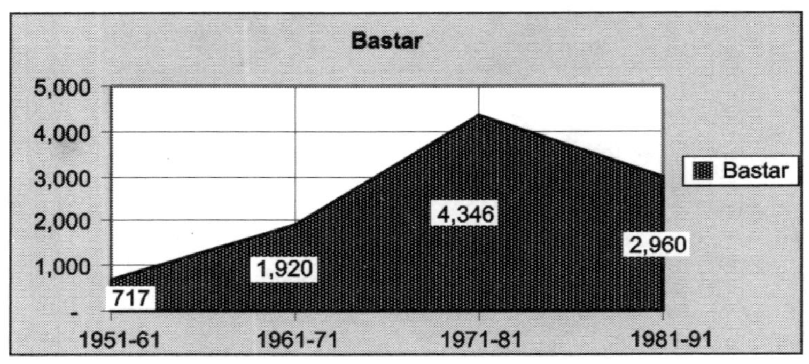

REFERENCES

1. Member of the Protestant Church called 'The Church of North India'.
2. Please see Arun Shourie (2000) *Harvesting our souls - Missionaries, their design, their claims.*, ASA Publications, New Delhi.
3. He said *"Paisa Khuda Nahin Hota, Lekin Khuda se kam nahin"*.

7

The Hinduisation of Tribals: A Special Reference to the Oraons in Chhotanagpur

Joseph Marianus Kujur

Controversial though it is to talk of the concept of the 'civilizational pull', it is still helpful in analyzing the processes of Hinduisation of the tribals in India. Hinduism in the Indian subcontinent is a dominant culture and religion and as such exercises a pull on those who are outside the Hindu fold. Tribals, for example, are surrounded by Hindu culture. There was not much contact with or exposure to the Hindu environment as long as the tribals lived in relative isolation in the forests. The pull of Hinduism then on the tribal was negligible. Things started changing with the nationalist movement against the British. Nationalism implies a certain cohesiveness in society, which develops aspects, such as socio-cultural relationships, political consciousness, and there is also the question of nationhood and national identity. National identity is greatly influenced by civilisation, which is Hinduism in the context of India. This is clear from the fact that from the east to the west, from the north to the south, one finds the presence of innumerable Hindu temples. Therefore the process of nation building in India necessarily has certain implications. This politically identity is special in terms of geographical areas and cultural distinctiveness. Politically there is a system of control of one authority, viz. that of Hinduism. Hence the tribal society is caught in this process of entering into relationship with the dominant Hindu group which has inherited power from the British. By virtue of the Hindu domination there is a perception of India as a Hindu nation irrespective of the secular credentials of the Constitution. This perception tries to facilitate a process of the unification of different groups. If one is not careful, there is also a tendency of assimilation, which is nothing but a slow co-option. More over, if the BJP is at the helm of power with the support of the Hindu zealots, the collapse of the intercommunal social fabric of India is sure.[1] Hence, *Hindutva* poses a serious threat to multi-cultural democracy.[2] Juergensmeyer,[3] in this connection argues that religious nationalism is more than just religious fanaticism and there is an attempt to reformulate the modern languages and strategies of politics in order to provide a new basis and legitimacy for the nation-state.

However, as we are in the 21st century, we have a different type of consciousness, that is the process of transformation of various groups, there is the process of nation building. The question is: who will have an upper hand in the building up of the state, the Hindu minorities or the tribals? There is certainly an effort of the dominant Hindu group for socio-cultural, religious and political hegemony. In spite of the efforts of the dominant Hinduism for domination, there are articulations and expressions of assertion of different identities, nations and cultures in India. In other words, there is an assertion that the experiences of many local cultures are prior to those of the building of a Hindu nation. There is an assertion that "the future of India does not lie either in BJP's Hindutva or Indian Constitution's guarantee of secularism. It lies in the people of India and their co-existential traditions notwithstanding their miseries, conflicts and tribulations".[4]

Consequently, there is a clash between the experience at the grass roots land and general type of cultures by the tribals and that of the nation-state being built by the elite. The greater the identity of the local groups the deeper the conflict is seen if attempts of unification and homogenisation are made either covertly or overtly. On the basis of this conflict there are two nations of what a nation and a state is the first nation promotes one state, one culture, one language, one religion, which is the concept of the Hindutva organisation. The second nation is more spatial, ecological or geographical. It takes into consideration in the composition of the national or state identity a diversity of constituent elements such as cultures, religions, regions. This concept is very rich as it is inclusive of a number of cultures and values which come together and constitute one nation, which is the basic principle of federalism.

Further, we focus on the contestation that Hinduism is not a proselytising religion. We need to clear the myth that there is no proselytisation in Hinduism. In fact, religions like Islam and Christianity are always exclusively considered to be proselytising religion but not Hinduism. However, Pati's work shows how Hinduism de facto has been a proselytising religion all along and that it does so either in a subtle or aggressive way.[5]

The present paper will try to analyse the way in which the processes of Hinduisation have taken place among the Oraon tribal in Chhotanagpur in three parts: Evolution of the Oraon identity; Hindutva formulation of the Oraon/Tribal identity; and conclusions.

Evolution of the Oraon Identity

In common parlance, the term 'Oraon' is used to refer to a group of people with a common culture. The term is also used to designate the language of the group. Roy[6] holds that linguistically and ethnologically the Oraons belong to the Dravidian stock. Dalton,[7] in his Descriptive Ethnology of Bengal treats the Oraon as one of the tribes that had preserved the rudiments of their language and had some connection with the Dravidian tongues such as Tamil and Telugu. The Oraon community is scheduled as a 'tribe' in the Constitutional list of the Scheduled Tribes but this is restricted to the Oraons living in some of the states. The Oraons' homes are spread over different parts of the country today. They are found in Jharkhand, Chhattisgarh, West Bengal, Bihar, Orissa, Assam, Maharashtra and Tripura. They are also found in small numbers in Andaman and Nicobar Islands, Delhi, Rajashthan and other north Indian states.

Some of the recent works on the Chhotanagpur tribes in general[8] and on the Oraons[9] in particular, though different in focus have at least one theme in common the changing identity of the tribe. Scholars are conscious of the fact that the tribes now are what they were a few decades ago[10] one can study the identity of the Oraons observing changes in the areas such as (i) social life—language, eating habits, dress patterns, life style. (ii) economic life-mode of living; (iii) religious beliefs and practices; (iv) political behaviour, and so on. The perception of the Oraon identity today either by the Oraons or non-Oraons is not what it used to be in the past. In this section I have tried to trace the shaping of the identity of Oraons at two levels; (i) at the level of 'self-identification', and (ii) at the level of identification by the 'other'.

Self-Identification as Kurukhars or Kurukh

The nomenclature 'Oraon' is marked by controversies. It is not how the people speaking Kurukh addressed themselves originally.[11] Rather, they described and identified themselves as Kurukhars, speaking the Kurukh tongue.[12] It is quite possible that the term Kurukh was derived from a word of Dravidian origin meaning, 'man', which has become obsolete now. Dehon[13] observes that the original meaning of the word 'kurukh' was "hillman" Roy is of the opinion that the name Kurukh may well have been "given to the mythical king Karakh just in the same way as the name Adam was given to the Hebrew progenitor of mankind". According to the Kurukh tradition the Oraons prided themselves of having ruled the Karusa country. It is during this time that they seem to have affirmed the distinctive name of the 'Kurukhar' or 'Kurukh'.[14]

Identification of the Oraons by the 'Other'

The nomenclature used by various tribes of India to address themselves is "nothing else but the word which means 'men'".[15] Contrary to the self-identification of the Oraons as Kurukhs, groups and people other than Oraons had identified the Oraon tribe by different names until their identity was stabilised as 'Oraons'. Mullick argues, "present names of most of the tribes in India have been given to them by the invading societies". This is the case for example, in the nomenclature "Naga". The latter is used to refer to mean "the naked people" for a group of people in the north-east. Such is also the case of the nomenclature "suar" (swine) for the Shavaras in Orissa, "panias" (slaves) for a group in South India, and in the description of the Oraons from time to time both from the insider's and the outsider's point of view. We can trace those shifts in three different periods of time (i) Pre-colonial, (ii) Colonial, and (iii) Post-colonial.

The **pre-colonial construction** of the group we now call 'tribes' hinges on the construction prevalent during the Vedic period. The construct of the 'tribe' during the Vedic period was that of "a homogeneous and self-contained unit without any hierarchical discrimination".[16] These groups, which were by and large outside the Aryan civilisation , were considered "tribes". The nomenclature of the tribes crystallised in the Vedic period was based on such features as: (i) physical appearance, (ii) religious practice, (iii) attitude towards outsiders/aliens, (iv) names of the leaders, and (v) anagram and interchange of words.

In the **colonial period** too, the Oraons were identified and described by different names derived from such characteristics as physical features, general backwardness, occupation, belief and worship, social status and the Dhangar identity of the Oraons was linked with impurity. The name 'dhangar' was despicable and contemptuous. Walter Hamilton[17], in his description of Chhota Nagpur, writes: "The Khetauri, the keevi, and the Dhanggar still compose still compose the bulk of the inhabitant, and some of these are said not to speak the Hindi language". In Hamilton's description, the Oraons are not only perceived as 'dhangars' but also as 'impure' and 'unconverted mlechchas'.[18] Their Dhangar identity is due to the Other's perception of the Oraons as a cheap labour force.[19] The 'unconverted mlechchas', as indicated above, could have referred to the Oraons who were still not converted to Hinduism. Many of them were returned as 'Hindu' in the Censuses of India later. One of the reasons for this was that the Oraons did not know what their religion was. Besides, if they did not belong to any other category different from Hinduism, they were all clubbed with the Hindu population.[20]

Form of belief and worship was another criterion used by the colonial ethnologists and administrators for the nomenclature of the tribes. On the basis of their belief and worship the Oraons were returned as 'animists' in the censuses.[21] The Oraons were also distinguished from the adherents of the so-called established religions by virtue of their being nature-worshippers. But the procedure followed by the census enumerators to categorise the Oraons as animists was arbitrary. In this Connection, O'Malley[22] observes that when a person belonged to "an aboriginal tribe and had no recognised religion (i.e., was not a Hindu, Musalman, Christian, Buddhist, Sikh, Jain, Parsi, etc.), the name of the tribe was to be entered. All persons whose tribal name was entered in the schedules were taken to be animists". This is how their identity was assigned.

Social status had been one of the determining factors of nomenclature. Social status largely depended on the status of the purity/impurity of the tribe. Whether a tribe was pure or polluted was determined by its eating habits. The Oraons were looked down upon as inferior and as impure with low social status. Risley[23] gives a vivid description as to why the Oraons had such an inferior social position:

> In the eyes of the average Hindu the Oraons have no social status at all and are deemed to be entirely outside the regular caste system. In the important matter of the diet the tribes have as yet made no concessions to Hindu prejudice. Beef, pork, fowls, all kinds of fish, alligators, lizards, field-rats, the larvas of bees and wasps and even the flesh of animals which have died a natural death are reckoned lawful food. Oraons, in fact, will eat almost anything and are looked down upon as promiscuous feeders by the Bagadis, Bauris, and other dwellers upon the outskirts of Hinduism. A common charge is that they eat snakes and jackals. but this is only partially true, for the flesh of these animals is used solely for certain obscure medicinal purposes, and is not recognized as a regular article of diet.

One thing that becomes clear from the above observation by Risley is that the Oraons do not come under any Hindu caste category. They are an independent entity. the reason for the Oraons being outside the Hindu caste system is the former's eating habits, which the Hindus find abominable. Roy Chaudhury[24] also reports that the food of the Oraons was "pig, beef, goat's flesh, eggs, fowls, tiger, leopard, bear, all birds except vultures,fish, field-rats, and large bull frogs". In the 1901 census report, the section entitled 'Social grouping of the Dravidian Tract', classifies the Oraons as "scavengers and filth eaters" in the Hindu caste category, along with Dom, Hari, Ho, Kaur, Nagesia, Santal and others. Dhangar is mentioned as a lower artisan from whom a "Brahman will not take water".[25] They themselves were not clear about their own identity sometimes they were returned as 'Non-Hindus', at other times as 'Hindus'.

In the post-colonial scenario, the colonial hangover still persisted in India. This is evident in the identification and nomenclature of the 'tribe'. Consequently, the notion of tribe does not mean more than backwardness isolation inferiority, impurity, simple technology, practice of animism, etc. to majority of the citizenry in the country. Such a conceptualisation of the group is fallacious,[26] inadequate[27] and problematic.[28] In the post-colonial period the identity of Oraons goes through yet another shift from the colonial category of 'tribe' to the Constitutional category of the 'Scheduled Tribe'. We see the process of crystallisation of the new name for the Oraons and other such tribes in the Constituent Assembly Debates.[29] The identity formulation of 'tribe' in the CAD was argued along two different lines of thought: (i) the non-liberal Hindu line of thought, which did not necessarily represent the majority Hindus voices, but by virtue of being vocal it overshadowed other moderate voices, and (ii) the 'adivasis' (indigenous) line of thought which was in a minority in the CAD but represented the tribes across the country.

The protagonist of the tribals Mr. Jaipal Singh Munda was vehemently opposed to the term 'Vanjati' (literally, 'forest castes') for the 'tribes' proposed by the non-liberal Hindus. Mr. Munda, who claimed his people to be variously known as backward tribes, primitive tribes, and criminal tribes by the 'others', rejected the term 'vanjati'. Proud to be a 'jungli' (a derogatory term for the jungle dwellers),[30] Mr. Munda pleaded with the house not to "get behind the mind of the Adivasi".[31] He requested the House not to translate the Scheduled Tribes as 'Vanjati' (forest castes) because most of the tribes did not live in 'jungles'. Mr. Munda preferred the word 'adivasi' to vanjati to be incorporated in the Constitution because the word adivasi has grace and because the old abusive epithet of vanjati till recently meant an uncivilised barbarian.[32] The House instead of 'vanajati' preferred the word 'janajati' contrary to the demand of Mr. Munda.[33] K.M. Munshi disagreed with Munda in calling all the tribes 'Adivasis'. Munshi found "nothing common between one tribe and another", and hence he thought it would be fatal for the country to take them as one unit.[34] The reason why the term 'adivasis' was not accepted was explained by Dr. Ambedkar. Ambedkar was of the opinion that the word 'Adivasis was a "general term" without any "specific legal de jure connotation". The term Scheduled Tribe, however, as a translation for 'Anusuchit Janjati', had a "fixed meaning" because it enumerated the tribes[35] (Verma, 1990:11).

The Constituent Assembly (henceforth CA) specified the tribes as the "Scheduled Tribes" under which only those tribes could be included which were to be given "special treatment or facilities envisaged under the Constitution".[36] The Constitution does not really define nor does it lay down any criteria for specifying the "Scheduled Tribes". The President of India has the prerogative of specifying under Article 342 by a "public notification" the Scheduled Tribes Parliament, by law, can "include or exclude" from the Scheduled Tribes list any tribal community or part thereof in any State or Union Territory (ibid). One crucial clause included in the Constitution is that there is "no religious bar for specifying a person as a member of a Scheduled Tribe". In the case of the Scheduled Castes, however, "no person professing religion orther than Hinduism or Sikhism" can be deemed as a member of the Scheduled Caste.[37]

That the tribal identity was at stake is evident again in the context of the census enumerations. Mr. Munda drew their attention to this aspect when he said:

> Ever since the Hindu Mahasabha became a militant political organization, the census figures have never been reliable or accurate. We have yet to a stage where we want to get scientific facts in an honest way. Take, for instance. the Central Provinces. You compare the figures of Adivasis there, say in 1941; take the censuses of 1921, 1931 and 1941. You find in between 1911 and 1941; the figure gets reduced by 18 kakhs. I know particularly that the Adivasis are not a dying race and yet somehow or other one minute the Gonds are enumerated as Hindus and the next minute they come back as Adivasis: and that type of cooking of figures and misenumeration has gone on at every census and the sooner this country becomes honest about it and tries to find out statistics in an honest way. without any religious bias. the better it will be.[38]

It can be discerned that the administrative term 'tribe' which was first used in the colonial period has stuck to the Oraons as it has in the case of the other tribes though the new term 'Scheduled Tribe' is given to them Constitutionally. Xaxa[39] observes that however limited and problematic the term 'tribe' is,

> it has now been adopted by the tribals themselves to mean the dispossessed, depressed people of a region. There is no claim to being the original inhabitant of that region, but a prior claim to the natural resources is asserted vis-a-vis the outsiders and the dominant caste.

Xaxa further says:

> The identity that was forced upon them from outside precisely to mark out differences from the dominant community has now been internalized by the people themselves. Not only has it become an important mark of social differentiation and identity assertion but also an important tool of articulation for empowerment.[40]

It is the above observation by Xaxa which makes the identity articulation of the Sarna tribals crucial at this juncture of the history in Jharkhand. There is at present a process of affirmation and reinvention of its "tribal' identity by the Sarna community in the face of some forces denying the 'tribal' status to them. The dynamics of the Sarnas and the Hindutva forces is complex but it is interesting to see how these two groups perceive themselves and others and articulate their own as well as others' identity.

The issue of the identity of the tribals has been a bone of contention since the independence of the country. The Constitution guarantees certain privileges to the 'Scheduled Tribes'. Many groups in the country by virtue of their 'tribalness are 'scheduled' as 'tribes' irrespective of their religious affiliations. Hence, an imposition of the Hindu status on the Scheduled Tribes is not without nuances. There is thus a contestation by the Hindutva forces over both the 'tribalness' and the 'Scheduled Tribeness'. Not only that; there is also a challenge to the Mundaness, Oraonness and Kharianess if the tribals belong to the Munda, the Oraon and the Kharia communities respectively. Contestation of this nature has serious implications for the identity not only of the Sarna tribals but also for the tribes in general. We shall now examine the Hindutva formulation of tribal identity.

Hindutva Formulation of Oraon Identity

The main contentions of the Hindutva forces are: (i) tribals are Hindus, and (ii) the Oraon Christians are non-tribals. Here I examine the dynamics of suchcontentions. In order to do that I take 3 cases (i) the controversy over the tribals as 'Hindus' in Gazetteer; (ii) the Malti Oraons' participation in the Shivrait (Shivaratri) Puja; and (iii) the circulars and pamphlets reportedly issued by the Hindutva forces in Jharkhand.

Case -1 : Controversy over Tribals as Hindus in the Gazetteer Formulation

David Munzni[41] brought to the notice of the tribal intelligentsia the irregularities held in the recording of the tribals identity in the *Gazetteers*. Paul Hansda, Minister for Tribal Welfare in the Government of Bihar, wrote to the Minister in the Revenue Department in the Government of Bihar, in "protest against the inclusion of the scheduled tribes withthe Hindus in the revised by N. Kumar, the successor of P C Roy Chaudhury. The section 'Religion' of Chapter lll on 'people' reads as follows—"Religion: Hindus including Scheduled Castes and Scheduled tribes; Muslims; Christians; followers of other religions-5". In protest against such formulation Mr. Hansda wrote:

> If the editor intends to include scheduled tribes with the Hindus, he is distorting facts. All the well known anthropologists of the past who have on the tribes of the Ranchi District(Cfr. E.T. Dalton: S.C. Roy; F. Hahn; J. Hoffmann, etc;) have always considered tribal religion as distinct from Hinduism .... Since the tribals worship no major Hindu dcitics, and do not believe in important Hindu tencts like Karma and samsara, and since they are not served by Brahmins and do not occupy any caste groups, it is most misleading to call them Hindus .... Besides, the inclusion of the scheduled tribes with the Hindus will have far reaching political disadvantages to the former.[42]

In view of the above Hansda requested the Minister of the Revenue Department Government of Bihar to look in to the matter and forthwith to order a rectification" in the revision of the *Gazetteer*.

Munzni also wrote in protest at the distotion and suppression of the first draft of the *Ranchi District Gazetteer* prepared by P.C. Roy Choudhury. He pointed out that Roy Chaudhury, special officer and state editor, *Bihar District Gazetteer*, vacated his office at the end of April 1966. Till then Roy had completed two volumes of the revised *Ranchi District Gazetteer*. He had particular directives from the late Mr. Birchand Patel, Minister of Revenue and Shri S.K. Chakravarty I.A.S. Secretary Revenue Department, to go deep in to the history and culture of the people of Ranchi district particularly the adivasis. Mr. Roy had made extensive tours and had also deputed his resarch assistants to tour in different parts of the district. There were separate coverages for the different tribals and semi-tribals and all this formed the second volume of the revised district gazetter. These drafts had been looked into by the Minister, late Mr. Patel, and he had highly spoken of the drafts he used to say that he was proud of the *Ranchi Gazetteer* which was going to see the light of day very soon. The manuscript in two volumes had actually been sent to the government printing press at Gulzarbagh, Patna with the full concurrence of the gazetteer editor. Ministry would be no objection to printing a separate volume about the people of Ranchi.

The problem seemed to have arisen when N. Kumar, the successor of Roy Choudhury as the Special Officer, Revenue

Department and state editor did not want to publish the *Ranchi Gazetteer* in two volumes and got back the manuscripts from the press. It was not understood if this was done with the approval of the Revenue Secretary or not. Munzni demanded an enquiry as to how the chapters on history and on the tribals were being revised, distorted and changed at will by the very same research assistants allegedly at the bidding of Kumar and by Kumar himself. Munzni wanted to know on what basis the Scheduled Castes an Scheduled Tribes were clubbed together as Hindu. It was also pointed out that Kumar had avoided convening a meeting of the Advisory committee for the district gazetteers which was set up in 1966. Munzni prayed that the decision of the Supreme Court on the 6th March 1968, legitimising scheduled tribal status to the tribal Christians be included in the Ranchi District Gazetteer.

Case-2 : The Oraons' Participation in the *Shivrait puja*

One of the ways the Hindutva forces try to show the Sarna-Hindu affinity is to remind them of the Sarna participation in the Hindu feasts like *Shivrait* and the *Manda puja* (feast of the Sadan Hindus). Majority of the Sarna Oraons of Malti village, Mandar Block, Ranchi district in Jharkhand, were seen visiting the Shiv Temple, about eight kilometers north-east of the village, beyond another village called Ambatoli. Not only did the Oraons visit the temple, they also offered milk libation on the Shivalinga, besides fruits, flowers, and sweets. The Sarna Oraons devotedly participated in the puja rituals at the temple, seeking the blessings of Lord Shiva. It looked as if the Hindus and not the Oraons were offering the puja. In this event, the distinction between the Sarnas and the Hindus seemed to have narrowed considerably and the gap between the Sarnas and the Christians widened. There was, however, another side of the story. Among many counters which were opened for charitable work, like distributing water, medicine, and for giving information, there was one banner named 'Sarna Central Yuva Samiti, Mandar'. I had an appointment with the leader of the Samiti; Assured that I was an 'insider', he told me;

> Our people (Sarna) have becone Hinduized and we feel sorry that they are offering puja like Hindus. We cannot change the attitude of our people overnight. But we are here to slowly bring awareness in them about the distinctivaness and beauty of the Sarna religion so that those who have crossed over to Hinduism come back to the real Sarna.

Tribal religion became the latest subject of politicking in Jharkhand as reported in Indo-Asian News Service, (Ranchi, May 25, 2003). It stated that while sone BJP leaders insisted that "the State's tribals are Hindus", the main opposition party the JMM said that the stand of the BJP was an "insult to the independent tribal identity". Babulal Marandi's statement that "tribals are Hindus and they worship Hindu gods" sparked off sharp reactions. Some angry Santhal groups announced Marandi's boycott. The "independence" of the tribal religion was emphasised by the JMM and allies as opposed to the stance of Marandi. Ignoring the reactions of the Opposition leaders Arjun Singh Munda, the present Jhrkhand Chief Minister backed the view of his predecessor on the basis of "similarities between tribal religion and Hinduism". He contended that the tribals had adopted Hindu ways of worship in many tribal festivals. The JMM, the Congress and the allies accused Marandi and Munda of propagating RSS ideology. The BJP accused the Opposition of trying to draw "political mileage" out of this controversy. The debate on tribal religion came as a boon for the oppsition parties who had been trying project the BJP as 'anti-tribal', 'anti-poor' and 'anti-people'. Even the social anthropologists of the State seemed to be divided over the issue of tribal religion and identity. Some of them termed tribal faith as "offshoots of Hinduism" while others termed them as "independent religions" (*Hindustan Times*, May 26, 2003:8).

Case-3 : Circulars reportedly by the Hindutva Forces

During my fieldwork, I came across six photocopied circulars. It was difficult to ascertain the sources of the circulars. Clear instruction was given at the bottom of each circular that the document be kept "confidential and secret'. The sources vaguely acknowledged in some of the circulars were the "Hindu Dham

Sansad', 'Brahman Sevak Sangh', 'RSS', 'Vanvasi Nawjgran Yuva Sangh, Karra in Ranchi', etc. These documents were meant for the *pracharaks* (catechists). The administration could not but take note of these circulars. An official circular from the police Department confirmed such developments in parts of Jharkhand. All the concerned police officers in the State had been asked to take precautionary measures to diffuse the tensions caused by the RSS and its affiliated campigns.

The analysis of the content of these circulars point to a direct link with the identity question of the Adivasis (Sarna + Christian). The targeted groups in the pamphlets were the Dalits, the Adivasis, the Christians, the Muslims, and the Buddhists, especially the Ambedkarites. The document sought to promote of the Hindu caste boundaries and to eliminate the above groups physically, culturally, socially, and psychologically. The rationale for eliminating the Adivasis was the latter's refusal to accept the mainstream Hindu religion. The circular revealed a plan to trap innocent, illiterate tribal girls and initiate them into drugs so that they would be barren forever. It recommended the 'slow death' of the tribals by poisoned medication. It encouraged drinking and other bad habits among tribals. It also instructed the RSS *pracharaks* not to allow the filling up of the backlogs in government jobs. The circulars were against the development projects for the STs and Backward classes. Efforts for privatisation and disinvestment were appreciatedas they would remove the policy of reservation. The Adivasis were addressed as 'Vanvasis' (inhabitants of forest) and 'Van-bandhus ' (brothers living in forest). The policy also envisaged bringing in sexual immorality among tribals by initiating hostal girls into prostitution to incapacitate then from participating in competition. The circular encouaged the non-Adivasis to appropriate tribal land by hook or by crook and to use pressure tactics for this. The circular said, "Give them money and they will be ready to do anything". The documents encouraged the RSS cadres to create problems such as strikes, sabotage, etc. in Christian institutions in collaboration with goondas, anti-social elements and criminals.

Analysis

The emerging theme in the three case-studies above seems to be the clash between the forces seeking hegemony on the one hand and those asserting their separate and distinctive identity on the other.

The forces seeking hegemony promote the Hindutva ideology which believes in the process of homogenisation of fthe country. As part of this process the Hindutva forces assert that tribals are Hindus. It is in keeping with this ideology that the RSS Chief Sudershan appealed to the Sarnas of Jharkhand before the census of 2001 to return themselves as "Sarna Hindu". This was also the reason for the Hindutva intellectuals' efforts to disprove the theory of the "Aryan Invasion" and to promote the idea of a perfect, peaceful Co-existence of the Aryans and non-Aryans (Danino and Nahar, 1996; Frawley, 1998; Talageri, 1993), for the Hindutva forces underlining why they consider the tribals as Hindus. The tribal participation in the pujas like Shivrait also reinforces their belief that tribals are Hindus.

Surprisingly, it is on the basis of the same criteria, viz. belief system and practice, that the traditional Sarnas refute the suggestion that they are Hindus. While asserting their separate identity they claim that the Sarna religion is completely different from Hinduism. They underline the fundamental differences between the two as follows[43]: (i) Hinduism is theo-centric and is based on the hierarchy of the *varna* system; (ii) Hinduism being in the realm of the Great Tradition follows written Scriptures and the Sanskrit language for their ritualistic practices whereas Sarnaism has all its rites and rituals in the Adivasis languages; (iii) in Hinduism the Brahmin offers the puja. He belongs to the high caste in the system of hierarchy. In Sarnaism puja is offerred by an Adivasis *pahan* who can be any person authorised by the Adivasis community; (iv) in Hinduism women have a secondary place in many of the activities such as puja, cremation, etc. In Sarnaism, women enjoy equal rights with men and are allowed to participate in most of the activities with men; (v) dowry has spread as an evil in Hinduism, as contrary to the bride price given to the girls' parents in Sarnaism; (vi) in Hindu religious rituals *agni* (fire) has special significance and *Yagnya*, hawan, etc. cannot be offered without agni. In Sarnaism, however, there is worship of nature and agni has no significance; (vii) in Hinduism there is the practice of cremating the corpse. In Sarnaism there are specific burial sites for the deceased.[44]

What I find important in the above illustration is not the strength of the 'argument' as such but the assertion of the Sarnas of their distinct identity and separateness from Hinduism. It is in view of promoting awareness among the Sarnas that the Sarna Samitis take up the responsibility of educating the Sarna masses about their real identity. The stand of the Samiti has been consistent with their cultural revivalism. It is only by asserting their identity that the Sarnas hope to have bargaining power. If they give in to Hinduism and are subsumed by the Hindu identity as designed by the Right wing, they lose their 'Sarna' identity. By losing their identity they also lose their 'tribal' identity and are deprived of any Constitutional benefits meant for the tribals. It is true that despite the Sarnas getting Hinduised they still get the Constitutional benefits. But the loss of the tribal identity of the Sarnas due to Hinduisation is likely to affect them adversely in the long run. The loss of tribal identity of the Hinduised Sarna is likely to arise specially due to the fact that the Hinduism being a caste hierarchy is opposed to the tribals' 'casteless' and egalitarian system. The Hinduised tribals can be absorbed in the Hindufold only at the bottom and as 'outcastes'. If the Sarnas are 'sufficiently' Hinduised to lose their surnames, society, this alienation of the Sarnas from the parent community may make the Constitutional benefits inaccessible to them.

The Hindutva forces, besides attempting the homogenisation of the Sarnas, try to de-recognise the tribal Christians as 'tribals'. The Hindutva forces have always looked upon the Christians as their arch enemies. One finds this idea in the book called *Bunch of Thoughts* by the RSS ideologue Golwalkar (1980 : 233-265). He identifies Muslims, Christians and Communists as the three threats to India. Sarkar (1999:73), referring to the RSS ideology and its modus operandi, points out that it is not new for the Sangh Parivar to target a minority community. It has always needed "one or more enemies" to consolidate into an "aggressive bloc the 'Hindu community' which it claims to represent and seeks to constitute" (ibid.).

However, while the Hindutva forces emphasise the Sarna-Christian 'separateness' the Christians reiterate their 'sameness' and 'oneness' with the larger Oraon society. This is manifest in the reaction of the tribal Christians to the activities of the Hindutva forces to de-schedule them. For example, in Munzni's[45] reaction to the formulation in the *Gazetteer* in the 1960s, there was a demonstration of how the tribal Christian intelligentsia had been articulating tribal identity. Such a sense of identity was the outcome of education which also brought about political and social consciousness among the tribals. Without such a consciousness, it would not have been possible for the tribals to fight cases in the Supreme Court against Kartik Oraon's demand for de-scheduling the tribal Christians from the Scheduled Tribes' list. It is this type of consciousness of the 'distinctiveness' of the *Adivasiness* that motivates the present generation of tribal leadership to articulate their identity as different from that of the 'Hindu'.

Conclusion

In this paper I have discussed the way various groups of people have described and given identity to Oraons over the years. Though the present day Oraons originally addressed themselves as Kurukhars/Kurukh, the 'others' identified them differently and at different points of time. The pre-colonial identification of tribes in general and Oraons in particular took shape during the Vedic period, and this continued with the coming of the British. During this phase, groups outside the Aryan civilisation were called 'tribes'. They were so identified on the basis of their distinct physical, social, cultural and religious features. The Aryans gave those groups derogatory nicknames such as Dasa, Dasyu, Rakshasas, etc. During the colonial period the British administrators and ethnologists described the Oraons as the Kols, Dhangars, Kodas, Kisans, Modis, Rakshasas, Oraons, etc. These nicknames in the course of time became part of their consciousness. In the post-colonial articulation, the name 'tribe' was further crystallised in the "Scheduled Tribes" nomenclature, which is a Constitutional category. The Oraons, both Sarnas and Christians are seen today as a "Scheduled tribe" having access to all the Constitutional provisions meant for the STs. Thus the identity of the Oraons as 'Oraon' had been an imposition from outside. It did not resonate with the self-identification of the group itself. Ironically, it has been the identity-tag 'given' that has been internalised by the Oraons, and has persisted even to this day.

Notwithstanding the historical distinctiveness from the Hindus, the Hindutva forces asserted that the tribals were indeed Hindus. The Sarnas, however, drive home the point that they were distinct from the Hindus. Xaxa[46] in this regard observes that despite the fact that tribes are in transition as in the case of Oraons who speak various tongues and practice different religions, have variety of occupations, etc. they continue being Oraons "in some socially significant sense" without losing their distinctive identities.

The larger question in the whole argument is not whether the 'Sarnas' are 'Hindus', but whether the 'Oraons' are 'Hindus'. Sarna is a generic name for the religion practised by the Sarna Adivasis. An adherent to the Sarna faith cannot simultaneously practise another religion. A Sarna can be an Oraon, a Munda, a Kharia, a Ho, a Santhal, or any other ethnic group with similar social, cultural and religious characteristics. An Oraon can embrace Islam, Hinduism or Christianity. But he remains an Oraon until the new system assimilates him so completely that there is no trace of the old one that he once identified himself with. To say, therefore, that a Sarna is a Hindu is like saying that a Hindu is a Muslim, or a Christian is a Hindu, etc.

The argument is that there is a civilisational pull, and this progressively brings people together. There is the power centre that tries to pull the weaker groups to itself. The Bhartiya Janata Party and its Hindutva alliances have become that power centre trying to assimilate into itself groups other than Hindu. Though the current of assimilation and homogenisation by the authoritarian groups is strong, resistance by the local is also part of the political process of democracy. Insofar as the power structure is concerned, there is a clash between the ideology of domination and equality. The ideology of domination represented by the elite that is of mono-culture and monoreligion is vehemently resisted by the ethnically diverse groups, asserting their own identity. The dominant groups try to co-opt other groups, buy them, force them or use other unfair means to make the dominant culture as the culture of everybody else. Social consciousness of the local, however, continues slowly but steadily.

REFERENCES

1. Partha Ghosh, 1999, *BJP and the Evolution of India Nationalism: From Periphery to Centre.* New Delhi: Manohar.
2. C.P. Bhambri, 2003, *Hindutva: A Challenge to Multi-cultural Democracy*. Delhi: Shipra Publications.
3. Mark Juergensmeyer, *Religious Nationalism Confronts the Secular State*. Delhi: Oxford University Press.1994.
4. Ghosh, ibid, 404–05.
5. Biswamoy Pati, 2003, *Identity, Hegemony, Resistance: Towards a Social History of Converstone in Orissa, 1800-2000*. New Delhi: Three Essays Collective.
6. Sarat Chandra Roy, 1915, *The Oraons of Chhota Nagpur*, Ranchi: Man in India Office.
7. E.T. Dalton ,1872, *Descriptive Ethnology of Bengal*. Calcutta Office of the Superintendent of Government Printing, pp. 243–45.
8. Lachman M. Khubchandani, 1992, *Tribal Identity; A Language and Communication perspective*. Shimla/New Delhi: Indian Institute of Advanced Study/Indus Publishing Company.

   Sachchidananda, 1999, *The Changing Munda*. New Delhi: Concept Publising Company.

   K.N. Sahay, 1986, "Christian Impact on the Uraon: A Theoretical Perspective" in *Christianity and Culture Change in India*, New Delhi: Inter-India Publications.

   Mangobinda, Banerjee, 1993, *An Historical Outline of Pre-British Chhotanagpur from Earliest Times to 1765*. Ranchi: Educational Publications.
9. Mangobinda Banerjee, 1993, *An Historical Outline of Pre-British Chhotanagpur from Earliest Times to 1765*, Ranchi: Educational Publications.
10. See Shereen Ratnagar, 2000, "Our Tribal Past", in *Social Scientist*. Vol. 31. No. 1-2 January-February.

Virginius Xaxa, 1999, "Tribes as Indigenous People of India." In *Economic and Political Weekly*. Vol. XXXIV, No. 51. December 18, and, Banerjee 1993 Ibid.

11. H.H. Risley, 1981. The Tribes and Castes of India, Vol. II Calcutta: Firma Mukhopadhyay, p. 113.
12. *Imperial Gazetteer of India* 1909, p. 251, Roy, 1915 Ibid, p. 10, *District Gazetteer of Ranchi*, 1969, p. 137.
13. P. Dehon, 1906 "Religion and Customs of thc Uraons" communicated by E.A. Gait. I.C.S. in *Memoirs of the Asiatic Society of Bengal*. Vol. 1. No. 9, pp. 121–181 (The particulars in this article were derived from the *Catholic Herald of India* for July 5th, 1905).p. 122.
14. Ibid.
15. S.B. Mullick, E. Jajdas, A. Akkara, and A. Jaydas, (Eds), 1993. *Indigenous Identity*. New Delhi: Navdin Prakashan Kendra, p. 6.
16. R.C. Verma, 1990, *Indian Tribes Through Ages*. New Delhi: Publications Division. Ministry of Information and Broadcasting. Government of India, p. 4.
17. Walter Hamilton, 1828. "Chuta Nagpoor:" in the *East-India Gazetteer: Containing Particular Description of Hindustan*. Vol. 1. London: Parbury, Allen and Co., p. 415.
18. Ibid.
19. They had been transported to the tea gardens of Assam, Bhutan and to the difficult terrains of Tripura. Arunachal Pradesh and other remote places for road construction. The Oraons labour force still out migrates seasonally from time to time to work in brick kilns. A recent phenomenon in Delhi is the fact of tribal girls in migrating from Orissa, Chhotanagpur, Bihar, Jharkhand, Madhya Pradesh, Chhattisgarh, West Bengal, and so on, to work in *kothis* (big houses) as domestic working girls. Any stranger to the tribals when encountered with these girls gets the impression of the tribals as impoverished. In the regional Sadri language such are called 'dhangarin', the female for 'dhangar'. In chaste Hindi, the word *'aaya'* is used for them, a term which is not liked by the girls themselves.
20. Ibid.
21. Risley and Gait, 1903, *Census of India. 1901. Vol. 1 A. India. Part-II Tables, 17- Population by Religion*. Calcutta: Office of the Superintendent of Government Printing. and Gait,1913, *Census of India, 1911, India, Part-1, Report*. Calcutta: Office of the Superintendent of Government Printing, India.
22. L.S.S. O' Malley, 1907. *Bengal District Gazetteers*, Calcutta: The Bengal Secretariat Book Depot.

23. H.H. Risely, 1981, *The Tribes and Castes of India*. Vol. 2, Calcutta; Firma K.L. Mukhopadhyay.
24. P.C. Roy Chaudhury, 1961 *Bihar District Gazetteer. Palamau.* Patna: Printed by the Superintendent Secretarial Press.
25. Ibid.
26. Suranjan Sinha, 1993 "Construction of Identity," in *Seminar* 412. December.
27. A.R. Desai, 1960. "Tribes in Transition" in *Seminar*.
28. Xaxa, Op.cit., pp. 35–39.
29. The Constituent Assembly Debate (CAD) started before Independence and continued after it.
30. Constituent Assembly Debates (CAD-1:143).
31. (CAD-IX : 991).
32. (CAD-IX : 992).
33. (CAD-IX : 993).
34. (CAD-IX : 997-998).
35. arma, Op cit. p. 11.
36. CADp.10
37. Ibid.
38. (CAD-IX : 652-653).
39. Xaxa, Op. cit.
40. Ibid.
41. David Munzni. Ex M.P. Pthalkudua. Ranchi (Bihar), to the Chief Minister, Bihar, Patna.
42. This is the copy of the letter sent to the following on March 11, 1968 by David Munzni: (i) The Minister of Education, Central Government. New Delhi; (ii) The Editor, Gazetteers Education Ministry, Central Government. New Delhi; (iii) Shri Ashok Mehta, Minister of Social Welfare, New Delhi; (iv) His Excellency Dr. Zakir Hussain, the President of India, New Delhi. (for reference).
43. The data here is taken from a leaflet reportedly by a group of the Sarnas trying to counter the efforts of the Hindutva forces in the Hinduisation of the tribals. At the bottom of the leaflet it is written "Both the religions, namely the Sarna and Hindu are completely different but still there is a conspiracy to make us Sarnites 'Hindu' forcibly".
44. It should be noted that the Sarnas also cremate their deceased under certain circumstances.
45. Munzni, in his letter, speaks of his enclosure about the "gazetteer" which is meant for Sri Zakir Hussain. President of India. New Delhi. He wants Dr. Ekka to go through the copy of the letter.
46. Xaxa, OP. cit.

Note on Contributors

Virginius Xaxa is Professor of Sociology at Delhi School of Economics, University of Delhi, and is currently holding the Rajiv Gandhi Chair for Contemporary Studies at North-Eastern Hill University, Shillong. He is the author of *Economic Dualism* and *Structure of Class: A Study in Plantation and Subsistence Settings in North Bengal* (1997), and co-author of *Tea Plantation Labour in India* (1996).

Nandini Sundar is Professor of Sociology, Delhi School of Economics, University of Delhi, and Co-editor, Contributions to Indian Sociology. She has previously worked at the Centre for the Study of Law and Governance, Jawaharlal Nehru University; Institute of Economic Growth, Delhi and the University of Edinburgh. She has authored *Subalterns and Sovereigns: An Anthropological history of Bastar 1854-2006*, Delhi, Oxford University Press, 2007.

Thingnam Kishan Singh is Assistant Professor of English in Manipur University. He taught earlier at Shyam Lal College, University of Delhi and D.M. College of Arts, Imphal. He is the author of *Rethinking Colonialism*. He is the editor of *Alternative Perspectives.*

Joseph Marianus Kujur is Head, Department of Tribal and Dalit Studies, Indian Social Institute, New Delhi His specialisation is in Religious Conversion and Tribal Identity. He has written many research papers for national and international journals.

Moirangthem Prakash is a member of People's Research Society (PRS), Bhopal and currently working as a researcher in the Tribal and Dalit Unit of Indian Social Institute, New

Delhi. He has been working on 'Social Conflict'. His articles have been published in various journals.

Yemuna Sunny is a social scientist and has been for more than a decade involved in examining social geography. She has worked in Eklavya and is a member of People's Research Society (PRS). Her interest is to understand the political nature of human relations. This has helped in articulating a critique of education that ignores modern political values of equality and justice.

Dharmendra Kumar is Assistant Professor in Political Science in Government J.H. College. He is a member of People's Research Society (PRS). He has worked on impact of Globalisation on Working Class Politics from an Open Marxist Perspective.

Kumar Sanjay Singh teaches history at Shradhanand College, University of Delhi, Delhi. He has extensively worked on the question of National Self Determination and Identity Politics in India. He has been actively involved with various radical political formations.

Rajendra Sail is a Human Rights Activist. He has been the first secretary of PUCLDR (People's Union for Civil Liberties and Democratic Rights). One of his major concerns is the plight of Bonded Labourers. He has been the Organising Secretary of Indian Social Action Forum (INSAF).